THE LITTMAN LIBRARY OF JEWISH CIVILIZATION

EDITORS:

David Goldstein
Louis Jacobs
Lionel Kochan

This Library is dedicated
to the memory of

JOSEPH AARON LITTMAN

Hasidic Prayer

LOUIS JACOBS

SCHOCKEN BOOKS · NEW YORK

BM
669
2.J3
1978

134870

May 1986

Contents

Contents

Preface

There is no lack of literature on the practical aspects of the Hasidic movement and on its history, tales and legends. Little has been done, however, to examine Hasidic thought in a systematic way. (The works of G. Scholem, I. Tishby, J. G. Weiss and Rivka Schatz Uffenheimer are, of course, honourable exceptions.) The obstacles to such an investigation are many. The Hasidic masters generally expressed their ideas unsystematically; their language is a complicated amalgam of rabbinic Hebrew and Aramaic and is full of kabbalistic terms and allusions; the Hasidic literature frequently seeks to convey the flavour of an experience rather than transmit bare ideas; it is hard to distinguish among different, even contradictory, emphases and to determine the authenticity of teachings attributed to particular leaders. Yet the task is not a completely impossible one and is worth attempting, as the work of the scholars we have mentioned abundantly shows.

This book is a study of one very important aspect of Hasidic thought; the attitudes of the Hasidic masters to prayer. While the stress is on the theoretical side, the practical manifestations of Hasidic prayer have also been noted. The book seeks to portray the major tendencies among the Hasidim in the matter of prayer from the earliest period down to the present. But the subject is so vast that it would be futile to pretend that the book possesses the kind of comprehensiveness a much larger volume might have had. None the less, it is hoped that a fairly clear picture is given of Hasidic prayer and its originality as well as its role in the history of Jewish prayer and worship.

This book, it need hardly be said, is not a manual of prayer. It purports only to be a critical examination in which Hasidism is neither denigrated nor praised to the heavens. I am not a Hasid and have tried to see Hasidism from the outside, with a degree of affection for this fascinating movement but with an attempt to be objective and unbiased one way or the other. If the book manages to illumine in some small way an overlooked corner of Jewish life and thought it will have fulfilled its purpose.

Note on Names and Dates

The letter 'R' before a name stands for 'Rabbi', e.g. R. Shneor Zalman = Rabbi Shneor Zalman. The names of the Russian and Polish towns in which the Hasidic masters lived are given not in their correct form as in the atlases but as normally pronounced by the Hasidim (see M. Buber, *Tales of the Hasidim* (New York, 1947–8), vol. 2, p. 343), e.g. Koznitz for Koziniec; Lizensk for Lezajsk; Pulnoye for Polennoje, Zlotchov for Zloczow. The names of Talmudic tractates are given in the notes in the abbreviated form familiar to students of the Talmud, e.g. M.K. for Moed Katan. The dates of the Hasidic masters are given only where relevant to the argument. For this reason they are sometimes given more than once.

The biblical translations are those of the Jewish Publication Society version of 1917; the numbering of the verses may differ slightly from the Authorized Version.

Hasidic Prayer

CHAPTER I

Hasidism

At precisely the same time that the wider Gentile world saw the emergence in Europe and America of revivalist movements, the Hasidic movement was born in the forsaken Jewish communities of Volhynia and Podolia. Despite the fiercest opposition on the part of the Jewish establishment, Hasidism spread with startling rapidity. Fifty years after the death of its founder, R. Israel b. Eliezer (d. 1760), known as the Baal Shem Tov ('Master of the Good Name [of God]'), the movement had succeeded in winning to its banner half the Jewish population of Russia and Poland, the great centres of Jewish life in the eighteenth to nineteenth centuries. Indicative of its hold over the masses is the fact that the upholders of the *status quo* were very soon referred to as *Mitnag-gedim* ('opponents'), implying that they, and not the Hasidim, were obliged to be on the defensive. Thanks chiefly to Martin Buber's *Tales of the Hasidim*, the Western world in general has become acquainted with the sayings of the Hasidic masters. Their maxims are now to be found in anthologies of religious literature, where the Hasidic anecdote vies with the Zen *koan*.

The term *Hasidim* (sing. *Hasid*) is found in the Bible and is derived from the frequently occurring *hesed*, generally translated into English as 'lovingkindness', 'mercy', 'love', 'loyalty', even 'grace' or 'charm'. It is important, however, to appreciate that the idea of 'saintliness', later associated with the term *hasid*, is not found in the Bible. Unlike the English word 'saint', from the Latin *sanctus*, the term *hasid* in its original (i.e. Biblical) usage possesses no overtones of consecration or dedication to a special life of extreme holiness and piety. The Biblical *hasid* was certainly no charismatic personality. He was simply one who practised *hesed*, one whose heart and mind were suffused with a rich intensity of goodness (the root of the word *hesed* suggests intensiveness), resulting in complete devotion to God and unqualified love of his fellow-men. God Himself is described in the Book of Psalms (Ps. 145: 17) as *hasid*. To speak of the Creator as 'good' is understandable, as 'saintly' is merely grotesque.

There are many references in the Book of Psalms to the *hasidim*. Who were these men? Is the term *hasidim* no more than a generic term for the righteous and godly, or does it designate a special group of men dedicated to some common purpose? It is impossible to answer this conclusively. When the Psalmist, for instance, refers to God speaking peace to His people and to His *hasidim*, are the words 'to His *hasidim*' in apposition to 'to His people' or do they refer to a special group of *hasidim* among the people? Many Biblical scholars are inclined to the view that in some of the psalms the *hasidim* are none other than the men of that name who fought with the Maccabees against Antiochus. Psalm 149 in particular speaks, apparently, of a group of fighting 'saints'.

The Biblical *hasid*, then, is not a specially consecrated individual, one set apart from his fellows. He is not a 'type' at all, merely an exceptionally good and pious man. It is possible, however, that in the period of the Psalms pious individuals formed themselves into groups for the purpose of defending their faith. If this is correct, these men—the *hasidim*—may be the group of that name in the time of the Maccabees or they may be the group out of which the latter emerged. Of one thing we are certain, that in the revolt against Antiochus a company of men joined the ranks of the rebels and were known as *hasidim*.

The earliest definite references we have to a group of devoted men calling themselves *hasidim* are in the Books of the Maccabees, where it is stated that these men (*Asidaioi* in Greek) attached themselves to the Maccabees (1 Macc. 2: 42–4; 7: 8–18) or, according to another version, were the group of which Judas Maccabeus was the captain (2 Macc. 14: 3–6). Scholars have long noted that there is internal evidence (the use of Greek words, for instance) that the Book of Daniel was composed during the Greek period. It is a plausible suggestion that the book was written during the Maccabean revolt to encourage the Jews to remain steadfast in their loyalty to the faith of their fathers. This conjecture finds strong support in the account of Daniel's vision of the 'fourth beast' who made war 'with the saints' (Dan. 7: 19–22).

The spiritual heirs of the Maccabean *hasidim* were the Pharisees, who showed the same devotion to the Law, and the Essenes. (It has been conjectured by Schürer that the word 'Essenes' may even be a Greek form of the word *hasidim*.) The Essenes lived a monastic life in which possessions were shared. They dwelt chiefly in the neighbourhood of the Dead Sea. The Dead Sea Scrolls, according to many scholars, appear to have been produced by members of this sect or one very like it. When not working, these saints— Philo says that they were about four thousand in number— engaged in religious study and prayer. Philo (p. 217) writes of them:

> In fact they do constantly assemble together, and they sit down with one another, the multitude in general in silence, except when it is customary to say any words of good omen, by way of assent to what is being read. And then some priest who is present, or some one of the elders, reads the sacred laws to them, and interprets each of them separately till eventide; and then when separate they depart, having gained some skill in the sacred laws, and having made great advances toward piety.

There are a number of references in the rabbinic literature to the 'Pious Men of Old' (*hasidim ha-rishonim*). These may have been the Essenes (of whom, incidentally, there is curiously no direct mention in the Talmudic literature) or, possibly, the earlier Maccabean group. Of these men it is said that they would wait one hour before their prayers in order to direct their minds to God; that they would insert the fringes to be worn on the corners of the garment (Num. 15: 37–41) as soon as three handbreadths of the garment has been woven (although the law does not demand that these be affixed until the garment is to be worn); and that they would only consort with their wives on a Wednesday in the belief that conception on any other day might result in a birth on

3

the sabbath, which would involve a certain amount of sabbath desecration (this was allowed by law but the exceedingly pious took the most extreme steps in order to avoid even a licit desecration of the sabbath). The same scrupulous regard displayed bv these men in connection with their religious duties was shown in their sense of social responsibility. It was their practice to hide their thorns and broken glass in the midst of their fields at a depth of three handbreadths and so guard against the possibility of anything belonging to them doing harm to others. Although one or two of the details may be later embellishments, there is no reason for doubting the authenticity of these accounts; from which there emerges the picture of a group of men careful, with a scrupulosity extending far beyond the letter of the law, in matters of prayer, of sabbath observance, of ritual in general and of social welfare. The looser Biblical term is now used of the members of a special pietistic group. The fact that the group is referred to in the rabbinic literature as the 'Pious Men of Old' makes it clear that the group was no longer in existence in the rabbinic period. In this period the term *hasid* denotes the exceedingly pious individual, outstanding for his love of God and man and his punctiliousness in the observance of his religious and ethical duties. The *hasid* is now the equivalent of the saint.

Some rabbinic sayings about the *hasid* afford an insight into how the rabbis saw this religious type. The late first-century teacher R. Jose the Priest is described as a *hasid*. His rule of life is recorded as, 'Let the property of thy fellow be dear to thee as thine own; and fit thyself for the study of the Torah, for it is not thine by inheritance; and let all thy deeds be done for the sake of Heaven.' Here the essence of saintliness is apparently good neighbourliness and disinterestedness. An anonymous teacher, whose views, like that of R. Jose, are recorded in the ethical treatise *Ethics of the Fathers*, described saintliness as intensity of virtuous behaviour. Of the four characters among men the *hasid* is he who says, 'What is mine is thine and what is thine is thine.' Of the four kinds of tempers the *hasid* is he who is hard to provoke and easy to pacify. Of the four types of almsgiver the *hasid* is he who gives and wishes others to give. Of the four who frequent the House of Learning the *hasid* is he who goes and also practises.

We saw that the idea of intensity belongs to the root of the word *hesed* and in the examples of the *hasid* just quoted intensity and extremes of goodness are advocated. In the Hasidic movement, too, this phenomenon is to be observed. It seems, indeed, to be typical of the saintly character in all religions. William James, in his *Varieties of Religious Experience* (p. 339), after surveying examples of extreme saintly conduct, remarks on this:

> Our survey of the phenomena of saintliness has unquestioningly produced in your minds an impression of extravagance. Is it necessary, some of you have asked, as one example after another came before us, to be quite so fantastically good as that? We who have no vocation for the extremer ranges of sanctity will surely be let off at the last day if our humility, asceticism, and devoutness prove of a less convulsive sort. This practically amounts to saying that much that it is legitimate to admire in this field need nevertheless not be imitated, and that religious phenomena, like all other human phenomena, are subject to the law of the golden mean. Political reformers accomplish their successive tasks in the history of nations by being blind for the time to other causes. Great schools of art work out the effects which it is their mission to reveal, at the cost of a one-sidedness for which other schools must make amends. We accept a John Howard, a Mazzini, a Botticelli, a Michael Angelo, with a kind of indulgence. We are glad that they existed to show us that way, but we are glad there are also other ways of seeing and taking life. So of many of the saints whom we have looked at. We are proud of a human nature that could be so passionately extreme, but we shrink from advising others to follow the example. The conduct we blame ourselves for not following lies nearer to the middle line of human effort. It is less dependent on particular beliefs and doctrines. It is such as wears well in different ages, such as under different skies all judges are able to commend.

In the rabbinic literature the difference between the formally religious—the *zaddik*—and the *hasid* is that the *hasid* goes beyond the letter of the law. (In the chapter in this book on the prayers of the Zaddik we shall see why, in the Hasidic movement, the roles were reversed.) R. Huna (late third century) contrasted the two parts of the verse, 'The Lord is righteous [*zaddik*] in all His ways' and 'and gracious [*hasid*] in all His works' (Ps. 145: 17). At first God acts with sinners according to their just deserts but in the end He is gracious to pardon, i.e. He goes beyond the letter of the law. There was a widespread belief, shared by the rabbis, that the parings of fingernails could be injurious to the health of a pregnant woman who stepped over them. The man who throws away his nail-parings is wicked, he who buries them is a *zaddik*, but the *hasid* burns them, i.e. he avoids the remotest possibility of their doing any harm. The third-century teacher R. Judah said that he who wishes to be a *hasid* must fulfil the laws dealt with in the Order *Nezikin* (treating of damages and how to avoid injury to others). Raba (299–352) said that he must fulfil the matters dealt with in *Ethics of the Fathers*. Others say that he must fulfil the matters dealt with in tractate *Berakhot*, which has prayer for its subject. Thus special stress is laid on saintliness (*hasidut*) in prayer, in self-improvement and in care for the goods and property of others.

In the rabbinic period, then, the *hasid* was the man of special sanctity, altruism and holiness, particularly noted for his desire to go far beyond the letter of the law. With the addition of mystical and ascetic elements of various kinds the *hasid* in subsequent Jewish life and thought belongs to this rabbinic type. By virtue of their education the Hasidim in the eighteenth century were thoroughly familiar with the rabbinic literature and its descriptions of saintly behaviour, upon which they tried to model their own conduct.

The *hasid* as an ideal type persisted throughout the Middle Ages. Many individuals were given the title by their fellow-Jews. The type appears frequently in Bahya Ibn Pakuda's classic work *Duties of the Heart*, in which, incidentally, the title is also given to Gentile saints whom Bahya holds up for admiration, the Sufis, for example. More significant is the emergence in medieval Germany of a group of ascetics belonging to the school of R. Judah the Saint (*hasid*) of Regensburg (12th–13th centuries) who were styled 'The Saints of Germany' (*haside ashkenaz*). The book produced in this circle is called 'The Book of the Saints' (*Sefer Hasidim*), a work which became extremely popular in Jewish pietistic circles. The Hasidim of Germany, whose life, as Baer has shown, if not directly influenced by Christian monastic ideals, bore striking resemblances to them, introduced a strong ascetic tendency into Jewish life. They had, for instance, an elaborate series of penances for sin, of a kind hitherto unknown in Jewish thought. Among these were prolonged fasts, rolling naked in the snow in winter and sitting naked in summer smeared with honey in order to be stung by bees.

The influence of the Hasidim of Germany on the followers of the Baal Shem Tov was indirect rather than direct. Professor G. Scholem rightly remarks in his *Major Trends in Jewish Mysticism* (p. 118), speaking of the relationship between the two groups of Hasidim separated by several centuries:

> There is little to connect these old Hasidim of the thirteenth century with the Hasidic movement which developed in Poland and the Ukraine during the eighteenth century . . . The identity of name is no proof of real continuity. After all, the two are separated by two or three great epochs in the development of Kabbalistic thought. The later Hasidism was the inheritor of a rich tradition from which its followers could draw new inspiration, new modes of thought and, last but not least, new modes of expression. And yet it cannot be denied that a certain similarity between the two movements exists. In both cases the problem was that of the education of large Jewish groups in a spirit of mystical moralism. The true Hasid and the Zaddik of later Hasidism are related figures; the one and the other are the prototypes of a mystical way of life which tends towards social activity even where its representatives are conceived as the guardians of all the mysteries of divinity.

In the Kabbalistic tradition to which Scholem alludes and which influenced beyond measure the Hasidic movement, there are two great schools of thought. The first is represented by the 'Bible' of the Kabbalists, the Zohar, which appeared in Spain at the end of the thirteenth century. The second is the sixteenth-century school of the Kabbalah which flourished in Safed in Palestine, the most outstanding figure of which was R. Isaac Luria (d. 1572), known as the *Ari* ('Lion'). We shall have glimpses in this book of how the Hasidic masters used the Kabbalistic ideas and adapted them in their mystical approach to prayer.

The followers of the Baal Shem Tov, it is important to realise, did not invent the term Hasidim as applied to themselves. It is not as if, looking for a name by which to describe themselves, they adopted this one. The truth is that in Poland and the Ukraine in the eighteenth century, groups of Hasidim (who used the term as developed in the previous centuries) were to be found. These men were generally Kabbalists and ascetics, the Lurianic Kabbalah containing powerful ascetic elements. Not to be discounted is the influence of the Sabbatian movements on some of the members of these groups. The pseudo-Messiah Sabbatai Zevi (1626–76) had at first a vast following among the Jews of many lands who hailed him as the true Messiah. Even after his conversion to Islam, there were large numbers of crypto-Sabbatians, 'believers' as they called themselves, who kept their faith with Sabbatai Zevi even after his apostasy, on the grounds that the Messiah was obliged to descend into the realms of impurity in order to redeem the 'holy sparks' (of which much will be said later in this book). Another heretical Jewish group active in this period was that of the Frankists, followers of Jacob Frank (1726–91), who developed the Sabbatian ideas about 'holy sin' in an even more bizarre form and who was eventually converted to Catholicism. We shall have occasion to note how all this made its impact on Hasidism proper. There were also to be found *Baale Shem* ('Masters of the Name'), miracle-workers and healers who operated chiefly by the magical use of the divine names. (By the way, the popular opinion that Israel b. Eliezer was called 'The Master of the *Good* Name' in order to distinguish him from the other Baale Shem, who were less 'good', is unfounded. 'Good' in the title does not qualify 'Master' but 'Name'.) It was against such a background that the Baal Shem Tov and the Hasidim appeared. They were, at first, one of a number of groups of Hasidim and the Baal Shem Tov one of a number of Baale Shem. But the emphases of the Baal Shem Tov and his followers were different.

The particular doctrine of the Baal Shem Tov and his followers has sometimes been called 'pantheistic'. This is a misnomer. No attempt was ever made by the Hasidim to identify the universe with God. The more correct description of the doctrine is 'panentheism', the belief that all is *in* God. Such ideas were certainly not the invention of the Baal Shem Tov (nor, except in the Habad group, were they developed by the Hasidim in a systematic way), but he and his followers gave them fresh emphasis and applied them in their daily life. Since all things are in God and 'there is no place empty of Him', the Baal Shem Tov taught that rather than practise asceticism in order to find God, man should use the things of the world to bring him nearer to God. But the idea (popularised by Zangwill in his essay on the Baal Shem Tov in *Dreamers of the Ghetto* and later by Buber and justly attacked by Scholem) according to which Hasidism teaches that the worship of God is to be realised in the concrete forms of the 'here and now' is erroneous. To be sure, the Hasid meets his God in the 'here and now'. The Hasid is not normally in favour of asceticism (though some of the Hasidic masters were ascetics), nor is he a hermit. But the things of the world are, for Hasidism, only the means by which he can grasp divinity. The true aim of the Hasid is to penetrate beneath appearances to see only the divine vitality which infuses all things. His ultimate aim is the attainment of what Hasidism calls *bittul ha-yesh*, 'annihilation of the self'. The ego is left behind as man's soul soars aloft through his contemplation of the tremendous theme that all is in God. The Neoplatonic element in Hasidic thought (which came to Hasidism through the Kabbalah), and the striking resemblances to Far Eastern views on the illusory nature of the world of the senses, cannot be overestimated.

Who was the Baal Shem Tov? Legend is so inextricably mixed with fact in all that is told of him that any attempt to answer this question is saved from sheer speculation only with difficulty. The cantankerous E. Deinhard, a foe of the Hasidim, even advanced the quite preposterous opinion that the Baal Shem Tov never existed. What seems undeniable about the Baal Shem Tov is that he was a powerful charismatic personality who was orphaned at an early age and so escaped in large measure the fate of being compelled by his parents to adopt the conventional scheme of Jewish learning, which might have stifled his originality. It would seem that the Baal Shem Tov did, in fact, manage to acquire more than the rudiments of a Talmudic education. That he was an outstanding Talmudist is only maintained by uncritical admirers whose chief argument, that he must have been a great scholar in order to attract scholarly disciples, displays a complete lack of understanding of religious psychology. It is said, with justice, of the Baal Shem Tov, that in the Carpathian mountains, where he lived in seclusion, he learned to reflect on the beauties of the creation and that his mystical bent was nourished there in private meditation far from the haunts of men. He was one of those who did see every common bush afire with God and he took off his shoes. We know very little about his wife except that she was a sister of a famous scholar in Brody, R. Gershon of Kutov, who later became an ardent follower of his brother-in-law. When the Baal Shem Tov eventually came out of his seclusion to 'reveal' himself, he gathered around him in the town of Medziboz a circle of followers. Some of these, however, were associates rather than disciples. The names of some of these men have come down to us: Phinehas of Koretz, Nahum of Tchernobil, Nahman of Kosov, Jehiel Michal of Zlotchov, Rafael of Bershad, Arye Laib of Spola, Laib son of Sarah, Meir Margaliot, Zevi the Scribe and Wolf Kitzes. The Baal Shem Tov's only son, Hirsh, did not become his successor and occupies no real place in the development of Hasidism. His daughter Adelle, the subject of numerous Hasidic legends, was the mother of Moses Hayim Ephraim of Sudlikov and Baruch of Medziboz.

The two chief disciples of the Baal Shem Tov were R. Jacob Joseph of Pulnoye (d. 1782) and R. Dov Baer, the Maggid of Meseritch (d. 1772). Although the institution of Zaddikism has its antecedents in the life of the Baal Shem Tov himself, it was these two—the former by his writings, the latter by his organisational talents—who developed, as the central feature of the new movement, the doctrine of the Zaddik, the saint and miracle-worker, who acts as a 'Guru' to his followers, who prays on their behalf and who leads them to God. The new role of this type of religious leader is expressed in the saying, attributed to the Baal

Shem Tov, that the purpose of the Torah is that man should himself become a Torah, and in the saying of one of the Maggid's disciples that he did not journey to the Maggid in order to study Torah but to see how the master tied his shoe-laces. Eventually, the idea that the son of the Zaddik, conceived as he was in holiness, inherited his father's sanctity, was developed so that 'dynasties' of Zaddikim flourished. Some of the Zaddikim, especially in the later period, had 'courts', to which thousands of their followers would flock to receive the blessing of the holy man, and to hear his inspired 'saying of Torah'.

R. Jacob Joseph of Pulnoye was the author of *Toledot Ya'akob Yosef*, the first Hasidic work to be published (in 1780, both in Medziboz and Koretz). In this and in his other works, R. Jacob Joseph quotes many sayings he has heard from the Baal Shem Tov (generally with the formula, 'I have heard from my master') as well as sayings of the Baal Shem Tov's associates. R. Jacob Joseph's work is still studied assiduously by the Hasidim (he is known by them not by his name but as the *Toledot*) and is among the most important sources we have for Hasidic ideas.

R. Dov Baer became the successor of the Baal Shem Tov and the leader, organiser and mystical teacher of the new movement. For part of his life R. Dov Baer lived in Meseritch, hence his name 'the Maggid [preacher] of Meseritch'. He became acquainted with the Baal Shem Tov only towards the end of his life and to some extent was independent in his treatment of the Hasidic ideas. There is no doubt that the success of the movement depended on the organisational ability of R. Dov Baer and the impression he made on extremely gifted men who became his disciples. His teachings are recorded in the works of these men. His addresses on the sabbath were put into written form by Solomon of Lutzk and published under the title *Maggid Devarav Le-Yaakov* or *Likkute Amarim* (Zolkiev, 1792).

The Maggid became the teacher of a remarkable galaxy of Hasidic saints, celebrated in Hasidic legend, each of them becoming in turn a pioneer of the movement in the Ukraine, Poland and Lithuania. The doings and wise sayings of these colourful personalities are recorded in scores of Hasidic collections in Hebrew and

Yiddish, and in English in Buber's *Tales* and Newman's *Hasidic Anthology*. Among the most famous are Levi Yitzhak of Berditchev, Elimelech of Lizensk, Abraham of Kalisk, Hayim Haikel of Amdur, Zeev Wolf of Zhitomer, Zusya of Hanipol (brother of Elimelech), Solomon of Karlin, Mordecai of Tchernobil, Menahem Mendel of Vitebsk, Shmelke of Nikolsburg and Shneor Zalman of Liady. The last-named was the founder of the *Habad* group, with greater emphasis than all the other Hasidic groups on intellectualism.

As examples of how the Hasidic dynasties took shape after the Maggid we can refer to the following. R. Elimelech of Lizensk brought Hasidism to Poland, where four of his disciples became Hasidic masters, each with his own large following. To him the Hasidim apply the verse, 'And a river went out of Eden to water the garden; and from thence it was parted, and became four heads' (Gen. 2: 10). 'Eden' is the Baal Shem Tov. The 'river' is the Maggid of Meseritch. The 'garden' is R. Elimelech and the four 'heads' or tributaries are: R. Menahem Mendel of Rymanov; R. Israel, the Maggid of Koznitz; R. Meir of Apt; and R. Jacob Isaac of Lublin, known as the 'Seer' because of his clairvoyant powers. The Maggid's son Abraham, known as the 'Angel' because of his holy life, had a son who became a Hasidic master, R. Shalom Shachna of Probishtch (d. 1803). R. Shalom's son was R. Israel of Ruzhyn (d. 1850), who had six sons, each of whom led a new Hasidic community. R. Mordecai of Tchernobil (d. 1837), disciple of the Maggid, had eight sons, each of whom became a Hasidic master in the Ukraine. R. Shneor Zalman settled in Liady in White Russia. His son, R. Dov Baer, became his successor as the leader of the Habad group in the town of Lubavitch in the same district. He was succeeded by his son-in-law (who was also his nephew) R. Menahem Mendel of Lubavitch. R. Menahem Mendel's great-great-grandson is the present leader of the Lubavitcher Hasidim with his headquarters in New York and followers in every part of the Jewish world. The Baal Shem Tov's great-grandson, R. Nahman of Bratzlav (d. 1810), son of Adelle's daughter, settled in Uman. His way is in many respects different from that of the other Hasidic leaders and no successor was appointed when he died. The Bratzlaver Hasidim have no living Zaddik to guide them but owe allegiance solely to their departed master, hence they are sometimes known as the 'dead Hasidim'.

Hasidic literature, it has been estimated, numbers at least three thousand items. Much of this material was destroyed during the Nazi period but most of the Hasidic classics have been reprinted after the war in Israel and the United States. The majority of these classics were not actually written by the masters to whom they are attributed but by their disciples. The usual procedure was for disciples to record after the sabbath the discourses they had heard from the master on the sabbath and which they submitted to the Zaddik for his approval.

As we have seen, the Hasidic leader was known as the Zaddik. But another name given to him from the earliest times was 'Rebbe' ('Master'), to distinguish him from the Rav (the traditional Rabbi). Thus today one speaks of the Belzer Rebbe, the Lubavitcher Rebbe and so on. Some few Hasidic masters were also the formal Rabbis of the towns in which they resided but this was unusual. A later title given to the Zaddik in indirect speech was Admor, an abbreviation of: Adonenu, Morenu Ve-Rabbenu ('Our Master, Teacher and Rabbi'). The plural of Admor is Admorim. There exists in the United States a professional organisation of 'wonder-rabbis' known as 'The Association of Admorim'!

It can readily be seen from the above how absurd it is to expect uniform ideas among all the Hasidic masters. The influence of the Zaddik's surroundings, his individual temperament, the traditions of his teachers and his understanding and application of them, all made for a degree of originality in each Hasidic court. There was a good deal of rivalry, sometimes leading to bitter insult and even to blows, among the Hasidim of different masters, each group claiming supremacy for its own views. Habad and Bratzlav both developed more or less independently of the other groups. Especially in the earlier period, the teachings of the Baal Shem Tov are interpreted in various ways so that, for example, the school of the Maggid is not necessarily in agreement with the opinions of the other associates and disciples of the Baal Shem Tov. That is why one will look in vain for any comprehensive and systematic treatment of Hasidic doctrine acceptable to all the Hasidim. For all that, certain basic themes and a certain mood, founded on the panentheistic belief, are fairly constant. Among the ideas stressed in every variety of Hasidic thought are: the love and fear of God; *devekut*, 'cleaving' to God at all times; *simhah*, 'joy' in God's presence; *hitlahavut*, 'burning enthusiasm' in God's worship; and *shiflut*, 'lowliness', 'humility', construed as a complete lack of awareness of the self.

Hasidism met with much opposition from two groups of Jews: the Mitnaggedim, the rabbis and community leaders who followed the older traditional pattern of Jewish life; and the Maskilim, the 'enlightened'. The Maskilim were the advocates of Western culture for the Jews. These men in the early nineteenth century, full of missionary zeal for the new learning and anxious to combat the backwardness, as they saw it, of the Eastern European Jew, looked upon Hasidism as a reactionary movement to be fought with the weapons of satire and ridicule. The Hasidim, they protested, fed on the credulity of the masses, opposing secular learning of any kind, believing in reincarnation, demons, amulets and other forms of superstition, encouraging mystical flights as an escape from the pressing social and economic problems the Jews had to face if they were to survive.

The Mitnaggedim were extremely suspicious of the new movement on other grounds. Especially in Lithuania, the stronghold of traditional rabbinic learning, the opposition to Hasidism was bitter in the extreme, led by the towering rabbinic figure of Elijah, the Gaon of Vilna (1720–97). The anathemas published by the Mitnaggedim against the Hasidim urge that none should intermarry with the Hasidim and that they be driven out of the communities until they repent of their evil ways. The alarm felt by the Mitnaggedim was due to attacks on scholars in works like *Toledot* so that the Hasidim were accused of lack of respect for Torah learning and its practitioners. The Hasidic emphasis on constant attachment to God was held to demote the study of the Torah from the prominent place it had occupied in Jewish life. Could one really study if, instead of concentrating on the passage studied, one's mind was on God? The ruthless Hasidic stress on

Torah study 'for its own sake' and the contempt expressed in Hasidic works for scholars who studied in order to acquire fame and the like was suspected of leading eventually to indifference to Torah study as the supreme religious value. If only a saint could really be considered a Torah student then, since saints were few, students would be few. The Hasidic substitution of the Lurianic Prayer Book for the traditional Prayer Book (of which much will be said later in this book); the special dress adopted by the Hasidim; the bizarre antics some of the Hasidim got up to in prayer; the Hasidic preference for specially honed knives for killing animals, which affected, among other things, the dues paid by the ritual slaughterers to the community chest; all these were also a source of great offence to the Mitnaggedim. On the theological level, the Hasidic doctrine that all is in God and that 'strange thoughts' (of which, too, more will be said later) should not be rejected but 'elevated' in prayer, was held by the Mitnaggedim to be rank heresy. The story has often been told how, none the less, Hasidism triumphed; indeed, as opposition movements generally do, it throve on the attacks made upon it. Eventually Mitnaggedim and Hasidim made common cause, though reluctantly, against their common foes, the Maskilim.

The only complete history of Hasidism was written by Simon Dubnow, *Toledot Ha-Hasidut*, 'History of Hasidism'. It was Dubnow's aim to study Hasidism objectively and his lead was followed by several scholars. No one has done more to encourage the scholarly investigation into Hasidism and Jewish mysticism generally than Professor G. Scholem. The school he established at the Hebrew University in Jerusalem continues to make outstanding contributions in this field.

The ghastly holocaust, in which a third of the Jewish people were destroyed by the Nazis and their helpers, brought to an end the pulsating life of the Hasidim in the great centres of Eastern Europe. But Hasidism still lives on. Among the more famous Hasidic groups today are those of Lubavitch, Sotmar, Vishnitz, Bobov, Gur and Belz. That the movement has severely declined, partly through the external causes we have mentioned, partly through its inability really to cope with the challenges of a new world, is undeniable. Yet Judaism is the richer for having given birth to this astonishing revival of Jewish mysticism and for the fact that there are still many thousands of Hasidim following the old ways and continuing to tell the ancient tale of how God sent down from heaven the lofty souls of the Baal Shem Tov and his disciples to illumine the darkness of exile.

CHAPTER II

The Nature of Hasidic Prayer

An early Hasidic text[1], speaking of the dialogue of the Baal Shem Tov (d. 1760), the founder of the Hasidic movement, with his own soul, remarks:

> The soul declared to the rabbi, may his memory be for a blessing for the life of the world to come, that the reason why the supernal matters were revealed to him was not because he had studied many Talmudic tractates and Codes of Law but because of his prayer. For at all times he recited his prayers with great concentration. It was as a result of this that he attained to an elevated state.

There is no doubt whatsoever that prayer occupied a central place in early Hasidic life and has continued so to do down to the present. Speaking of the doctrines of the Maggid of Meseritch, the disciple of the Baal Shem Tov, Rivka Schatz[2] rightly observes:

> Contemplative prayer became the spiritual message *par excellence* of Hasidism. A Hasid who did not pray with the aim of divesting himself of corporeality, detaching himself from this world, and rising above nature and time in order to attain complete union with the divine "Nothing", had not really achieved anything of spiritual value.

She is not, however, correct when she goes on to say[3] that Hasidism has assigned an exclusive role to prayer 'giving it—*in keeping with the Jewish tradition*—pride of place in the religious life' (italics mine). The Hasidic elevation of prayer over other religious duties, even over that of study of the Torah, is not in keeping with the Jewish tradition. The Hasidim here were innovators. In the

17

rabbinic tradition the obligation to pray is rabbinic, not biblical.[4] In the Talmud[5] one rabbi can rebuke another who prolongs his prayers unduly by protesting 'they leave aside eternal life [= the Torah] to engage in temporal existence' [= prayer]. Scholars like R. Simeon b. Yohai, we are told, whose sole occupation was study of the Torah, would not interrupt their studies in order to pray.[6]

The Hasidic teachers were not unaware that their elevation of prayer over all other duties was a departure from what, at least, was held to be the tradition and they sought to justify their innovation by seeking to demonstrate, as religious innovators are wont to do, that the tradition, rightly understood, was really in line with their attitude. Thus R. Shneor Zalman of Liady (1747–1813), founder of the Habad group in Hasidism, in a letter addressed to Alexander of Shklov,[7] makes the point explicitly:

> Those who argue that prayer is only binding by Rabbinic law have never seen the light. It is true that the forms of the prayers are Rabbinic, and that prayers must be recited three times a day, but the concept of prayer and its essential idea belong to the very foundation of the Torah, namely, to know the Lord, to recognise His greatness and His glory with a serene mind, and, through contemplation, to have these fixed firmly in the mind. A man must reflect on this theme until the contemplative soul is awakened to love the Lord's name, to cleave to Him and to His Torah and greatly to desire His commandments. Nowadays, all this can only be achieved by reciting the verses of praise and the benedictions before and after the Shema with clear diction and in a loud voice so as to awaken the powers of concentration. All this and then perhaps! It was otherwise with regard to R. Simeon b. Yohai and his colleagues. For them the recitation of the Shema alone was sufficient for them to attain all this. It was all achieved in a blink of the eye, so humble was their heart in its covenantal loyalty. But, nowadays, anyone who has drawn near to God and has once tasted the fragrance of prayer, knows and appreciates that without prayer no man can lift hand or foot to serve God in truth, rather than as the commands of men who learn by rote.

Similarly, R. Kalonymus Kalman Epstein of Cracow (d. 1827) writes:[8]

When the Jew draws near to the form of worship that is prayer it is to the greatest thing in the whole world that he draws near, as the holy book tell us. The Talmud states explicitly that prayer is greater than good deeds.[9] In our generation, especially, the chief method by means of which a man can refine his character, so as to approach the divine and serve God, is prayer. From the time of his coming, the holy Baal Shem Tov, may the memory of the holy and saintly be for a blessing, caused the tremendous sanctity of prayer to illumine the world for whoever wishes to draw near to God's service. However, in order for a man to attain to pure prayer it is necessary for him to engage in much service of the sages, to labour long, night and day, in the study of the Torah and in performance of good deeds so that, as a result, he may learn how truly to pray with fear and great love, as those who have discernment know full well.

Here we clearly see how an influential Hasidic author strives to reconcile the traditional view of the supremacy of Torah study with the new Hasidic emphasis on the supremacy of prayer. His solution is that, indeed, the study of the Torah and the performance of good deeds are essential and that without them prayer is futile. But—and a complete transvaluation is involved in the qualification—these are essential as aids to prayer. They are the guarantee that the worshipper will be capable of offering his prayers 'with fear and great love'. In another passage[10] R. Kalonymus Kalman, commenting on Jacob's dream, notes that a Midrash reads homiletically that Jacob awoke from his learning (*mi-mishnato*, instead of *mi-shenato*, 'his sleep'). The Midrash, of course, suggests that Jacob saw his vision of the divine because he was learned in the Torah. But R. Kalonymus Kalman boldly turns the Midrash on its head to suggest that, on the contrary, once Jacob had experienced true prayer he saw that his learning was only a dream in so far as he had imagined that by it he could come to love God. Jacob, remarks our author, had hitherto known only that man can draw near to God through the study of the Torah. When, however, he prayed to God in the place of his dream, he experienced such a powerful feeling of nearness to God that he came to realise that the true awakening of the spirit is through prayer alone. Jacob, speaking of prayer, then declared, 'Surely the Lord is in this place; and I knew it not'. After remarking that both Torah study and prayer are essential and that one without the other is inadequate, R. Kalonymus Kalman goes on to say that a man cannot perfect his soul by the study of the Torah alone:

> There is no doubt that a man who studies the Torah for its own sake can attain to great sanctity, provided always that he studies for its own sake and attaches all his vitality, spirit and soul to the letters of the Torah. For all that, the only way he can attain to real fear and love of God, to the longing for the worship of God, and to comprehension of His divinity, is through prayer offered with self-sacrifice and burning enthusiasm. All this is well known and is stated in all the holy books.

The early Hasidic master R. Meshullam Phoebus of Zhabaraz, disciple of the Maggid of Meseritch and of R. Jehiel Michal of Zlotchov, adopts a different way of reconciling the traditional demand for the supremacy of Torah study with the new Hasidic claims for the supremacy of prayer. He declares that indeed the study of the Torah is the highest value, but argues that true Torah study is only possible if it is attended by a proper life of prayer, that is by prayer as understood by Hasidism. In his little book *Derekh Emet*[11] this author accuses the learned of his day as totally lacking in real religious fervour even though they are well versed in both the 'revealed' Torah and the Kabbalah. Of the scholars he attacks he remarks:

> They know nothing of what attachment [*devekut*] to God means and nothing of what love and fear mean. For they imagine that their studies themselves constitute attachment to God and that these are themselves the love and fear of God. But how can this be? It is well known that many of the scholars are guilty of fornication, Heaven spare us, and they are notorious sinners. It is also true that many Gentiles study our Torah. How, then, can this be considered attachment to God? For one who is attached to God in love and fear cannot possibly commit even the slightest sin, to say nothing of a severe sin, God forbid, and to say nothing of attachment to some lust, God forbid. For, behold, God is holy and separate from all materialism. Consequently, it does not need saying that the love and fear of God are quite a different matter and they have to do with the heart, that a man's heart should be constantly in dread and awe of God and that the love of God

should burn always in his heart. . . . No one can attain to this state except by virtue of the study of the Torah for its own sake. And the prior, essential condition is prayer with attachment [devekut], with burning enthusiasm [hitlahavut] of the heart, with a coercion of all man's psychological faculties in the direction of clear and pure thoughts on God constantly, and in separation from every pleasure. It goes without saying that there must be separation from light and severe sins and that all the laws must be obeyed scrupulously and that all the limbs of the body must be clean and protected by the special kind of sanctity appropriate to each of them, as the moralistic works have recorded, and especially the author of Reshit Hokhmah [Elijah de Vidas]. But how can there possibly be attachment [devekut] by means of the Torah in the way they conduct themselves in that they despise prayer? The truth is that they only learn by rote in order to be considered wise.

The Hasidic attitude towards prayer and the reason for the significance of prayer in Hasidic thought cannot be understood without reference to the basic Hasidic idea of devekut, attachment to God, to which R. Meshullam Phoebus alludes and which has been explored in a famous article by Gershom Scholem.[12] Briefly stated, the doctrine means that ideally man should always have God in his thoughts, seeing beneath appearances only the divine vitality which infuses all things. For Hasidism, though with varying emphases, the only true reality is God. The material world, and, for that matter, the 'upper worlds' as well, only seem to enjoy reality. They are a kind of screen, which hides God from human eyes, but through which He can be seen if man's spiritual gaze is properly directed. The Hasid can learn to restore all things to their Source and to see only the infinite, divine power as this is manifested in creation. This is the Hasidic doctrine of panentheism, that all is in God. The Hasid is expected to attain to the state described in Hasidic thought as bittul ha-yesh, 'the annihilation of somethingness', that is an awareness that God alone is true reality and that all finite things are, as it were, dissolved in His unity. Bittul ha-yesh includes the annihilation of selfhood, the soul soaring to God with the ego left behind. This attitude is especially to be cultivated at the time of prayer, so that in Hasidism prayer is essentially an exercise in world-forsaking and abandonment of self.

In a passage[13] from the work *Maggid Devarav Le-Yaakov* (otherwise known as *Likkute Amarim*), containing the teachings of the Maggid of Meseritch, the disciple of the Baal Shem Tov, the process is described as follows:

It is stated that when a man studies the Torah or when he prays he should think to himself that he is, as it were, in the Garden of Eden, where there is neither envy not lust nor pride, and by so doing he will be spared from motives of self. But one has to understand the meaning of this. For how can a man think that this is so when he knows only too well that, in fact, he is in this world among persons he can identify? The matter is as follows. When a man studies or prays with fear and love, attaching himself and binding himself in his thoughts to the Creator, blessed be His name, and when he considers that the whole world is full of His glory and that no place is empty of Him, all being filled with the divine vitality, then all he sees in whatever he observes is the divine vitality which is drawn down into the object of perception. For example, when he sees other human beings, he observes that their appearance, their voices which he hears, their speech and their wisdom, all stem from this divine vitality. And this applies to whatever he sees or hears. For everything has that form and purpose to which it is suited. The same applies to that which he sees and that which he smells. It is all the vital power of the Creator, blessed be His name. It follows that when a man studies or prays with fear and love he gains much from it in that he becomes bound in his thought to the Creator, blessed be He. Such a worshipper sees nothing and hears nothing except the divine vitality that is in all things. For everything is from Him, blessed be His name; only it is clothed, as it were, in various garments. How, then, can motives of self, worldly desires, enter his mind, if all he sees before him is the vitality of the Creator alone and the spiritual delight that inheres in all things?

In another early Hasidic text[14] it is similarly taught:

In what way is a man better than a worm? For the worm serves God with all its might and mind, and man, too, is a worm, as it is written, 'But I am a worm, and no man' [Ps. 22: 7]. If God had not endowed man with intellect he could only have worshipped Him as a worm does. Consequently, he has no more worth up above than does a worm and certainly not more than other men. He should think to himself that he and the worm and all minute creatures are all companions in this world, for all are God's creatures and have no power except that which the Creator, blessed be He, gives them. This should always be in his thoughts.

The Hasidic attitude to prayer as an exercise in self-transcendence created for the Hasidim an especially acute problem. Prayers of adoration could effectively produce the desired aim; the Hasid could, by their aid, lose himself in reflection on the divine majesty. But what of petitionary prayer? In this type of prayer man entreats God to satisfy his needs, both spiritual and material. He prays for knowledge and wisdom, for bodily health and sustenance, for forgiveness of sin and redemption. This would seem to frustrate the whole purpose of prayer, since consciousness of need implies self-awareness. If man's aim in prayer is to see only the divine vitality, how can he petition God to attend to his own needs? Far from this type of prayer leading to the desired aim of loss of self it encourages concentration on self. The logical conclusion of the Hasidic doctrine would have been to reject all petitionary prayer as a hindrance to the attainment of self-annihilation. But such a solution was not open to the Hasidim who believed, like their contemporaries, that the traditional liturgy, which contains numerous petitionary prayers, was divinely inspired and divinely ordained.

The quietistic and radical way out of the dilemma generally adopted by the early Hasidim is that petitionary prayer is not, in fact, a request to God to satisfy man's needs but to satisfy His own needs. In the language of Hasidism, petitionary prayer is for the sake of the Shekhinah ('Divine Presence'). In the Kabbalah, upon which a good deal of Hasidic teaching is based, the Shekhinah is a kind of female element in the Godhead; female because it is the passive aspect of Deity, the manifestation of the divine power which vitalises all creation. God's purpose, the Kabbalistic doctrine runs, in creating the world is to benefit His creatures. True, if there were no creatures no loss of benefit or good would be experienced by anyone, but it is the nature of the All-good to have recipients for His bounty so that, as it were, He can fulfil Himself. Moreover, since man is created in God's image, since he is the microcosm of which the universe is the macrocosm, his deeds have a cosmic effect. When man is virtuous he sends up on high spiritual impulses which help to promote harmony in the realm of the Sefirot, the various potencies in the Godhead. God's purpose of benefiting His creatures as worthy recipients of His goodness can then be fulfilled. There is harmony above and so grace and blessing can flow through all creation. Man's wickedness, on the other hand, arrests the flow of the divine grace, producing disharmony in the Sefirotic realm. This is the cause of all death and destruction, of chaos and catastrophe, of evil and man's lack of all he requires for his continued existence and wellbeing. The Shekhinah is one of the Ten Sefirot. It is known as Malkhut ('Sovereignty') because through it God's rule over His creatures is established. In mythological language—and the whole of the Kabbalah is highly-charged mythology—when man lacks anything the lack is in the Shekhinah since then God's purpose remains unfulfilled. The Hasid, it is therefore taught, should not ask for his needs to be satisfied because they are *his* needs but because ultimately they are the needs of the Shekhinah. Even when praying for himself his true aim is for God. Even petitionary prayer serves his aim of self-transcendence.

The whole doctrine of prayer influencing the 'upper worlds' was accepted without qualification by the Hasidic teachers. R. Jacob Joseph of Pulnoye, disciple of the Baal Shem Tov, writes[15] that this is why the prayers have to be recited verbally and it is not sufficient for man simply to have the prayers in mind. Although God knows all thoughts, when a man gives verbal expression to his prayers he provides a 'vessel' through which the divine grace can flow to the material world, otherwise it would only be capable of flowing into the spiritual 'vessels' provided by thought. In his *Toledot Yaakov Yosef*,[16] the first Hasidic book to be printed, R. Jacob Joseph remarks that a prayer for man to cleave to God (where the question of the divine flow of blessing is not involved and is purely spiritual) can be simply thought of in the mind and requires no verbal expression.

The theme of prayer for the sake of God—more specifically, for the sake of the Shekhinah—is treated with variations in the classical Hasidic writings, of which a few examples should here be quoted.

All these are from early Hasidic works, but even at this early stage in the development of Hasidic thought there are differing emphases, so that one will look in vain for a consistent, systematic treatment acceptable to all the Hasidic masters.

R. Moses Hayim Ephraim of Sudlikov, grandson of the Baal Shem Tov, reports,[17] in the name of his grandfather, a comment on the Mishnah[18] that one should serve God without conditioning for reward. In some texts the reading is 'conditioning for no reward'. The Baal Shem Tov is reported as saying that both versions are correct and refer to different stages in the prayer life of man. There is an ebb and flow in man's life of prayer. It is not possible for him always to have the highest motives and conduct himself on the most elevated plane. The two versions are interpreted as referring to prayer but to two different stages, one higher than the other. Both versions refer to those who pray for the sake of God, not for themselves. One worshipper declares that God's will, not his own, be done. While he acknowledges that tradition demands that he entreat God to satisfy his needs, he accepts in love that God may not answer his prayers. His service is without conditioning for reward. It is simply his duty to pray, leaving the rest to God. The second stage in the life of prayer is still higher. Here the worshipper 'conditions for no reward'. He, too, prays for his own needs, since he is so obligated to do by the tradition, but he does not want his request to be granted. His true desire is always to be in a state of need so that he can come again and again before God to present his petition. The particular things he needs form only the excuse he has for praying to God. What really matters for him is the joy of approaching his Maker.

This parable can be given. A man is possessed of a powerful desire to commune with the king, his heart burning in longing for it to happen. The king decreed that whoever presents his requests to him will have them answered. This man, whose desire and longing it is to converse with the king, is apprehensive that, when he comes to present his request, the king will grant it and he will then have no further excuse for conversing with the king. He prefers that the king should not grant his request so that he will have good reason for coming again to the king and having once again the joy of conversing with him.

Another report in the name of the Baal Shem Tov[19] speaks of petitionary prayer as answered automatically:

> The main thing in prayer is the belief that God, blessed be His name, fills the whole earth with His glory. A man should also believe that his request is answered immediately as soon as he utters the formal words of the prayers. If you ask, how is it, then, that the request is not, in fact, granted? The answer is that the prayer is always answered but sometimes in a way hidden from men. For example, even though a man's particular request was for his own pain to be removed his prayer may be answered for the pain of the world to be lessened. And, in reality, it is for his own good or to cleanse him from sin and the like. For if a man has the intention of waiting for his prayers to be answered he introduces something corporeal into his prayers, whereas the proper thing is for them to be purely spiritual, for the sake of the Shekhinah and not for the sake of worldly things.

In this passage the magical power of petitionary prayer is stressed. No prayer goes unanswered but the answer is not necessarily personal. It may have an effect on the well-being of the world as a whole while, for various possible reasons, having no direct effect on the life of the petitioner himself. Since this is so, then it is futile for the worshipper always to expect a definite personal answer to his petition. Moreover, it is really undesirable for him to expect a personal answer. By so doing he introduces the note of selfhood and this frustrates the whole aim of prayer. The additional *motif* here is that the granting of the request for the world in general does not involve any catering to the ego. Consequently, petitionary prayer is not an exercise in futility and yet, at the same time, it is for the sake of God whose desire it is to benefit His creatures.

'For this let every man that is godly [*hasid*] pray' (Ps. 32:6). This verse was used[20] to summarise the aim of Hasidic prayer. 'This' (*zot*) represents the Shekhinah. Man should consider that whatever happens to him happens, as it were, to the Shekhinah. The events of the Hasid's personal life call attention to that which the Shekhinah lacks. If the Hasid finds himself to be sick in health, for example, he should reflect that God wants him to be well again, and until he recovers from his illness God's will is unfulfilled. His purpose, then, in praying for good health and a speedy recovery should be so that the Shekhinah will lack no more. The further mystical meaning of *zot* is said to be that the word represents the whole Sefirotic realm. The word *zot* is formed from the three letters *zayin, alef, tav*. Of the Ten Sefirot there are three 'higher' and seven 'lower'. The three 'higher' are: Keter ('Crown'), Hokhmah ('Wisdom'), Binah ('Understanding'). The seven 'lower' are: Hesed ('Lovingkindness'), Gevurah ('Power'), Tiferet ('Beauty'), Netzah ('Victory'), Hod ('Splendour'), Yesod ('Foundation') and Malkhut ('Sovereignty'). The three 'higher' Sefirot have to do with the divine thought; the seven 'lower' with the divine emotions, as it were, as manifesting that thought. Malkhut, or the Shekhinah, is the link between the Sefirotic realm and the worlds beneath. Into Malkhut there flows the divine grace so that, including itself, it is said in the Kabbalah to be called 'Bathsheba' (= *bat sheva*, 'daughter of seven') and from Malkhut the flow of blessing is transmitted to all creatures. Thus *zot*, containing the letters *zayin, alef, tav*, represents not alone the Shekhinah but the Shekhinah in its relationship with the whole of the Sefirotic realm as well as with the whole of creation. This is because the numerical value of *zayin* is seven, representing the seven 'lower' Sefirot, while *alef* and *tav*, the first and last letters of the Hebrew alphabet, represent the Shekhinah as the alpha and omega of all finite being. These letters are, in the Kabbalistic scheme, not mere symbols but the form assumed here on earth by those spiritual forces on high that God uses in His creative activity. The purpose of prayer is to elevate these spiritual forces inherent in the letters, to bring them back to their Source and by so doing restore all creation to the divine 'Nothing' whence it came. When this takes place all is blessed unity. Complete harmony is promoted in the Sefirotic realm and the divine grace can freely flow. The *alef* and the *tav* are united with the seven Sefirot and the Shekhinah becomes whole. 'For this [*zot*] let every Hasid pray.' The Hasid should have this in mind when he prays and his prayers will then be for the sake of the Shekhinah. Furthermore, he should have in mind that the letter *tav*, the final letter of the alphabet, represents the ultimate extent of the Shekhinah's influence, while the letter *zayin* represents the seven stages of the Sefirotic flow. All this should be connected in the mind of the worshipper with the letter *alef* (the middle letter of the word *zot*). This represents *En Sof*, the Limitless, God as He is in Himself, the Ground of all being from which the Sefirot emanate. The letters of the word *alef* (*alef, lamed, pe*), when transposed, form the word *pele*, 'marvel'. Thus the whole of creation is raised, as it were, to its source in *deus absconditus*, the Marvel and Mystery behind all things and in which all things have their being.

The implications of this intricate but not untypical comment are that, whatever prayers are offered, the worshipper should not be concerned at all with the personal aspects of his petition but with the power of the letters through which unity and harmony is achieved. The worshipper is engaged in assisting God's creative processes. From this way of looking at it, unlike the other descriptions of prayer for the sake of the Shekhinah, petitionary prayer is virtually rejected except for its formal letters which, in fact, mean something quite other than the plain meaning of the words formed from them. It must be repeated that early Hasidic thought is not in the nature of a complete system. More than one way of coping with the basic problems is found in the early Hasidic writings.

For all the various interpretations given to it, however, there is no reason to doubt that the basic doctrine of prayer for the sake of the Shekhinah is an authentic doctrine of the Baal Shem Tov. R. Moses Hayim Ephraim of Sudlikov reports this, as we have seen, in the name of the Baal Shem Tov and he returns to the theme again and again, as do other Hasidic writers, in the name of the Baal Shem Tov. Elsewhere[21] R. Moses Hayim Ephraim writes:

> The matter has to be understood on the basis of the saying of my master, my grandfather, his soul is in Eden, may his memory be for the life of the world to come, that all things derive, as it were, from the Shekhinah. A man should know that whatever he lacks is a lack in the Shekhinah, blessed be He and blessed be His name. With breadth of knowledge he (the Baal Shem Tov) illumined our eyes in this matter. Consequently, all prayer should have as its aim that the Shekhinah's lack should be filled, as it were, and man's own needs will automatically be satisfied. This is the

meaning of the saying that the righteous are the deputies of the Matrona, for when the righteous experience any lack they know that, corresponding to their own, there is a lack in the Shekhinah, and they cause the Shekhinah to attain to complete unification.

This is how the Baal Shem Tov is said to have solved[22] the contradiction between two passages in the Zohar. In one passage it is said that whoever does not pray for his sustenance daily is of little faith. But in another passage scorn is poured on those who bark like dogs begging for food. The solution is that man should not beg for his food solely for his own sake. Man's experience of lack of food is due to his vital soul. Since this vitality is, in reality, that of the Shekhinah, he should pray for the pain experienced, as it were, by his vital soul, which is only another way of saying that he should pray for the sake of the Shekhinah.

A realistic note is sounded in the writings of R. Jacob Joseph of Pulnoye in the name of R. Menahem Mendel of Bar.[23] A man's troubles may be so heavy that he cannot rise above them to forget himself in praying solely for the sake of the Shekhinah. At such times, rather than pretend to himself that he is indifferent to his own pain, a man should be honest enough to offer his petitionary prayers in their plain and simple meaning, that is for his own needs to be satisfied. R. Menahem Mendel of Bar was an associate of the Baal Shem Tov, evidently a member of the latter's circle, but with independent views. It seems that the doctrine of prayer for the sake of the Shekhinah was taught in the circle of the Baal Shem Tov, with each subsequent teacher interpreting the doctrine in his own way, so that in some early Hasidic writings the prayer for personal needs was ruthlessly rejected while in others some concession was made to human frailty.

The Maggid of Meseritch, disciple and successor of the Baal Shem Tov, when dealing with the theme of prayer for the sake of God, gives[24] a curious turn to the verse, 'He will fulfil the desire of those who fear Him' (Ps. 145: 19). The word *yaaseh*, translated as 'fulfil', can mean 'He will make'. The Maggid translates the verse 'He will make the desire of those who fear Him' to yield the thought that the righteous have no will of their own. Selfhood is so little pronounced among the righteous that they have no desires. But since God wishes the righteous to pray to Him, He puts into their hearts a desire for worldly things which otherwise they would never have, so that they might turn to Him.

> God makes those who fear Him to have a desire, for prayer is called 'desire'. God puts this desire to pray for something into man's heart, for of himself the God-fearing man would have no desire to pray at all to ask God for anything since 'there is no want to them that fear Him' [Ps. 34: 10]. The God-fearing man says 'enough' to whatever God gives him. Consequently, God puts the thought of prayer into man's heart for He desires man's prayers. Therefore, the verse concludes: 'and He hears their cry and saves them' [Ps. 145: 19].

Elsewhere[25] the Maggid is reported as teaching:

> Behold, when a man prays, God forbid that he should direct all his desire towards that corporeal thing for which he asks but he should rather have the following in mind. Our Rabbis say that the cow wishes to feed the calf more than the calf wishes to be fed. This means that a giver has a greater desire to give than the beneficiary of his bounty has the desire to receive. So it is with God. His delight in benefiting His creatures is greater than that of the creatures He benefits.

In other words, petitionary prayer should be to please God in His role as Giver. The worshipper, knowing that God has this desire to give, should ask but not for his own sake. The paradox of petitionary prayer is that the request is real and the satisfaction of man's needs guaranteed. But the true worshipper sees it all as the fulfilment of God's purpose. In the act of receiving, or requesting to receive, the righteous man becomes a giver because he assists God to attain His desire to be a Giver.

A further elaboration of the theme found in early Hasidic writings is that, since the righteous pray for the sake of the Shekhinah, then their prayers for different particular things such as health, sustenance and wisdom are not for the different satisfactions of their own needs but are all for the lack in the Shekhinah evidenced in their own needs. The result is that all petitionary prayer, no matter how varied in relation to its particular requests, is basically one simple prayer, that the lack in the Shekhinah be filled. R. Zeev Wolf of Zhitomer, disciple of the Maggid of Meseritch, finds this idea[26] in the verse, 'One thing have I asked of the Lord' (Ps. 27: 4).

> You can see that, since a man's chief aim when he pours out his speech in prayer and supplication is only for the sake of the exile of the Shekhinah, it follows that he has only one request.
> Even when many evil events and happenings befall him, yet the many requests for them to be eased are only a single request. This is that he experiences in all these evil happenings the clothing of the limbs of the Shekhinah. It is to this that his aim and his efforts are directed, to elevate them to their source, and he senses nothing of his own needs. It is otherwise when a man senses his own physical sorrows in all the many details of the events and happenings which befall him. His requests are numerous in proportion to the different kinds of sorrow he experiences all the time.

Reference must here be made to the valuable analysis of this theme of prayer for the sake of the Shekhinah by Rivka Schatz Uffenheimer.[27] She rightly sees in the doctrine the strong element of quietism in early Hasidic thought and she points to similar ideas in Christian quietism. Father Ronald Knox, for instance, in a chapter on Quietism, describes the very same problem:[28]

> But it is more important to ask, in view of the Quietist controversy, what is the attitude of the mystics towards the prayer which asks favours, temporal or spiritual, for ourselves? Here a new principle emerges. The prayer of petition does, in any case, tend to disappear, or rather to be merged in the stream of contemplation. But, more than that—in proportion as the soul becomes united to God, its will becomes united to his, and the objects of ambition (spiritual, no less than temporal) are seen rather as something that must be left to him by an exercise of holy indifference than as something we must secure from him at all costs.

The passivity of the mystic appears to be a universal tendency but the Hasidim were Orthodox Jews and traditionally Judaism is activist and, as we have noted, petitionary prayer occupies an important place in the traditional liturgy. That is why there is so much tension in this matter among the Hasidic masters, the ideal of mystical contemplation and loss of selfhood pulling one way, the demands of the tradition pulling the other.

Rivka Schatz Uffenheimer sees the most extreme attitude of quietism in the Maggid of Meseritch. Although, as we have seen, many of the early Hasidic masters favour the doctrine of prayer for the sake of the Shekhinah, nowhere is personal need more negated than in the teachings attributed to the Maggid, even though some of his disciples tend to soften his rigours. The fact is that nowhere in the works containing the teachings of the Maggid himself do we find any leniency. It is simply forbidden for a man to ask for his own needs, only for the needs of the Shekhinah. Nowhere in the works of the Maggid do we find the kind of distinction made by R. Jacob Joseph of Pulnoye that when a man is weighed down with sufferings he should have his own personal needs in mind when he prays.

The Hasidic ideal then is contemplative prayer in which the Hasid practises self-annihilation. Petitionary prayer is not only accepted but is binding by the tradition. Yet this aspect of prayer is so interpreted by many teachers that it, too, is an important part of contemplative prayer. On this they are virtually all agreed. Where they differ is in the extent to which selfhood can and should be transcended in the prayer of petition.

Thus far we have been examining early Hasidic thought on prayer. In later Hasidism all these ideas are somewhat softened or even overlooked entirely. There is no longer any detailed consideration of whether prayer should be active or passive, with selfhood or without it. The later Hasidic teachers were familiar with the ideas presented in the classical Hasidic texts, but tended to suggest that many of these were only intended for the spiritual supermen of 'those times', not for the spiritual pygmies of 'our day'. But purity of intention is still insisted upon even in the much later Hasidic works and the ideal of self-annihilation in prayer is never completely abandoned.

In the interesting document *Tzav Ve-Ziruz*, compiled by R. Kalonymus Kalman Spira of Piatzina, a Hasidic master who flourished in pre-war Poland and who was murdered by the Nazis, the rabbi gives his young followers advice on how to purify their hearts for God's worship. He advises them to offer, from time to time, a private prayer to God to assist them in their task. While he is averse to writing such private devotions for them, he gives the following as an example.[29] In this private devotion we have as good an example as any of how the ideal of prayer finds its expression in more or less contemporary Hasidism.

Sovereign of the universe! Thou hast created me out of nothing and Thou hast formed all my body, my spirit and my soul. Thou seest how great is my longing to stand in Thy presence with a pure and refined soul which senses Thy will and meditates on Thy thoughts. In the innermost recesses of her heart Thy voice is heard. But how great is the sickness of my heart within me because of her coarseness. She experiences foreign sensations and desires gross things. Instead of becoming a golden bell whose sound is heard on entering the holy place, the voice of a wicked man is heard in her, towards which she rises and bestirs herself. Even when I rise and strengthen myself to drive away every unworthy sensation and desire and to silence the voice of the wicked which springs out to call, it is only from my mind and my heart that I succeed in driving them away, but they remain in my soul.

Sovereign of the universe! Pure and Purifying! How exceedingly does my heart melt within me when I consider that if it is only his house or his courtyard that a man cleanses yet does he throw out the rubbish and places it far away from where he resides. Yet when I try to purify my whole essence and being, to sate my soul with delights, to bathe her and cleanse her before the the Lord of eternity, the Pure, whose ministers are pure, higher than all names and attributes, I succeed only in hiding the filth on the surface but it still pushes in to enter my innermost self. I become loathsome and filthy in my own eyes because of the ugly stock that has accumulated in my innermost self. My soul swells and is puffed out ready to burst so as to drown me, God forbid, in the waters of presumptuousness, when the time comes. Even at this moment this thought or that lust (it is proper to mention this explicitly) has bestirred itself within me. It is very bitter to me when I reflect that even though I can prevail over it, with Thy help, and refuse to allow it to achieve its aim, yet my soul has not been cleansed and it will appear again from time to time, whether as a thought or as a lust. O Lord purify my soul! Remove the evil inclination from me! Cast away the evil part of my soul to a place in which it will not be mentioned and not visit me and never enter my heart again, not now and not when I grow old.

Especially when I attain to a state of greatness of soul at the time of studying the Torah and prayer and so forth, when my soul has the merit of ascending to the Throne of Thy Glory, let my soul be clean and pure to become clothed with the pure white garments provided by the light of the precepts, and to fly aloft in yearning and longing to be annihilated and embraced by the unity of the One God.

In view of all that has been said, the opinion, encouraged, unfortunately, by popular works on Hasidism, that the movement hailed the prayers of the unsophisticated offered in simple faith, needs to be drastically revised. It is true that there are Hasidic tales about the Baal Shem Tov and his followers refusing to reject the prayers of the untutored, but such tales are not peculiar to Hasidism and are found even among the Lurianic Kabbalists who certainly favoured, as we shall see later, highly sophisticated techniques of contemplation in prayer.[30] These tales mean no more than that the leaders of the movement, with their stress on inwardness and concern for the masses, believed that God accepted every true prayer even if it was confused and in error. But this was because nothing higher could have been expected from the heroes of these tales. The Hasid, if he was capable of it, was expected to rise to much higher realms in his prayers and for him the simple prayer was most emphatically not enough.

For instance, the story is told[31] of the Baal Shem Tov that it once happened that there was a severe drought. The people fasted and cried out to God, but all to no avail. The Baal Shem Tov noticed, however, that 'a certain person belonging to the ignorant and the simple folk' was reciting the Shema and when he recited the verse 'and He shut up the heaven, so that there shall be no rain' (Deut. 11: 17), he said it 'with great concentration'. The Baal Shem Tov asked him what he had in mind when reciting the verse. The man replied that he thought the verse meant 'and He shall squeeze out the heaven, so that there shall be no rain (left there)'. Because of this prayer all the prayers of the people were answered and the rains came.

For the Creator, blessed be His name, searches the heart and knows all its secrets and it is the heart that He wants. That is why the words of this man were so pleasant to Him since his prayers were recited with such great concentration of the heart and were so true and inwardly sincere, and his prayers were answered.

In this and in all such similar tales it is emphasised that the hero was an ignorant but devout man, one who could do no better. It is nowhere suggested that the Hasid with spiritual aspirations dare rest content with simple, untutored prayer. On the contrary, as we have seen, Hasidic prayer belongs to the group of mystical exercises of a most rigorous nature through which the self is transcended.

CHAPTER III

The Hasidic Prayer Book and Prayer House

One of the chief complaints of the Mitnaggedim, the opponents of the Hasidic movement, was that the Hasidim, in their conventicles, used the Lurianic Prayer Book instead of the older Prayer Book hallowed by tradition in the Ashkenazi communities of Russia and Poland. In this chapter we must examine what the Lurianic Prayer Book is, how it differs from the standard Prayer Book and why the Hasidim adopted it.

R. Isaac Luria (1534–72), the famous Safed Kabbalist and originator of a new Kabbalistic system, placed great stress on the doctrine of *kavvanot*, 'intentions'. According to the Kabbalah, God's creative processes are all by means of numerous combinations of the divine name. Since, in the Kabbalah, it is man who can affect the cosmic processes by his deeds and thoughts, it follows that if man has these divine names and their combinations in mind when he prays he performs the tremendous task of sending upwards those impulses which help to promote greater harmony in the Sefirotic realm, and by so doing he succeeds in bringing down the resulting flow of divine grace and blessing. The words of the Prayer Book, composed, as the Kabbalists and traditional Jews generally saw it, by divinely inspired men, mean, say the Kabbalists, much more than appears on the surface. In reality, they are put together so that the initiate is able to have in mind, when he recites them in his prayers, the various combinations of divine names. Now the members of the Lurianic school altered to some extent the Sephardi Prayer Book then in vogue in Palestine in such a way that all its words would give the fullest expression to the Kabbalistic mysteries. The worshipper was then able to use the Lurianic Prayer Book with the correct 'intentions' in mind and so dwell in his mystical contemplation on the whole complex scheme in which the divine names are hinted at in the words of the prayers. These are the *kavvanot*. To what extent the Hasidic masters themselves practised the *kavvanot* will be discussed in a later chapter. Here it should be said that whether they practised them or not, i.e. whether or not they had them in mind when reciting their prayers, all the Hasidim believed that the words, and the *kavvanot* implied in them, did have the effect attributed to them in the Lurianic Kabbalah; hence their need for a Prayer Book containing the right words in the right order from the Kabbalistic point of view. Consequently, they preferred the usage of the Lurianic Prayer Book to the standard Ashkenazi Prayer Book used by the Jews of Russia and Poland. The Mitnaggedim themselves generally believed in the efficacy of the *kavvanot* but objected to the usage of the Hasidim on three main counts. First, it was, they held, forbidden to depart from tradition, and the Ashkenazi tradition held fast to the Ashkenazi Prayer Book. Secondly, the use of a different Prayer Book in separate conventicles encouraged the spirit of division in the community. Thirdly, and most important of all, the Mitnaggedim were prepared to tolerate the use of the Lurianic Prayer Book by small groups of real Kabbalistic initiates, but believed that it was nothing less than overweening pride and arrogance for that Prayer Book to be used by the masses, as the Hasidim advocated.

Obviously sociological motivations were involved on both sides of the fierce debate; the Kahal, the body of community leaders, anxious for its authority to be accepted unquestioningly, and the Hasidim equally concerned to throw off the yoke of the Kahal's domination. But theological justification was required for what was in those days a radical departure from tradition. The justification was attempted by the Maggid of Meseritch, the organising genius of the Hasidic movement. But the Maggid was by no means the first to adopt the Lurianic rite. From all the accounts it appears certain that the associates of the Baal Shem Tov prided themselves on this innovation. Hasidic legend[1] tells how one of these, R. Nahman of Kosov, once entered a synagogue and led the prayers, without asking permission to do so, and he used the Lurianic version. The people protested at R. Nahman's daring in changing from the version 'in which our fathers and their fathers prayed and they were the great men of their generation'. R. Nahman replied, 'How do you know that they are in the Garden of Eden?' The Maggid, however, was the first, so far as we know, to attempt an elaborate theological justification for the departure from tradition.

Prayer, the Maggid is reported as teaching,[2] is the ladder with its feet on earth and its head reaching to the heavens. Each tribe has its own gateway to heaven. That is to say, there are twelve different ways of combining the words of the prayers to produce various divine names and since there are twelve tribes there are twelve different versions of the Prayer Book. The effects to be produced on high depend in large measure on the particular quality of soul of the worshipper and this depends in turn on his descent from this or that tribe. A man descended from the tribe of Reuben is obliged to use the *kavvanot* implied in a given order of words suitable to the nature of a Reubenite soul and so forth. The ideal, then, is for each tribe to use its own version of the Prayer Book. This was, in fact, the original situation and explains why there are so many different versions of the Prayer Book. But, nowadays, no one knows to which tribe he belongs. The Lurianic Prayer Book can help him here because this was so drawn up that it provides a general gateway to heaven through which the souls of members of all tribes can ascend. The Lurianic Prayer Book is the thirteenth gate through which all the tribes can enter.[3]

The Hasidic Prayer Book[4] is, in fact, composed of three elements: (1) the Polish Ashkenazi version in use at the time of the rise of Hasidism; (2) the Lurianic Prayer Book; (3) the older pre-Lurianic Sephardi Prayer Book used in Palestine in Luria's day upon which the Lurianic Prayer Book is based. Luria adopted the Sephardi Prayer Book for the purpose of the *kavvanot*. But the

Hasidim, who lived in an Ashkenazi *milieu*, were obliged to adapt the Lurianic forms to the Ashkenazi Prayer Book, which differs from the Sephardi Prayer Book in both the versions of the prayers and in the arrangement of the prayers. Thus it came about that the Hasidic Prayer Book differed from the older Sephardi rite, from the original Lurianic rite and from the older Ashkenazi Prayer Book. The ideal Hasidic Prayer Book would have been a careful blending of all three elements to suit the purposes of the new movement. But the truth is that these three elements were never combined in a consistent way and there is, in fact, no uniform Hasidic Prayer Book. Nor can we overlook the numerous printing errors which crept into editions of the Hasidic Prayer Book. Among the Prayer Books used by the Hasidim in the early period were: the *Kol Yaakov* of R. Kopel of Meseritch; the *Siddur* of R. Shabbetai Rashkover; and the *Siddur Ha-Rav* of R. Shneor Zalman of Liady. This latter was the first Hasidic Prayer Book proper. Later Hasidic masters tried their hand at producing Hasidic Prayer Books. Some kept to the Ashkenazi rite with very few changes, others introduced many Sephardi elements even when these were not demanded by the doctrine of the *kavvanot*. The late Hasidic master R. Hayim Lazar Spira of Munkacs (1868–1937)[5] complains bitterly of the introduction of Sephardi elements over and above those appertaining to the *kavvanot*. This author writes:[6]

> Therefore, I cannot discover the reason why some Zaddikim and some Hasidim changed a good deal of the Prayer Book. This applies also to some of our teachers and elders who preceded us, may their merits shield us, who added much in the prayer of the Eighteen Benedictions and took no care with regard to the number of words. Most of these additions are taken from the version of the Sephardim who are known as the Franks. In reality we never accepted this. On the contrary, it is forbidden for us Ashkenazim to change over to the afore-mentioned Sephardi version. It is only that we have a tradition from our masters, the disciples of the holy Baal Shem Tov, may his merits shield us, to pray in accordance with the Lurianic version . . . It is permitted to change over from any other version to this one . . . But it is not permitted to add from the version of the Sephardim (the Franks) where the *Ari* [Luria] of blessed memory did not command us so to do.

The substitution of the Lurianic Prayer Book for the traditional one is a constant cause of offence to the Mitnaggedim. The complaint appears in practically all the anti-Hasidic documents.[7] The Mitnaggedim were prepared to tolerate the use of the Lurianic rite for the few mature Kabbalists. In the anti-Hasidic proclamation issued at Brody in Galicia in 1772 an express exception was made for the Kabbalists in the *stiebel* (conventicle) in the *klaus* of Brody. But for the immature, argued the Mitnaggedim, it was strictly forbidden both to set up such conventicles and to use the Lurianic Prayer Book. For the light it throws on the whole polemic the Brody proclamation (written in Yiddish) must be quoted in part:[8]

> These people [the Hasidim] who create new customs for themselves build for themselves high places[9] so as to be apart from the holy community. They form separate *minyanim*[10] and do not pray with the rest of the community in the synagogues and houses of learning set aside for public use. They depart from the coinage of prayer, coined by the great Codifiers responsible for the order of prayer in these lands. And these same people taunt and insult the the angels of God [the rabbis]. They allow the correct time for the recitation of the Shema and the Prayers to go by. Especially, do they change the version of the Prayer Book to one that is not in use in these lands. This prayer Book [the Ashkenazi] has been instituted by the great scholars of old so that it is forbidden to turn aside from it either to the right or the left. Nowadays, one finds these wicked men, sinners with their bodies, of incomparable wickedness. They cast off the yoke, forsaking eternal life only to indulge all day in song. They form themselves into groups and sects. They despise the Oral Law in general and declare that they study only the Kabbalah. They use in their prayers the Prayer Book of the man of God, the holy *Ari*, of blessed memory, and, without doubt, they are guilty of lopping off the branches. . . .[11] Therefore, the above-mentioned holy community issues a great and terrible anathema . . . that from this day onwards God forbid that any change should be made from the Ashkenazi version of the Prayer Book in any synagogue or in any of the *minyanim* which are allowed in private houses by the laws of our community. It goes without saying that no one must have the temerity to use the Prayer Book of the godly *Ari*, his memory for the life of the world to come, or of any of the other Kabbalists into whose secret counsel the souls of these wicked men have not been admitted.

God forbid, too, that any man should use in his prayers any other Prayer Book than that of the Ashkenazim, which we have by tradition from the scholars of old, with the exception of the remnant called by God, who pray in the first *stiebel* at the side of the *klaus* in our community. It is clear beyond doubt that the men who have set aside that place for their prayers are full of the revealed learning, the Talmud and the Codes, and they have made progress, too, and have acquired fame in the secret learning of the Kabbalah. These have used the Prayer Book of the *Ari*, of blessed memory, for many a long year, and they followed their custom in the presence of the rabbis of old, the famous great scholars of our community, who did not prevent them from following their custom because it was known that from their youth they studied, in the main, Talmud and Codes. And they were outstanding in piety, knowing their Master and having the correct intentions [*kavvanot*]. These famous men referred to are permitted to pray, as is their custom, out of the Prayer Book of the holy man of God, the *Ari*, may his memory be for a blessing, but no one else is allowed so to do. Outside that *stiebel*, God forbid that any *minyan* should alter even one letter of the Askkenazi version of the Prayer Book. They should have nothing at all to do with the secret wisdom. Nor should they follow any of the Sephardi customs, only the customs of this land. God forbid that we should change any of the customs of our fathers. Furthermore, our concession [to the men of the *stiebel*] only applies to men of thirty years and over. But God forbid that any under the age of thirty should attach themselves to the above-mentioned *stiebel*.

The Hasidic reply was forthcoming in a letter by R. Eleazar son of the Hasidic master R. Elimelech of Lizensk, disciple of the Maggid of Meseritch. This letter was first published as an Appendix to the first edition of R. Elimelech's *Noam Elimelekh* (Lemberg, 1788) and has appeared in all subsequent editions of the work.[12] The part of the letter relevant to our theme reads:

I asked my master, my father, my teacher and mentor, may his light shine, to tell me the reason why we have altered the standard version of the Prayer Book. This was his reply. Behold, the *Bet Yosef*,[13] of blessed memory, who is the foremost of the Codifiers, of blessed memory, quotes these versions [of Luria]. Afterwards, the *Rama*,[14] of blessed memory, who is also first of all the Codifiers, came and he investigated and introduced all the rules for the generality of Israel. He saw what a great illumination is contained in this version [of Luria], so great that the world is unworthy to use it, so that he established for us the Ashkenazi version which applies to all men of our degree. But he certainly did not intend to prevent the Zaddikim, who have cleansed themselves from filth and who are strict with themselves to a hair'sbreadth, from using the version recorded by the *Bet Yosef,* of blessed memory. And both these and these are the words of the living God.

It can be seen that R. Elimelech is more circumspect than his teacher, the Maggid. While the Maggid declares that it is the Lurianic version that is applicable to all (*davar ha-shaveh le-khol nefesh*), R. Elimelech uses this very same term of the Ashkenazi version. It is, basically, according to R. Elimelech, only the Zaddikim who are worthy of using the Lurianic version. But in that case, R. Elimelech goes on to ask, what justification is there for the ordinary Hasidim to use the Lurianic version? 'If you will ask, behold, there are many people who have not reached the degree of which I have spoken and who, none the less, use this version in their prayers and who attach themselves to the elevated Hasidim and they themselves are called Hasidim?' His reply is that Israel believed in the Lord and in His servant Moses (Exod. 14: 31). By believing in Moses ordinary folk have a share in the elevated stage of prophecy to which Moses had attained. By the same token those who have faith in the Zaddik and are attached to him have a share in his sanctity and are, therefore, allowed to use the Lurianic version even though, basically, its use is only sanctioned for the Zaddikim. Thus the use of the Hasidic Prayer Book served to advance the cause of Zaddikism, of which R. Elimelech was one of the most vigorous exponents.

However, R. Eleazar is evidently not too convinced of the force of his father's argument. He continues that if anyone does not accept this notion of sharing the Zaddik's sanctity he can still use the Lurianic version if he purifies himself from sin, and R. Eleazar gives detailed instruction on how this may be achieved. He concludes that once a worshipper has tasted the fragrance of the Lurianic version he will never again be able to use any other. Even though people will contend with him for using this version he will ignore them and suffer rather than give it up.

Because of their opposition to the ideas of the general community and their adoption of the special Prayer Book, the Hasidim were forced to congregate in their small *stiebels*. This was a constant offence mentioned in the trenchant diatribes of the Mitnaggedim, as we have seen. [15] Eventually, the Hasidim made a virtue of necessity. To this day the Hasidim, on the whole, prefer prayer in the homely and informal *stiebel* to prayer in a large synagogue. A further reason for the later use of the *stiebel* was that the Hasidim of a particular dynasty would be found in small groups in many of the larger towns and, not being able to afford to purchase a large synagogue, which in any event would be too large for their needs, preferred to hire a small room where like-minded folk could worship together.[16] In the 'court' of the Zaddik a large synagogue was far from being an unusual feature.

Although the traditional preference is for prayer to be recited in the large synagogue of the town and is opposed to worship in small conventicles, the Hasidim were able to point to a Responsum by the famous sixteenth-century legal authority R. David Ibn Abi Zimra in which the importance of like-minded persons worshipping together overrides the advantages of worship in a large congregation.[17] This responsum deals with a group which separated itself from the general community to pray, together with their teacher, in a synagogue of their own. The Hasidim were able to use the fortuitous references to the 'teacher' and adapt these to the Hasidic Zaddik. The responsum has such an uncanny resemblance to the particular needs of the Hasidim that, were it not for its undoubted authenticity, one would imagine it to have been invented by a contemporary Hasid.

The Responsum in question declares:

> We read in the Talmud that one should not rise to offer prayer when one has been joking or in a frivolous state of mind or gossiping or quarrelling or in a bad temper. We read further that R. Hanina would refuse to pray on a day on which he had lost his temper. We read further that no man should offer his prayers unless his mind is serene. We read further that Samuel would not pray in a house in which there was beer because the smell of the beer would disturb him and prevent him from concentrating on his prayers. From all this you can learn that a man should offer

his prayers neither in a place in which his thoughts are disturbed nor at a time when his powers of concentration are set at naught. Consequently, if an individual or a number of persons are in a state of enmity or bad temper or hatred or contention with the community, their prayers are unacceptable and it is forbidden for them to pray there [in the synagogue of the community] since his [the individual worshipper at loggerheads with the community] thoughts are disturbed and he is unable to concentrate on his prayers. It applies all the more if they [the members of the community] are always in the habit of vexing him to his face and all the more if the cause of the vexation concerns the leaders of the congregation. Were I not afraid I would go so far as to say that it is better for a man to recite his prayers in private than to pray together with people with whom he cannot get on. There is another reason, too, why a man should only pray in a place which his heart desires. The reason for this is that when a man gazes at someone with whom he is on friendly terms his soul is awakened to concentrate adequately, his mind is enlarged and his heart is gladdened. The spirit of the Lord can then rest upon him, as prophecy declares. In the books of wisdom it is further declared that when a man has his teacher in mind and directs his heart to him then his soul becomes bound to the soul of his teacher and some of the flow of grace that belongs to the teacher rests upon the disciple. The disciple then acquires an additional soul, which they [the Kabbalists] call 'the mystery of impregnation while both master and disciple are alive'. This is referred to in the verse, 'But thine eyes shall see thy teacher' [Isa. 30: 20] and this is the meaning of, 'That they may stand there with thee . . . and I will take of the spirit which is upon thee, and will put it upon them' [Num. 11: 17]. And so our holy master [R. Judah the Prince] used to pray that if he could only have seen the face of his teacher he would have reached a most elevated stage. All the more if the teacher has the same intention so that one calls to the other, this one to give, the other to receive. It is for this reason that R. Jose said that a man does not have the merit of learning the Torah from everyone. On the basis of this the rabbis permit a man to go away to study the Torah even if his father forbids him to go, so that by going he disobeys his father. For a man does not have the merit of learning the Torah from everyone. This very reason applies to prayer. For when a man looks at his friend or his relative or his teacher or one who pleases him, his soul is awakened to an elevated degree of concentration and an additional spirit from on high rests upon him. This matter is attested to by the intellect.

Many of the Hasidim, especially in the early days of the movement, attended the courts of the Zaddikim or associated with the Hasidic groups in defiance of both their parents and the community leaders. It must have been encouraging to the rebels to find an acknowledged legal authority of the standing of R. David Ibn Abi Zimra giving them a clear dispensation to form their own congregations for prayer even when this involved separation from the community and disregard of the fifth commandment.

CHAPTER IV

Preparations for Prayer

Preparation (*hakhanah*, plural *hakhanot*, 'preparations') for prayer occupies an important role in Hasidic life. Precisely because prayer had so important a role to play it should not be engaged in, taught the Hasidim, without eager anticipation beforehand. Prayer had to be preceded by a period of preparation during which the mind would be cleared of unworthy thoughts and the body cleansed of impurities. The Hasidic preparations were arduous in the extreme. The thoughts of the worshipper were to be directed to God through prior contemplation, and the bowels were to be evacuated. Among the earliest Hasidim the use of tobacco was advocated to achieve both these aims. For many of the Hasidim all this was so important that the Talmudic rules regarding the special times for prayer were overlooked. These teachers held that unless a prayer was preceded by adequate preparation it was no prayer at all so that, as Hasidic legend has it, the Hasidim could argue that while they offered their prayers at too late an hour, and so offended against the law, the offence of the Mitnaggedim was worse in that they did not pray at all. If the Hasidim were guilty of prayer without time, the Mitnaggedim were guilty of time without prayer.[1]

The idea that prayer requires preparation is found in a number of Talmudic passages. The Mishnah[2] states that one should only pray in a serious frame of mind and that the Hasidim of old used to wait an hour before praying in order to attune their hearts to God. The fact that the term Hasidim is used in the Mishnah for these pious men of old must have encouraged the followers of the Baal Shem Tov in their practice of special preparation for prayer. The cleansing of the body before prayer is also strongly advocated in the Talmud.[3] There it is said that if a man needs to ease himself and yet recites his prayers without doing so, his prayer is an abomination. A proof-text is quoted, 'Prepare to meet thy God, O Israel' (Amos 4: 12). The verse 'Guard thy foot when thou goest to the house of God' (Eccles. 4: 17) is interpreted to mean, 'Guard thy orifices at the time when thou art standing in prayer before Me'. These rules were formulated in the standard Code, the Shulhan Arukh.[4] Both Hasidim and Mitnaggedim knew of these sources, of course, and relied on them. Where the Hasidim differed was in the extremes to which they took these measures to the consternation of their opponents. On the other hand, the Talmud states explicitly that immersion in a ritual bath (*mikveh*) is not required before prayer,[5] but the Hasidim attached great importance[6] to ritual immersion, especially as a preparation for prayer.

Mention must also be made of the donning of a girdle around the loins for prayer. Quoting the above-mentioned verse, 'Prepare to meet thy God, O Israel' (Amos 4: 12), the Talmud[7] states that it is proper to wear a girdle around the loins when praying. The French medieval scholars, the Tosafists, in their comment on this passage, remark, that the reason is so that there should be a division between the heart and the genitals. Consequently, they conclude that 'nowadays,' i.e. in medieval France, since in any event a belt is worn around the trousers, no special girdle is required for prayer. None the less, the Shulhan Arukh[8] rules that even if one does wear a belt one is obliged to wear a special girdle for prayer on the basis of the verse in Amos. The general custom in Russia and Poland was, however, to follow the ruling of the Tosafists, and a special girdle for prayer was not normally worn. Eventually, all the Hasidim took to wearing a special girdle for prayer (nowadays fashioned from twined silk), though it is not at all clear when the practice was first introduced. There does not seem to be any reference to it in the early Hasidic sources, nor is it mentioned in the anti-Hasidic polemics. In a work attributed to R. Menahem Mendel of Rymanov (d. 1815)[9] the Hasidic practice is said to be hinted at in the verse, 'And righteousness shall be the girdle of his loins, and faithfulness the girdle of his reins' (Isa. 11: 5). Two girdles (i.e. the ordinary belt and the special prayer girdle) are necessary, the second representing 'faithfulness', the Hasid's special reminder of his faith as he stands to pray.

In the matter of dress for prayer it was also an early Hasidic practice to avoid wearing any garment made of wool. The reason behind this curious custom was that a garment containing both wool and flax (*shaatnez*, see Deut. 21: 11), if worn by the worshipper, prevented his prayers from soaring heavenwards. In order to avoid the slightest suspicion or risk of this happening the Hasidim took to wearing at prayer only garments containing no wool. Wertheim[10] quotes a number of comparatively late sources in which this Hasidic custom is recorded but conjectures that the practice is much earlier. In fact, R. Avigdor ben Hayim of Pinsk, the fiery opponent of Hasidism, in his counts against the Hasidim presented to the Russian Government in 1800–1, accuses the Hasidim of departing from the Jewish tradition 'in their prayers and even in the garments they wear, for they do not wear wollen garments', and that is why, he remarks, they are referred to as a 'sect' (*kat*).[11]

The exaggerated preparations for prayer by the Hasidim were attacked in many of the anti-Hasidic polemics.[12] For example, the following is said in the pamphlet with the typically flowery title *Zemir Aritzim Ve-Harevot Tzurim* ('The Song of the Terrible Ones and Knives of Flint'), published in Alexsnitz near Brody in 1772:[13]

'They (the Hasidim) do not awaken the dawn with their prayers for they say that their throat is parched[14] and that they cannot offer their prayers until they have removed their dunghill to cleanse themselves from their filth so that their prayer should not be an abomination, and until they have placed incense in their nostrils[15] and the herb which produces as much smoke as the smoke of a furnace.

The same pamphlet quotes from a letter written in Vilna in 1772 in which it is said,[16] 'They [the Hasidim] wait many hours before reciting their prayers until the correct time for reciting the Shema and even the prayers [which can be recited at a later time] has passed by and they spend all their days in the smoke which proceeds from their mouth.' It was not only with regard to the morning prayer that the Hasidim allowed the proper time to go by. Some of them, at least, used to recite the afternoon prayer after nightfall. David of Makov, the preacher against Hasidism, complains in his *Zemir Aritizim* (1798), of the Hasidic leader R. Israel of Koznitz that he used to recite the afternoon prayer after the stars had come out.[17] The same writer complains of R. Isaac, the 'Seer' of Lublin, that on the Days of Awe he disregarded the times of the afternoon prayers.[18]

R. Hayim of Volozhyn (1749–1821), disciple of the chief opponent of Hasidism, the Gaon of Vilna, compiled his *Nefesh Ha-Hayim* as a counterblast to the Hasidim. On the subject of excessive preparation for prayer, R. Hayim writes:[19]

Now see the ways of the evil inclination and be wise here, too, to see how clever he is to do evil under the guise of doing good. Today he will tell you that any study of the Torah or prayer without attachment [*devekut*] is worth nothing and that it is essential for you to prepare your heart before performing any good deed or offering your prayers by elevating your thoughts until they are the purest of the pure. The result will be that you will be so occupied with preparation for the good deed before you carry it out that the time for the performance of the good deed or the prayer will have gone by. He will then produce arguments to demonstrate that any good deed or prayer that is carried out with tremendous concentration, in holiness and purity, even though it is carried out in the wrong time, is more precious than the fulfilment of a good deed in the correct time if it lacks concentration. Once your evil inclination has persuaded you to become accustomed to the idea that it does not matter so much if you alter the time for the performance of a good deed or of prayer, since you are occupied in purifying your thoughts and in a prior attempt to attune the heart, then, in the course of time, he will lead you astray step by step with his smooth talk and you will be unaware of it. Eventually, it will appear axiomatic to you that you can allow the time of prayer or the good deed to go by even when your heart is occupied with futility in idle thoughts. He will then push you completely from the way and there will be left to you neither the actual deed in its proper time nor the good thought.

R. Hayim is almost certainly thinking of Hasidic practice when he remarks:[20]

> O reader! Do not imagine that I have made this up. I have experienced it all and tested it after I had decided to investigate. Mine own eyes have seen many who desire to be near to God but who stumble in this very matter. I saw for myself in a certain place some men who had become so accustomed to this for so long that they had virtually forgotten the time of the afternoon prayer as ordained by our Sages. On the contrary, so accustomed had they become to it that it seemed to them that the law demands, in fact, that the afternoon prayer be recited chiefly after the stars have come out. And when one of these men says to his neighbour, 'Let us recite the afternoon prayer', the other replies, 'Let us first observe whether the stars are to be seen in the sky'. May God forgive them and may He pardon those who sin unwittingly and foolishly.

How did the Hasidim justify their extreme emphasis? R. Jacob Joseph of Pulnoye quotes[21] the verse, 'To Thee silence is praise, O God' (Ps. 65: 2) and remarks that the silence during which a man does not offer his prayers, because he is engaged in preparation for them, is itself praise of God.

> The Psalmist means that it sometimes happens that a man is unable to study the Torah or to pray as soon as he rises from his sleep, because he needs first to evacuate his bowels so as to be able to study in purity. This may take some time but if he does it for the sake of his Maker then, 'To Thee silence is praise' [i.e. if it is 'to Thee' or 'for Thee' that he delays]. Or it may be that he delays his prayers because he wishes to purify his thoughts, so that he reflects on before Whom he intends to pray or study, before the King of the kings of kings, blessed be He, the Principle and Root of all worlds. When he has this and similar thoughts in mind it is quite proper' [to be silent and postpone the recitation of the prayers].

Whereas R. Jacob Joseph defends the 'silence' (from prayer) caused by the need to purify body and soul, the Maggid of Meseritch permits even recourse to frivolous behaviour before prayer on the basis of the typical Hasidic notion that all things on earth are a pale reflection of the supernal mysteries. Man can therefore be led

on, from the delight he takes in telling jokes and listening to them
and the like, to the Source of all delight and the only true delight.

If a man is unable to pray he utters joking remarks in order to
awaken the love in his psyche. Then he says to himself: If I have
delight in this nonsense how much more should I delight in the
King of kings, blessed be He, the Delight of delights! As a result
he recites his prayers in love and fear.[22]

If Solomon Maimon is to be believed, the Maggid's thoughts in
this connection were more than mere theory. In his Autobio-
graphy,[23] Maimon describes his visit to the court of the Maggid.
There he witnessed the Hasidim, urged on by the Maggid, playing
tricks on one of their number whose wife had given birth to a
girl. For his 'sin' in having a girl rather than a boy the Hasidim
gave the unfortunate Hasid a good drubbing, after which the
Maggid declared, 'Now, let us serve the Lord with joy'.

R. Mordecai of Tchernobil (d. 1837), son of R. Menahem
Nahum of Tchernobil, disciple of the Maggid, describes preparations for prayer in these terms:[24]

When a man gets up in the morning he should rise energetically to
serve his Creator, blessed be He, to be a faithful servant to Him.
As the Shulhan Arukh rules, he should first evacuate his bowels in
order to push the waste away so as to give the 'wicked man'[25] his
portion so that he should not be envious and seek to enjoy the
holy. It is also to avoid vapours ascending from the dung to the
mind since when this happens the mind can become contaminated
with strange thoughts of unbelief and fornication and these
invalidate the sacrifices of the brain, the Temple of the soul. He
will then find it easy to purify the brain and to turn away from all
thoughts that are outside the place of the world and outside its
time.[26] For then is the time for man to take upon himself the
recognition of God as God and to don the yoke of His service,
blessed be He, to serve Him by the sanctification of hands and feet,
namely, to wash his hands, as the Shulhan Arukh rules. Washing
the hands means cleansing oneself from evil loves, Heaven spare us,
and elevating oneself in perfect faith, which is the mystery of the
two thighs of truth. This means that man should believe that there
is a God, One and Unique, and that no other can be compared to
Him. Man should reflect on the greatness of his Creator and on
His exaltedness, blessed be He, for all worlds, above and beneath,

without limit and without end, and the angels, the Seraphim, the Holy Beasts and the Holy Ophanim, all serve Him in dread and trembling and perspiration so that the River of Fire is formed from their perspiration. As a result of such contemplation there can descend upon man great awe and dread and trembling because of the dread of the Lord and the splendour of His majesty.

Eventually, and possibly under the influence of the Mitnaggedic complaints, some of the Hasidic masters rejected much of the more extreme emphasis on preparation for prayer, especially where this was a cause of offence. Typical of this later tendency are the remarks of R. Solomon of Radomsk (d. 1866).[27] R. Solomon comments on a Talmudic passage in which it is stated that if honey were to be mixed with the other ingredients of the incense (Exod. 30: 34–8) in Temple times the fragrance would be so powerful that no man could have endured it. Yet the Torah forbids the use of honey in any offering made by fire unto the Lord (Lev. 2: 11). A practice, such as that of preparation for prayer, may be most fragrant in itself and yet it must be rejected if it leads to something the law forbids.

A man may at times imagine that he does a good deed or offers his prayers with exceptional holiness and cleanliness of body but forgets that, as a result, he transgresses, on the other hand, a command of the Torah. Even though in such circumstances his motive is worthy and no man can endure its fragrance yet, for all that, the Torah says: Do not bring it.

To this day Hasidic groups are divided on the question of 'preparations'. While practically all the Hasidim believe in the practice, they differ on whether the preparations should be so lengthy as to involve the recitation of the prayers later than the time fixed for them in the Talmud and the Codes.[28] There is a marked tendency among some later groups to advocate greater strictness in adhering to the law. But other groups still follow the Hasidic tradition in which the Hasid who prays is transported to a world that is 'above time' and he cannot, therefore, be expected to keep the times of the prayers.[29] R. Israel of Ruzhyn (d. 1850) gives the illustration of the king who has set times for the audiences he gives and no one can be admitted at any other time. A beggar demands admittance, and it is granted, outside the set times, on the ground that he does not come to ask something for himself but to give the king a message of vital importance to the well-being of the king himself.[30] R. Noah of Lechovitz (d. 1834) remarks:[31]

> The Zaddikim, all of whose affairs such as eating, drinking and sleeping, were higher than the world, their prayers, too, were higher than the world and higher than time. But when one's spiritual degree is not of this order, when his eating and drinking and so forth belong to the world, then his prayers, too, must be in the world and he is obliged to observe the set times for the prayers.

R. Menahem Mendel of Kotzk (d. 1859) was one of the Zaddikim at whose court the set times for prayer were overlooked. R. Menahem Mendel is said to have given two illustrations in defence of his custom. A workman employed to chop wood is paid not only for the actual chopping but also for the time he spends on keeping the chopper sharp. When a man is on his travels he observes a strict schedule in which each thing is done at a set time but once he comes near his home he drops the tight schedule.[32]

CHAPTER V

Gestures and Melody in Prayer

Gestures in prayer and a special posture for prayer are known at an early period in Judaism. The Biblical record refers to bending the knees while praying (1 Kgs. 8: 54; Isa. 45: 23); prostration on the face (Exod. 34: 8; Ps. 29: 2); the spreading of the hands heavenwards (1 Kgs. 8: 23; Isa. 1: 15); and, possibly, the placing of the face between the knees (1 Kgs. 18: 42). In the rabbinic period bowing the head and body was advocated at the beginning and end of the Eighteen Benedictions[1] and this became the standard practice. In another Talmudic passage[2] it is said that a layman should only bow at the places ordained but the High Priest should bow more frequently and the king more frequently still, though it is doubtful whether the passage reflects historical conditions in Temple times. The idea behind the passage may be, as Rashi, the famous Talmudic commentator, suggests, that the greater the rank the more there is need for abasement before God, or, it is possible that, on the contrary, rank brought with it the privilege of bowing more frequently. Of Rabbi Akiba in the second century it was said[3] that he would cut short his prayers in public but when he prayed alone he would bow and prostrate himself so much that he would begin his prayers in one corner and finish them in another corner. This statement about Rabbi Akiba was frequently quoted by the Hasidim in defence of wild Hasidic gestures in prayer. It is quoted, for example, by the disciple of the

Maggid of Meseritch, R. Shmelke of Nikolsburg (d. 1778).[4] R. Shmelke also quotes the instance of David dancing before the Lord (2 Sam. 6: 14–16).

Both the Zohar[5] and Judah Ha-Levi's Kuzari[6] refer to the Jewish practice of swaying the body while studying the Torah and it would appear that the practice was also widespread in the Middle Ages of swaying during prayer. R. Moses Isserles, in his notes to the Shulhan Arukh,[7] quotes earlier authorities who advocate swaying during prayer on the basis of the verse, 'All my bones shall say, Lord, who is like unto Thee?' (Ps. 35: 10), a verse that was to be frequently quoted in Hasidic discussions of the subject. However, the Kabbalist R. Isaiah Horowitz (d. c. 1630) remarks:[8]

> One who sways during his prayers causes his powers of concentration to be destroyed while to stand perfectly still without any movement at all assists concentration. As for the verse, 'All my bones shall say', this applies to the recitation of the songs of praise, to the benedictions of the Shema, and to the study of the Torah, but not to prayer. If any authority has declared that it applies to prayer as well it seems to me that his view should be ignored since experience proves that to stand perfectly still during prayer is an aid to concentration. Just see for yourself! Would a man dare to offer supplication to a king of flesh and blood if his body moves as the trees of the forest in the wind?

R. Abraham Gumbiner in his notes to the Shulhan Arukh,[9] after quoting authorities who favour swaying during prayer and others who denigrate it, concludes, 'It is correct to prefer either of these opinions provided that it assists concentration'.

With reservations here and there, the Hasidim favoured violent movements in prayer, believing these to be an aid to concentration as well as enabling man to put the whole of himself into his worship. Very revealing is the reply attributed to the Hasidic master R. Menahem Mendel of Kotzk[10] to the Mitnagged who asked him why the Hasidim run about during their prayers, since the Talmud[11] rules that when a man prays his feet should be placed together. The rabbi is said to have answered that the Talmud means that a man should figuratively have both feet together when he prays, not one foot in heaven and the other in hell!

R. Elimelech of Lizensk, disciple of the Maggid of Meseritch, teaches that every limb and organ of the Zaddik is under the control of his soul.[12] As his soul journeys in the higher realms in prayer, it influences the body to make gestures of an entirely uncontrived nature. Because of their spontaneity, the gestures of the Zaddik do not appear odd or grotesque. On the contrary, so attractive do they appear that they are not infrequently copied. Naturally, such imitation of the Zaddik's gestures is not authentic and invites ridicule.[13] R. Nahman of Bratzlav,[14] great-grandson of the Baal Shem Tov, states that the way to set the heart on fire for God is by motion, since rapid motion generates warmth. When wax is attached to an arrow the wax melts when the arrow is released from the bow at great speed. However, R. Nahman goes on to say that he refers not to the movements of the body but to those of the soul as it speeds from one contemplative idea to the other.

Some of the early Hasidim took the notion of physical movement in prayer to absurd extremes. It is reported that the followers of R. Abraham of Kalisk and R. Hayim Haikel of Amdur (both disciples of the Maggid of Meseritch, though their corybantism did not meet with the Maggid's approval) used to turn somersaults in their prayers.[15] The Hasidim of the Rabbi of Amdur, we are told, used to say, while engaged in these acrobatics, *Fun Gotts vegen un fun Rebbens vegen* ('For the sake of God and for the sake of the rabbi'). It is extraordinary, but such is the mystery of the *zeitgeist*, that at approximately the same time the 'Shakers' emerged in Manchester (where they were called 'Shaking Quakers') and later flourished in America.[16] The Shakers practised a rolling exercise which consisted in doubling the head and feet together, and rolling over like a hoop. It would seem that the practice of turning somersaults in prayer was derived in part by the Hasidim from their doctrine of self-annihilation, to which attention has been called in a previous chapter. The self was overturned, as it were, seeking nothing for itself and desiring only the glory of God. As part of the process the Hasid would deliver himself up completely to the Zaddik through whose prayers he would be led to God.

In a book published in Altona as early as 1768, only eight years after the death of the Baal Shem Tov, the fiery R. Jacob Emden writes of the Hasidic gestures in prayer:[17]

I trembled when I heard only recently that a new sect of foolish Hasidim had arisen in Volhynia and Podolia, some of whom have come to this country, whose sole occupation is to study moral and Kabbalistic works. They prolong their prayers for half the day, far longer than the Hasidim of old who used to spend no more than an hour[18] in prayer itself. Moreover, these men perform strange movements, weird and ugly, in the prayer of the Eighteen Benedictions. They clap their hands and shake sideways with their head turned backwards and their face and eyes turned upwards, contrary to the ruling of the rabbis[19] that the eyes should be directed downwards and the heart upwards. The Tanhuma only advocates that the eyes should be directed upwards when the Kedushah is recited and even then they should be closed.[20] R. Menahem Azariah in a Responsum forbids any movement at all in prayer.[21] I stormed the battlements time and again in order to discover some compromise whereby some slight and gentle motion of the body to and fro might be permitted, and this alone is permitted in order to bestir the vital powers. The teachers of old used to recite their prayers without any physical sensation. There is a maxim, based on the Zohar, 'When they stood, they let down their wings' [Ezek. 1: 24].[22] But these men make wings for themselves wherewith to fly in the heavens. Ask yourself if they would dare to do so in the presence of a king of flesh and blood. Why, he would have them thrown out so that their limbs would be shattered and their bones broken. Verily, if I ever see those who do these things, which our fathers, of blessed memory, the true Hasidim, never dreamed of doing, I shall break their legs with a bar of iron.

It is reported even of a Hasidic master like R. Shneor Zalman of Liady, founder of the intellectual movement in Hasidism known as Habad and opposed to the more bizarre antics of some of his colleagues,[23] that he used to bang his hands on the wall during his prayers so that blood would be found on his hands.[24] Eventually, the Hasidim were obliged to place soft hangings on the wall so that the rabbi would not come to harm. The letter written by the rabbi to Alexander of Shklov is interesting in this connection.[25] In the year 1787 the rabbis of Shklov issued a proclamation against the Hasidic manner of prayer, referring especially to the strange gestures in which the Hasidim indulged. Alexander of Shklov was at first a moderate Mitnagged but afterwards became a disciple of R. Shneor Zalman. He had evidently turned to the rabbi for advice after the attack on the Hasidim by the rabbis of Shklov. The letter of R. Shneor Zalman, part of which has been quoted in a previous chapter, begins:

Though I do not know you personally I have heard that the spirit of God has stirred you not to become involved in the counsel of the scoffers who pour scorn on those who desire to serve the Lord in truth in the service of the heart that is prayer.[26] Although they (the Mitnaggedim) have achieved much in the study of the Torah and through acts of mercy—would that they kept to this in truth all their days—now they have gone too far and have acted illegally when they have gathered together to attack me and to issue a decree of apostasy against prayer. They claim that we must pray as they do, that is, only hurriedly and without any bodily movements or raising of the voice just like those angels on high who have reached a stage than which there is no higher, as it is said, 'When they stood, they let down their wings' [Ezek. 1: 24]. But this is only said of the highest rank of angels known as the Seraphim and it does not apply to the other ranks, as it is said,[27] 'And the Ophanim and the Holy Beasts with a noise of great rushing'. Even of the Seraphim it is written, 'A noise of tumult like the noise of a host' [Ezek. 1: 24] and they make great movements as it is said in the Piyutim based on the Pirke Hekhalot.[28] Consequently, there is no proof from the saints of old who were greater than the ministering angels. But dare we, orphans of orphans, imagine that we can compare ourselves to them? It can only be that their heart is evilly disposed and falsehood is in their right hand.

It is interesting to find R. Shneor Zalman quoting the same verse from Ezekiel that R. Jacob Emden quotes. This can only be because it featured in the debates between the Hasidim and their opponents on the value of movement and gesture in prayer. R. Shneor Zalman is aware that the kind of violent movement and shouting aloud in prayer in which the Hasidim indulged was an innovation. He resorts to the defence that immobility and silent prayer was, indeed, once the ideal but it is an ideal only for the saints of old. For an orphaned generation, in which saintliness is lacking, the only way to awaken the powers of concentration is through gesture and strong verbal expression. R. Shneor Zalman's contemporary, R. Mordecai of Tchernobil, similarly remarks[29] that swaying in prayer is necessary so that all man's psychological powers and all his limbs, bones and sinews should move to awaken the supernal power, the power of En Sof that is contained in the letters of the prayers. This author writes that since the nations of the world have false beliefs, their adherents have no vitality in their prayers and that is why they stand in their houses of worship 'like a silent stone'. Nevertheless, he concludes, the Jew should learn from them to have decorum in the synagogue, 'for great is their respectful and bashful stance in their houses of prayer'.

It is clear from the many references to movement and gesture in the early Hasidic writings that the practice was an integral part of Hasidic behaviour from the beginning of Hasidism. It is notoriously difficult to establish how many of the sayings attributed to the Baal Shem Tov in Hasidic literature are authentic, but the fact that the early writings do attribute to him sayings in which the practice of violent movement in prayer is defended is itself significant in assessing the extent of such practice in early Hasidism. In one early source[30] it is said:

Rabbi Israel Baal Shem, on whom be peace, said: When a man is drowning in a river and gesticulates while in the water that people should save him from the waters which threaten to sweep him away, the observers will certainly not laugh at him and his gestures. So, too, one should not pour scorn on a man who makes gestures while he prays for he is trying to save himself from the waters of presumption, namely, from the 'shells' and strange thoughts which attempt to prevent him from having his mind on his prayers.

The 'shells' (kelipot) are, in the Kabbalah, the forces of impurity, so called because they surround the good and are nourished and sustained by it as the bark the tree and the shell the kernel of the nut. The strange thoughts, i.e. thoughts of gain and self-interest and of self in general, intrude to prevent concentration on God. They can only be driven away by physical movements of the body.

In some early Hasidic writings the defence of violent movements during prayer is expressed in crudely erotic terms to the
scandal of the Mitnaggedim and the 'enlightened' opponents of
Hasidism, the Maskilim. The mystical prayer is here described as
'copulation' (*zivvug*) with the Shekhinah. In two passages in
particular the erotic element is pronounced. In the first[31] it is
said:

> This is from the Baal Shem Tov, may his memory be for a
> blessing, 'From my own flesh I behold God'.[32] Just as no child can
> be born as a result of physical copulation unless this is performed
> with a vitalised organ and with joy and desire, so it is with
> spiritual copulation, that is, the study of the Torah and prayer.
> When it is performed with a vitalised organ and with joy and
> delight then does it give birth.

The second statement[33] is couched in even more direct terms:

> Prayer is copulation with the Shekhinah. Just as there is swaying
> when copulation begins so, too, a man must sway at first and then
> he can remain immobile and attached to the Shekhinah with great
> attachment. As a result of his swaying man is able to attain a
> powerful stage of arousal. For he will ask himself: Why do I sway
> my body? Presumably it is because the Shekhinah stands over
> against me. And as a result he will attain to a stage of great
> enthusiasm.

Joseph Perl, in his satire against Hasidism, *Megalleh Temirin*,[34]
gives these two passages, and others from the Hasidic writings, as
illustrations of the alleged obscene nature of some of the Hasidic
works. It is interesting that in the Hasidic anthology by Nahman
of Tcherin entitled *Derekh Hasidim*,[35] a bowdlerised version of the
second passage is quoted with instructions to the reader to consult
the work itself for further details. That man's love for God can
be expressed on the analogy of erotic human love is not, of course,
unknown in Jewish thought. Even so austere a thinker as Maimonides uses erotic imagery[36] and interprets the Song of Songs as
a dialogue between God and the individual human soul. Scholem[37]
remarks that the Zohar, on the other hand, while it frequently uses
erotic symbolism to describe the relationship between the Sefirot
of Tiferet and Malkhut, hardly ever uses this kind of symbolism

to describe the relationship between God and man, and that the older Kabbalists never interpret the Song of Songs as a dialogue between God and the soul. This latter was left to the later Kabbalists in sixteenth-century Safed. But of Moses the Zohar[38] does say that he had intercourse with the Shekhinah! Tishby[39] has, however, shown that there are, in fact, many passages in the Zohar in which erotic symbolism is used for man's relationship with God and not only with regard to Moses. For instance, the Zohar[40] states that when a man cannot be with his wife, for example, when he is away from home, or when he is studying the Torah, or when she has her periods, then the Shekhinah is with him so that he can be 'male and female'. There are similar developments in the Christian mystical tradition.[41] The Hasidic passages quoted are still extraordinary in their physical emphasis. It follows from the imagery of the Shekhinah as female and the worshipper as male that women are not normally within the full scope of the Hasidic doctrines on prayer. It is no doubt true that in certain areas Hasidism improved the status of the Jewish woman but, while Hasidic women offered their prayers, they occupied no place in the detailed life of prayer as discussed in the classical Hasidic writings.[42]

Joy and enthusiasm in prayer, mentioned in the first of these passages in connection with swaying, are essential ingredients in the life of prayer as understood by Hasidism.

> Prayer recited with great joy is undoubtedly significant and more acceptable to God than prayer recited in a melancholy fashion and with tears. There is a parable to illustrate the matter. When a poor man entreats and supplicates a king of flesh and blood, weeping copiously all the time, all that is given to him, in spite of his tears, is some small thing. But when a prince sings the praises of the king with great joy and, in the course of his praise, he introduces a petition, the king gives him a great gift suitable for an aristocrat.[43]

It is clearly in reaction to Hasidic stress on movements in prayer that R. Hayim of Volozyhn laconically remarks,[44] 'Swaying in prayer is solely for the purpose of keeping awake, as the *Shelah* observes.[45] But if one sways automatically out of powerful longing and purity of heart how good it is! Apart from this, the obligation is to put soul and sensation into the words' [i.e. and not into physical gestures].

It is not surprising to find a reaction to movement in prayer even among the Hasidim. Indeed, there is evidence of a certain ambivalence in this matter in the early sources themselves as can be seen from the following:[46]

> At times one should serve God with the soul alone, that is with thought. At times a man can recite his prayers with love and fear and powerful enthusiasm and yet without any bodily movements at all so that it seems to observers that he is reciting the prayers quite simply and without attachment. A man is capable of doing this when he is greatly attached to God. Then he can serve Him with the soul alone with great and strong love. This kind of worship is better, proceeds more speedily, and becomes more attached to God than prayer that can be witnessed externally through its effect on the limbs of the body. The 'shells' have no power to seize hold of such a prayer since it is all of inwardness.

In the passage about the 'shells' quoted previously (from the same work!) powerful movements are necessary in order to drive away the distracting thoughts. Here the exact opposite is stated. Inward prayer is too remote from the physical universe to be affected by external distractions. To be sure, Hasidism is not unaware that a worshipper may sway in his prayers with completely sham motives, such as in order to impress others with his piety. There is a saying attributed, though with very doubtful authenticity, to the Baal Shem Tov,[47] in the form of a comment on the verse, 'And when the people saw, they swayed, and stood afar off' (Exod. 20: 15). 'If a man sways in prayer in order that people might see him [i.e. in order to be admired for his piety] it is a sign that he is afar off, remote from God.'

One of the early Hasidic masters, R. Zeev Wolf of Zhitomer, disciple of the Maggid of Meseritch, is very critical of gestures and loud shouting in prayer, especially when such behaviour is not in accord with the Hasid's true feelings. Critical, here and elsewhere, of some of the Hasidic tendencies among his contemporaries, this author observes:[48]

We can see for ourselves that many are to be found who, at the time of Torah study or prayer, raise their voices too much so that they are heard at a distance. They smite palm to palm and make similar gestures with their limbs and dance on their feet as is the custom. Many of them are ignoramuses who imagine that the main idea of prayer depends on this. The truth is otherwise. It is proper for man to stand when praying in dread and fear. His legs should be straight, his voice should not be heard and only his lips should move. . . . In short a man is expected to weigh his actions in the balance of his mind when he raises his voice in prayer so that he should not raise it higher than the expression he needs to give to the love and fear of God that is in his inmost thoughts. For it is obvious that his heart and mouth must be in one accord, otherwise the letters he utters with his mouth have nothing of that freshness which comes from the illumination from on high that is drawn into them from preconceived thought . . . The principle is that before a man begins to pray to God he should be filled with love and fear. He should allow the thought of the majesty and greatness of En Sof to enter his mind and then he should recite his prayers with a clear enunciation of the words and gently withal, without any movements of the limbs in order to push away strange thoughts . . .

However, it must be said that in this lengthy passage, of which we have quoted only the gist, R. Zeev Wolf acknowledges that while the ideal is for the worshipper to be so pure that he has no 'strange thoughts'; if he has them, then the way to transcend them would seem to be in part by means of violent gestures and raising the voice.

The Lithuanian Hasidic master R. Abraham of Slonim (1804–1884) used to say his prayers silently and without any bodily movements whatsoever, yet, we are told, 'his face burned with fire so that whoever saw him became affected with a burning enthusiasm [hitlahavut].' In this connection an interpretation of R. Menahem Mendel of Kotz is metioned. R. Menahem Mendel interpreted the verse, 'If thou wilt return, O Israel, saith the Lord, yea return unto Me; and if thou wilt put away thy detestable things out of My sight, and will not waver' (Jer. 4: 1), to yield the thought that when a man rises above his physical nature he becomes so filled with the awe of God when he prays that he can only remain immobile in dread and he will not 'waver', i.e.

sway his body in prayer. It is further said that R. Elimelech of Lizensk said of a contemporary who remained completely immobile in prayer that he had such a great dread of God that he was unable to move any of his limbs.[49] Statements such as these demonstrate that by no means all the Hasidim imagined that gestures and bodily movements were essential in the life of prayer.

As for later Hasidism down to the present day, the majority of the Hasidim did perform gestures and movements in prayer and still do so, but some of them, especially the later masters, prepared with complete immobility. We have noted earlier in this chapter that R. Snheor Zalman of Liady, founder of the Habad group, favoured both gesture and vocal expression in prayer. His son, R. Dov Baer (1773–1827), however, adopted the opposite method. R. Shneor Zalman is reported as saying to his son,[50] 'For both of us the intellect is in control of the heart but for me it controls only the external heart; but for you it controls even the inner heart.' Jacob Kadanir,[51] disciple of R. Dov Baer, claims that he was an eyewitness to his master's prolonged prayer on the New Year festival and that for the three hours of its duration he made not the slightest movement of his body. Kadanir writes further that on such occasion R. Levi Yitzhak of Berditchev, while on a visit to R. Shneor Zalman, requested Dov Baer to recite the grace after meals in order to observe Dov Baer's powerful ecstasy in prayer about which he had heard so much. To R. Levi Yitzhak's astonishment, Dov Baer recited the grace without any overt ecstasy at all, as if he understood no more than the bare meaning of the words. When R. Levi Yitzhak expressed his surprise, R. Shneor Zalman replied that R. Dov Baer's worship was of a very high order of which he, R. Shneor Zalman, was envious. R. Dov Baer was filled with such an elevated love and fear of God that it could not be experienced at all externally. Only a lofty soul from 'the world of concealment' can experience this type of worship while still in the body. The successors of R. Dov Baer, the Hasidim of the Lubavitcher movement, to this day generally prefer immobile prayer and certainly eschew violent gestures.

It is reported of R. Menahem Mendel of Kotzk that he used to stand completely immobile in prayer. The only indication that he was engrossed in his prayers was his flushed face and burning eyes. So lost was he in prayer that it used to take him some time afterwards before he became aware of his surroundings.[52] On the other hand, of the Kotzker's disciple and brother-in-law, R. Yitzhak Meir of Gur (d. 1866), it is reported that his prayers were accompanied by loud cries and strange gestures, with his body bent double. After he had recited his prayers his clothes would be found to be bathed in perspiration. It once happened that in his burning enthusiasm he lost a tooth during his prayers and was unaware of it.[53]

Jiri Langer[54] describes his first personal encounter with prayer at the Hasidic court of Belz on a Friday evening in the second decade of this century. The old rabbi of Belz had advanced to the reading desk in order to lead the Hasidim in the recital of the psalms to welcome the sabbath.

> It is as though an electric spark has suddenly entered those present. The crowd which till now has been completely quiet, almost cowed, suddenly bursts forth in a wild shout. None stays in his place. The tall black figures run hither and thither round the synagogue, flashing past the lights of the sabbath candles. Gesticulating wildly, and throwing their whole bodies about, they shout out the words of the Psalms. They knock into each other unconcernedly, for all their cares have been cast aside; everything has ceased to exist for them. They are seized by an indescribable ecstasy . . . The old man throws himself about as though seized by convulsions. Each shudder of his powerful body, each contraction of his muscles is permeated with the glory of the Most High. Every so often he claps the palms of his hands together symbolically.

Herbert Weiner[55] describes his visit to the Hasidic centre, in the Meah Shearim district in Jerusalem, of the followers of the Hasidic master R. Arele Roth.

> 'Amen', shrieked the man next to me. He was doubled over, his face red, yelling at the top of his lungs, 'Amen—may His great name be blessed for ever, and ever, and ever'. For a moment I thought he was ill, but then I saw that all the worshippers were carrying on in the same way. The room resounded with a cacophony of shouts. My guide noticed my bewilderment. One of

R. Arele's teachings is that the response, 'Amen, may His great name. . .' be recited, as the Talmud suggests, in an utter abandonment of soul, as if one were willing at that moment to die in sanctification of the name.

R. Arele himself, in his ethical will, advised his followers on how to conduct themselves during their prayers.[56]

It is a fundamental principle in connection with prayer that a man should not be embarrassed, God forbid, because people laugh at it. For consider and reflect, my beloved child, that you are engaged in putting right the world, and all worlds and all angels desire every word and every utterance in which you express your nostalgia for the Creator in love and longing. Why should you be concerned with a foolish, brutish and stupid person who cannot discern between his right hand and his left! For all that, when you are among people who are unaccustomed to worship, then you must try to limit it as far as you can so as not to encourage scoffers to pour scorn. And you should not make any peculiar and crazy gestures, God forbid. All the members of our group are fully aware how strict I am about this, and this way is not our way, God forbid. What you should do is to toil with might and self-sacrifice, with the inner and outer organs, and to exercise the mind in toil, in the category of, 'Nay, but for Thy sake are we killed all the day' [Ps. 44: 23], which, as is well known, refers to prayer. But as for that which cannot be limited, do not bother to look at the whole world, God forbid, to prevent your giving satisfaction to your Creator. Thus have I seen it written in the work of one of the members of the king's palace, the disciples of the Baal Shem Tov, may his merit shield us and all Israel.

R. Arele's reference to the verse in Psalms is clearly intended to call attention to the Hasidic doctrine of self-annihilation in prayer.

R. Arele's letters of spiritual counsel have been collected and published. In one of them[57] he expresses his strong disapproval of peculiar gesticulation in prayer but not of swaying or of shouting aloud in prayer.

This was the reply I gave to a certain famous man, of the great and famous, who asked me about the peculiar gestures he had observed among some of my disciples. I replied that in reality this was not my way at all but it can be attributed to one of two things. Either the disciple who behaves in this way is a tyro in God's service and then one must allow him the freedom to pursue his own way if, beforehand, he was an inferior person and a sinner, God forfend [i.e. and he behaves in this way in order to escape from his past]. Or else he is an immature disciple who left me after having stayed only for a short time. He acquired some warmth through his association with our company and so forth, but he has not learned a sense of balance so as to be able to assess accurately the type of gesture he makes. This is intelligible. But after he has spent a year or two in beginning to serve God he must then choose a circumspect and moderate way, though inwardly it should be with a spirit of real self-sacrifice, uncomplicated and true. Now I do not mean by this any spirit of indifference, God forbid, such as to cancel out self-sacrifice and toil in prayer with all one's might. This must never be given up even if the whole world protests. For it is like a railway line, from which the train must not be derailed, God forbid. For it is this which brings sanctity and purity to body and soul and which draws down godly vitality to all the limbs and muscles. I refer only to a few imbeciles who make strange noises in their prayers and shake their heads about in a way different from that of the rest of the world, I mean of the world of those who worship God with self-sacrifice. I refer to such strange conduct as glazing the eyes or making odd gestures with other parts of the body. If one notices that sometimes a certain Zaddik does these things one should not copy him. for he does so at times because God's fire burns within him. However, as for swaying in the ordinary way, even with all one's strength and in a spirit of real self-sacrifice, and as for reciting the prayers in a loud voice and with effort, with regard to this it is said: 'Nay, but for Thy sake are we killed all the day' (Ps. 44: 23). Now how is it possible for a man to kill himself every day? The sacred books of old explain that the verse refers to prayer in a spirit of self-sacrifice and with all one's strength. As it is said [in those books]: How far should the power of prayer reach? Until one [virtually] expires. May the Lord help us to sacrifice ourselves to Him, blessed be He, and to sanctify His name continually. Amen.

As an aid to concentration and *devekut* in prayer, the Hasidim resorted to melody. Much has been written on the general Hasidic attitude to singing and dancing.[58] But this does not apply specifically to prayer. The Hasidim would sing as they sat around the table of the Zaddik, on festive occasions, or whenever the opportunity arose. We are concerned here only with the Hasidic use of melody in prayer.

The Jewish tradition knows of special melodies for the prayers. These have been handed down from generation to generation. The Hasidim used these but, in addition, composed original melodies of their own. Some of the Zaddikim composed melodies for particular prayers. In Habad Hasidism, with its strong emphasis on contemplative prayer, each Hasid would hum a melody of his own as he reflected on the mysteries of the upper worlds. R. Dov Baer, to whom we have referred earlier, in his *Tract on Ecstasy* observes:[59]

> One should begin by considering the subject of melody. What is the nature of melody? There is a well-known saying that the Faithful Shepherd [Moses] used to sing every kind of melody in his prayers. For his soul embraced the six hundred thousand souls of Israel and each soul can only ascend to the root of the Source whence she was hewn by means of song. This is the category we have mentioned of essential ecstasy in which the soul is rooted on high in the supernal delight. He who embraced them all was the Faithful Shepherd who therefore used to sing with every kind of melody, as we have written elsewhere. First, it is necessary to understand the nature of ecstasy produced by melody. This is in the category of spontaneous ecstasy alone, without any choice or intellectual will whatsoever. This is an ecstasy that is felt, and yet the one who experiences it is not himself aware of it, because it does not result from an intention of the self to produce ecstasy, but is produced automatically and comes of its own accord without its being known to him. Since it is as if it is not felt or known to him at that very moment, it can be said that there is a total lack of self-awareness. But, for all that, it is an experienced ecstasy.

R. Dov Baer uses the illustration of music to demonstrate the possibility of rapture in prayer without self-awareness, a contradiction on the face of it. It is possible, declares R. Dov Baer, for the self to have a profoundly ecstatic experience, as when one is moved by a melody, and yet to be so involved as to be lost in the music. The self of the Hasid can similarly experience the nearness of God to the extent that he is moved to ecstasy and yet be unaware of the self, so lost is he in God at that time.[60] It can justifiably be inferred from this that R. Dov Baer would have favoured the use of melody as an aid to contemplation. In fact, he had in his court an expert choir and orchestra, though, of course, the latter did not play during the prayers.

R. Elimelech of Lizensk speaks of some Zaddikim of his day who sang the sweetest spontaneous melodies as they prayed even though, normally, their voices were far from tuneful.[61] Hasidic legend tells of a visit to R. Elimelech by the Baal Shem Tov's cantor.[62] This man when young had no voice, but once the Baal Shem Tov had 'bound him to the world of melody' there was no one in the whole world who could sing so sweetly. R. Moses of Koznitz[63] reports in the name of his teacher, R. Meshullam Zusya of Hanipol (d. 1800), R. Elimelech's brother, that both worship of God with tears and weeping and worship of God with joy and song are acceptable to Him, but that worship in tears is capable of achieving only limited results while worship in joy and song can achieve results without limit. R. Meshullam Zusya paraphrases Psalm 126: 6 as, 'Though he goeth on his way weeping he beareth the measure of the seed, but if he goeth with joy he shall bear his sheaves.'

As we have seen, R. Dov Baer of Lubavitch devotes some of his work to the philosophy of melody in prayer. This theme is especially prominent among Habad writers. In the work *Magen Avot* by R. Solomon Zalman of Kopust (1830–1900), a great-great-grandson of R. Shneor Zalman, the founder of Habad, there are detailed theories regarding the role of melody in prayer.[64] R. Solomon Zalman observes[65] that the three colours of white, red and green can be expressed in melody. The meaning of this is that in the Kabbalah the colour white symbolises mercy (the Sefirah Hesed), red symbolises judgement (the Sefirah Gevurah), and green symbolises the harmony between the two (the Sefirah Tiferet). The three 'colours' of the melody are the way in which the worshipper, as he sings in his prayers, brings his contemplation to bear on these three aspects of the Sefirotic realm. Elsewhere[66] R. Solomon Zalman remarks that, in order to bring down the divine vitality from the upper worlds, the worshipper has to so sing in his prayers that it is as if his soul were ready to expire in longing for God.

CHAPTER VI

Contemplative Prayer

Concentration in prayer has a long history, of relevance to the Hasidic ideas on mystical, contemplative prayer. The word used in the rabbinic literature for concentration is *kavvanah*. The root meaning of the word is 'to direct'; in the context of prayer the meaning is to direct or adjust the mind to the act of prayer in which man is engaged. For the rabbis, *kavvanah* in prayer means that the worshipper is conscious that he stands in the presence of God and that his mind is aware of the meaning of the words he utters.

The Mishnah[1] tells of the 'Hasidim of old' who used to wait for an hour in contemplation before praying so that their 'heart would be directed to their Father in heaven'. In the chapter on preparation for prayer, we have noted that the followers of the Baal Shem Tov were influenced by this teaching about the 'Hasidim of old'. From another Talmudic passage[2] it emerges that the 'Hasidim of old' were only extraordinary in their lengthy preparations but that *kavvanah* in prayer itself was demanded of all worshippers. 'Our Rabbi taught: One who prays must direct his heart to heaven.' One of the rules regarding prayer derived from the narrative of Hannah is that *kavvanah* is required.[3] 'Now Hannah, she spoke in her heart' (1 Sam. 1: 13). The comment is, 'From this verse we learn that one who prays must direct his heart'. However, the difficulty of achieving sustained concentration, in prayers recited regularly no less than three times a day, was recognised and frankly acknowledged. 'One who prays must direct his heart in all of them [all the benedictions] but if he is unable to direct his heart in all of them he should direct his heart in [at least] one of them.'[4] The reference is to the Eighteen Benedictions, the main formal 'prayer' in Talmudic times. Ideally, a man should have *kavvanah* when reciting all of them, but at least he should have *kavvanah* when reciting one of them. The Talmud goes on to explain that the 'one of them' referred to is the the first and most important one, *Avot*, the benediction referring to the patriarchs. Elsewhere[5] it is said that a man should assess first whether he is able to achieve *kavvanah*. If he feels that he can he should pray; otherwise he should not pray. The Tosafists understand this to mean that if he can achieve *kavvanah* in at least the first benediction he should pray.[6] Because special *kavvanah* was required in prayer, workmen, although they were allowed to recite the Shema on top of a tree, were not permitted to recite their prayers there since it was practically impossible for them to have adequate concentration while they were in an awkward position, from which they could easily fall.[7]

During the Middle Ages the Jewish moralists and philosophers made a determined attempt to encourage greater inwardness in the carrying out of religious duties and, as a result, the doctrine of *kavvanah* in prayer was stressed especially by them.[8] Bahya Ibn Pakuda,[9] for example, observes:

When a man is employed in those duties in which both the heart
and the limbs are involved such as prayer and praising God,
blessed be He, he should empty himself of all matters appertaining
to this world or the next and he should empty his heart of every
distracting thought, after first cleansing himself and washing away
all stains and filth. He should keep himself far from every
unpleasant smell and the like. He should then consider to Whom
it is that his prayers are directed and what he intends to ask and
what he intends to speak in the presence of his Creator; pondering
on the words of the prayers and their meaning. Know that so
far as the language of prayer is concerned the words themselves
are like the husk while reflection on the meaning of the words is
like the kernel. The prayer itself is like the body while reflection
on its meaning is like the spirit, so that, if a man merely utters the
words of the prayers with his heart concerned with matters other
than prayer, then his prayer is like a body without a spirit and a
husk without a kernel, because while the body is present when he

prays his heart is absent. Of people such as he Scripture says, 'Forasmuch as this people draw near, and with their mouth and with their lips do honour Me, but have removed their heart far from Me' [Isa. 29: 13].

The main statement of Bahya was paraphrased as, 'Prayer without *kavvanah* is like a body without a soul' and in this form was widely known to Hasidim and Mitnaggedim alike.

Maimonides' understanding of *kavvanah* in prayer[10] is very similar to the Hasidic idea of *devekut*[11] and is, indeed, almost certainly one of the sources of the Hasidic doctrine.

> Know that all the practices of the worship, such as reading the Torah, prayer, and the performance of the other commandments, have only the end of training you to occupy yourself with His commandments, may He be exalted, rather than with matters pertaining to this world; you should act as if you were occupied with Him, may He be exalted, and not with that which is other than He. If, however, you pray merely by moving your lips while facing a wall, and at the same time think about your buying and selling; or if you read the Torah with your tongue while your heart is set upon the building of your habitation and does not consider what you read; and similarly in all cases in which you perform a commandment merely with your limbs—as if you were digging a hole in the ground or hewing wood in the forest— without reflecting either upon the meaning of that action or upon Him from whom the commandment proceeds or upon the end of the action, you should not think that you have achieved the end. Rather you will then be similar to those of whom it is said, 'Thou art near in their mouth, and far from their reins' [Jer. 12: 2]

Not that Maimonides imagines that *kavvanah* is easily attained. In a passage remarkable for its acknowledgement of the difficulties, Maimonides continues:

> From here on I will begin to give you guidance with the form of this training so that you should achieve this great end. The first thing that you should cause your soul to hold fast on to is that, while reciting the Shema prayer, you should empty your mind of everything and pray thus. You should not content yourself with being intent while reciting the first verse of the Shema and saying the first benediction. When this has been carried out correctly and has been practised consistently for years, cause your soul, whenever you read or listen to the Torah, to be constantly directed—the

whole of you and your thought—towards reflection on what you
are listening to or reading. When this too has been practised
consistently for a certain time, cause your soul to be in such a way
that your thought is always quite free of distraction and gives heed
to all that you are reading of the other discourses of the prophets
and even when you read all the benedictions, so that you aim at
meditating on what you are reading and at considering its
meaning.

Thus full concentration on all the benedictions is not to be
achieved except after *years* of continuous training and effort.

The Codes, following the Talmud, all stress the need for *kavvanah* in prayer. Basing himself on the various Talmudic statements on the subject, Maimonides[12] rules:

What is the meaning of concentration in the heart [*kavvanat
ha-lev*]? Any prayer that is recited without *kavvanah* is no prayer.
If a man recites his prayers without *kavvanah* he must recite them
again with *kavvanah*. If a man finds that his mind is confused and
his heart preoccupied he is forbidden to recite his prayers until his
mind is at ease again. Consequently, if he returns after a journey
and is tired or in a state of anxiety he is forbidden to recite his
prayers until his mind is at ease again. The Sages say that he should
wait for three days until his mind is at ease and has settled down
and then he should recite his prayers. What is the definition of
kavvanah? It means that he should empty his mind of all thought
and see himself as if he were standing in the presence of the
Shekhinah.

Elsewhere[13] Maimonides rules, 'If a man has recited his prayers
without concentration [*kavvanat ha-lev*] he should repeat them
with *kavvanah*. But if he did concentrate during the first benediction then this suffices.' The Tur[14] introduces a new idea, in which
the difficulty of achieving *kavvanah* is acknowledged to an even
greater extent. The Tur rules that 'nowadays', when we find it so
hard to concentrate adequately, the older rule, that if prayers have
been recited without *kavvanah* they have to be recited again, no
longer applies, since the likelihood is that the second time, too,
they will be recited without *kavvanah*.

In the classical sources, then, *kavvanah* means chiefly concentration on the meaning of the words of the prayers and the
realisation that one is in God's presence. In the Kabbalah, how-

ever, and especially in the Lurianic version, the whole doctrine of *kavvanah* receives, as we have seen in the chapter on the Prayer Book, a totally different meaning. Mystical contemplation is now the order of the day. The Kabbalist is expected to have in mind, when he prays, all the complicated combinations in the Sefirotic realm. Each word of the prayers has not only its surface meaning but represents one of the divine names in combination. By having these in mind the Kabbalist actually promotes harmony among the Sefirot. He sends upwards, as it were, the power of the divine names, he repeats the creative processes on high, and by so doing he assists the flow of divine grace through all creation. Of these thoughts that the Kabbalist is expected to have in mind, the plural *kavvanot* is used. Prayer involves for the Kabbalist both a profound knowledge of the whole Kabbalistic scheme and its application in severe contemplation during his prayers. Instead of *kavvanah* in the older non-mystical sense, the key-word is now *kavvanot*. The Lurianic Prayer Book was, as we have seen, compiled in order to place before the mystical adept the 'correct' words and order of the prayer, i.e. those representing the divine mysteries which he follows in the ascent of his soul. The Hasidim substituted the Lurianic Prayer Book for the older Ashkenazi Prayer Book precisely because of the doctrine of the *kavvanot*, though whether the Hasidim actually practised the technique of *kavvanot* is another question which we must now examine.

We are aided in this investigation by the excellent article on *kavvanot* in early Hasidism by J. G. Weiss[15] and by the pertinent observations of Rivka Schatz Uffenheimer.[16] It is not too clear whether the Baal Shem Tov himself practised the Lurianic *kavvanot*, though, as Weiss has suggested, it is most probable that he preferred the technique known as 'attachment of oneself to the letters'. What this means will become clearer from the following passages from the Hasidic writings. (Even if the early Hasidim did not actually practise the *kavvanot* there is no difficulty in the fact that they adopted the Lurianic Prayer Book because, as is frequently stated, they believed that, even without the worshipper having them in mind, the *kavvanot* were still, as it were, sent on high to have their effect.) What is certain is that in the school of the Maggid of Meseritch, the disciple of the Baal Shem Tov, the practice of the Lurianic *kavvanot* gave way to the use of prayer as a means of 'awakening love and fear' in which the technique of 'attachment to the letters' was used. In this school the practice of the *kavvanot* was a positive hindrance to the ideal of *devekut*. How could the worshipper become attached to God and have only God in mind if, at the same time, he was expected to engage in the very severe intellectual effort of retracing the details of the Sefirotic map? A new technique of contemplation was required and this was 'attachment to the letters'. In Weiss's words,[17] 'The metamorphosis which took place in the meaning of *kavvanoth* at the advent of Hasidism, and more explicitly after the Great Maggid, consists in this—that an originally intellectual effort of meditation and contemplation has become an intensely emotional and highly enthusiastic act.' It should here be said, however, that while this is undoubtedly true of the early Hasidim it is not true of the intellectual movement known as Habad. We shall see later that in Habad there is a return to severe contemplation in prayer, though this, too, differs from the older practice of *kavvanot* in the Lurianic sense. We must now examine the Hasidic sources on the idea of 'attachment to the letters'.

We begin with the famous letter (which is generally assumed to be authentic) written by the Baal Shem Tov around 1752 from Rashkov in the Ukraine to his brother-in-law R. Gershon of Kutov who was then in Palestine. The letter was published in the work *Ben Porat Yosef* by the Baal Shem Tov's disciple, R. Jacob Joseph of Pulnoye, at the end of the work, at Koretz in 1781. The section of the letter relevant to our theme reads:

> You must have the intention [*tekhavven*] of unifying a name whenever your mouth utters a word at the time you pray and study the Torah. In every letter there are worlds, souls and divinity, which ascend to become bound one to the other. Then the letters become bound and united one to the other to form a word and they become united with a true unification in the divine. You must allow your soul to become united with them at every stage of the above. Then all the worlds become united as one and they ascend so that there is immeasurable joy and delight. You know how great is the joy when bride and bridegroom unite

in this world of smallness and materialism. How much greater, then, is the joy at this lofty stage! God will undoubtedly help you and you will be successful and understand wherever you turn. Give to the wise and he will get further understanding.

The letters of the Hebrew alphabet are, as the Baal Shem Tov understands the matter, not mere symbols but the expression of metaphysical realities. They are the counterpart on earth of God's creative processes and are themselves endowed with creating power. The aim of the Hasid should be to assist the unification of these creative forces and in the process lose himself in the divine. As his mind dwells on each letter separately—Weiss calls this the 'atomization' of the letters—so that it embraces 'worlds, souls and divinity', his soul becomes absorbed in the unification process. The letters are then formed into words and, by reflecting on this, the mind of the Hasid is embraced in an ever higher unification process. Hasidic prayer is, then, an exercise in assisting the divine unification and participating in it, sharing the joy and delight which attend unification as all worlds and all souls become attached to God. The 'plain meaning' of the words of the prayers is entirely ignored. All that matters is the unification theme represented by the letters themselves and the way they are grouped together to form words. One can describe the difference between this kind of contemplation and the practice of the Lurianic *kavvanot* in the following way, apart from the fact that the former is intensely emotional while the latter is severely intellectual. Both techniques depart from the 'plain meaning' of the words, but while the Lurianic Kabbalist dwells on the 'higher' meaning of the words the Hasid is not interested in the meaning of the words at all, only in the unification process as represented by the letters and words they form.

An oft-quoted Hasidic comment in the same vein as the above is to the verse, 'A light shalt thou make to the ark' (Gen. 6: 16). The Hebrew word for 'ark' (*tevah*) is taken to mean 'word'. Thus . . .[18]

'A light shalt thou make for the word.' This means that the word should be illumined. For in every word there are worlds, souls and divinity. These ascend and become bound and united one to the other and with the divine. Then the letters become united and bound together to form a word and then they become truly united in the divine. A man must allow his soul to be embraced by each stage of the above-mentioned and then all the worlds become united as one and they ascend so that there is immeasurable joy and delight'.

Here again is the same theme. The letters of the Hebrew alphabet represent spiritual forces on high (e.g. the letter *alef* is a particular divine potency as it appears in the physical universe). In each letter there are represented the three stages of being: worlds, souls and divinity. The letters, in turn, combine to form words, expressing the further combination of all powers. Since man is the microcosm and the divine realm the macrocosm, then by contemplating the unification theme (the turning of the letters into words, etc.) in his prayers, man raises all these to their source in the divine and he assists the unification process. He repeats, as it were, in his own soul the divine creative activity and so restores the separated universe back to God.

In another passage[19] the technique is described in greater detail:

When he prays a man should put all his strength into the utterances and so he should proceed from letter to letter until he has forgotten his corporeal nature. He should reflect on the idea that the letters become combined and joined one to the other and this is great delight. For if in the material world unification is attended by delight how much more so in the spiritual realms! This is the stage of the world of formation. Afterwards he should reach the stage of having the letters in his thoughts alone so that he no longer hears that which he speaks. At this stage he enters the world of formation. Afterwards he should reach the quality of Nothingness at which all his physical powers are annihilated. This is the stage of the world of emanation, the quality of Wisdom.

This is a remarkable description of the Hasid's ascent of soul in his prayers until self-annihilation is attained. For the understanding of the passage something must be said of the Kabbalistic doctrine of the four worlds.

The doctrine runs that there are four worlds, one higher than the other. The highest of all is the *world of emanation* (*olam ha-atzilut*), the realm of the Sefirot. Beneath it and emerging from it is the *world of creation* (*olam ha-beriah*). Next there is the *world of formation* (*olam ha-yetzirah*). Lowest of all four is the *world of action* (*olam ha-asiyah*). This latter is the origin of the physical universe, which it embraces. The *world of emanation* is identified with the Sefirah Hokhmah ('Wisdom'). In Hasidic thought this Sefirah is called *ayin*, 'Nothingness', because of this stage of the divine process nothing can be said; it is utterly beyond all human comprehension. When a man attains to the stage of self-annihilation he can thus be said to have reached the world of the divine Nothingness. Emptied of selfhood his soul has now become attached to the true reality, the divine Nothingness. Thus in our passage the stages of the mystic's ascent in prayer are described in terms of the four worlds which, in fact, are mirrored in his own soul. He begins in the *world of action*, where he stands as he begins to pray. When 'he puts all his strength into the utterances' he abandons something of self and begins to ascend to the *world of formation*. The next stage in loss of selfhood is for him to lose the capacity to hear the words he utters. (The tradition of the rabbis has it that the words of the prayers must be voiced so that the Hasid, as an orthodox Jew, is prevented from taking the logical next step of completely silent prayer.) He continues to mouth the words, but his mind has become so preoccupied with the bare thought of the letters that he is no longer conscious of hearing the words he utters. He then reaches the *world of creation*. Finally, 'all his physical powers are annihilated'. He is no longer conscious even of his thoughts. He has attained to self-annihilation and is completely immersed in the divine Nothingness.

Reference must here be made to the idea, described in the chapter on the nature of Hasidic prayer, of prayer for the sake of the Shekhinah. We saw there that the Hasidic masters were bothered by the whole question of petitionary prayer in that this calls attention to the self and that their solution is that the Hasid should pray for the sake of the Shekhinah. On the face of it, this would seem to be in contradiction to the doctrine of 'attachment to the letters'. If the words of the prayers are only the means for the use of the technique described here, what difference does it make if in their 'plain meaning' they form prayers of petition?

The answer surely is that the 'plain meaning' is not entirely overlooked. Hence the 'plain meaning', too, must assist the true aim of the Hasid and this is said to be capable of realisation if the Hasid offers his petitionary prayers not for himself but for the Shekhinah. However, it would seem, none the less, from the descriptions we have recorded and others like them that, in fact, when the Hasid follows the technique of 'attachment to the letters' he eventually rises above even prayer for the sake of the Shekhinah and becomes entirely passive with not even this demand. But in these subtle matters there are, in all probability, different stages and no real consistency of outlook. It might also be noted here that occasionally we find in Hasidic literature a reaction against the doctrine of 'attachment to the letters' (apart from the Habad technique which differs, as we shall see, in any event). In a work attributed to R. Jacob Isaac of Lublin, the 'Seer', disciple of the Maggid of Meseritch, it is stated[20] that the Maggid's advice that man should put all his being into the letters only applies when time is short. But when there is no lack of time the worshipper should not concentrate on the letters. On the contrary, he should raise the words of the prayers heavenwards! This is one of many examples where early Hasidic ideas of a radical nature were later softened by subsequent teachers.

In this whole area of contemplative prayer the Hasid faces an acute problem posed by the tradition. Ideally the kind of contemplative prayer favoured by the Hasidim demands complete freedom from every type of distraction, but the tradition demands that the prayers be recited in a congregation of worshippers. The solution given in an early Hasidic work[21] is that the Hasid has no option except to do his best in congregational prayer (the implication is that God will assist his efforts) but that when he practises contemplation for the sake of attaining to *devekut* at other times, i.e. not during prayer, he should then avoid even the slightest distraction.

It is necessary for man, as he begins to pray, to have the sensation of being in the *world of action*. Afterwards, he should have the the sensation of being in the *world of formation*, the world of the angels and the Ophanim. Afterwards, in the *world of creation*, until he has the sensation in his thoughts that his thought has soared so high that it reaches the *world of emanation*. Just as a man strolls from room to room so should his thought stroll in the upper worlds. He should take care not to fall from his most elevated thoughts in the upper worlds but should strengthen himself with all the power at his disposal so as to remain above with his thoughts exceedingly high in the upper worlds. He should do this by having a bit and a rein on his thoughts so that he makes a kind of vow not to descend. If he wishes to do this in order to achieve *devekut*, at times other than those of prayer, it is essential that no other person should be present in the house. For even the chirping of birds can distract him and so, too, the thoughts of another person can distract him.

The idea behind the last sentence is that by a kind of telepathy the thoughts of another person in the same house can intrude into his thoughts and prevent him from soaring aloft or remaining lost in thought in the upper worlds.

As has been said, the Lurianic *kavvanot* were not only different from the Hasidic technique of contemplation. They were a positive hindrance to the Hasid. How can he lose himself in *devekut* if his mind is busily engaged in concentrating on the *kavvanot*? Eventually, in some Hasidic circles at least, the idea was put forward that the Lurianic *kavvanot* were for an earlier generation but that 'nowadays' the mind should be directed towards the attainment of self-annihilation, in the sense mentioned previously, and then the effects of the *kavvanot* would follow automatically through the recitation of the words of the prayers. This was stated explicitly by R. Kalonymus Kalman Epstein of Cracow in the name of his teacher R. Elimelech of Lizensk.[22]

> In our generation it is improper for a man to have in mind the *kavvanot* of prayer handed down to us in the Prayer Book of the Ari, of blessed memory, whether from the written text or whether he has learnt them and has them in mind by heart. So did I hear it from my master and teacher, the holy rabbi, the godly man, head of all the exile, our teacher Elimelech, may the memory of the righteous and holy be for a blessing. He said that a man should not have in mind thoughts or reflections on the *kavvanot* of the divine names. Instead he should bind both his external and his inner self, that is his vital force, his spirit and his soul, to En Sof, blessed be He. As a result, he binds all the revealed worlds and all

the inner aspects of the worlds to Him, blessed be He. His thought should be so attached to the pleasantness of the Lord that he has no time, not even for a moment, to have the *kavvanot* in mind. When a man's prayers are of this order the *kavvanot* and unifications are effected automatically.

It would be a mistake, however, to imagine that all the Hasidim gave up the practice of the Lurianic *kavvanot*. R. Hayim ben Solomon of Czernowitz and Mohilev (d. 1813), and somewhat outside the influence of the Maggid's school (he was a pupil of R. Yehiel Michel of Zlotchov), writes[23] that there are two types of prayer: simple prayer and prayer with the *kavvanot* in mind. Both are acceptable to God but prayer with the *kavvanot* is superior. Other Hasidim, too, used the *kavvanot* occasionally in their prayers. In the Prayer Book *Hare Besamim*, based on the comments of R. Isaiah Muskat of Praga, disciple of R. Israel of Koznitz, disciple of the Maggid, there are two types of *kavvanot*. The first is known as *kavvanot pashtiyot*, 'simple intentions', the second *kavvanot yesharot*, 'correct intentions'. The first are comments on the plain meaning of the prayers, the second are the Lurianic *kavvanot*. To give one example among many, on the verse, 'Then [*az*] sang Moses and the children of Israel' (Exod. 15: 1), which is part of the liturgy, these are the *kavvanot* recorded. The 'simple intention' is to have in mind the rabbinic comment that the Hebrew can be read as, 'Then Moses will sing' and the reference is to Moses singing at the resurrection of the dead. The 'simple intention' when reciting the verse is, 'I believe in perfect faith in the resurrection of the dead'. The 'correct intention' is to have in mind that the word *az* has the numerical value of eight (*alef* = 1; *zayin* = 7). This hints at the total number of letters in the two divine names (four in each) of Adonai and the Tetragrammaton. This is a far cry from the early Hasidic ideas on rejection of the *kavvanot* as a hindrance to *devekut*.

In the Habad system, contemplative prayer differs both from the Lurianic technique of *kavvanot* and from the early Hasidic technique of the atomisation of the letters as an aid to *devekut*. This system we shall examine in the next chapter.

CHAPTER VII

Contemplative Prayer (continued)

Contemplation, especially during prayer, is an essential feature of the Habad movement in Hasidism.[1] The very name Habad is formed from the initial letters of Hohkmah ('Wisdom'), Binah ('Understanding') and Daat ('Knowledge'). The first two, as we have noted in a previous chapter, are the names of two of the Sefirot, those representing the divine thought. In some Kabbalistic schemes Daat is also one of the Sefirot. In others it is not the name of a Sefirah but of a mediating principle between Hokhmah and Binah. Now according to the basic idea, stressed by Hasidism, that the divine processes are mirrored in man's soul, Hokhmah, Binah and Daat are descriptions, too, of man's contemplative life. Hokhmah is, in Habad thought, the first flash of intuitive knowledge and awareness, the emergence in the mind of a bare idea not as yet elaborated in thought. Binah denotes reflection on the elaborate details of the idea, the giving of form and content to it in the mind. Daat means an attachment of the mind to the idea so that it is fully grasped by the mind and acquires such a firm lodgement therein that, in turn, it is capable of arousing the emotions. Daat both follows on Hokhmah and Binah and is the motivating power, the essential interest, which propels a man towards Hokhmah and Binah.

As for the material of contemplation, Habad, here and in other areas, treads its own road. Essentially, the Habad Hasid is encouraged to reflect on the detailed Kabbalistic scheme by which creation unfolds. This follows the Lurianic pattern but as reinterpreted by the Habad thinkers. The Hasid has in mind the whole process by which all worlds proceed from En Sof through an increasing coarsening, as it were, of the divine light until the finite world we inhabit comes into being. The true Habad Hasid has to be, in fact, a Kabbalist and his contemplation in prayer consists of a review in his mind of the Lurianic mysteries in their Habad guise. This technique differs from that of the older Lurianic Kabbalists in that it is no longer a sustained reflection on each word of the prayers as referring to one or other of the divine names and their place on the Sefirotic map. Instead, the whole scheme is surveyed in the mind independently at appropriate stages of the prayers, especially when the Shema is recited.

Habad is, then, much more intellectual in its theory of contemplation than other Hasidic groups. It knows nothing of the early Hasidic idea, described in the last chapter, of the 'atomisation of the letters'. It differs from the few Hasidic Kabbalists who still preferred to use the Lurianic *kavvanot*. And it certainly differs from the tendency to be observed later among some groups of returning to the pre-Kabbalistic technique of simply concentrating on the 'plain meaning' of the prayers. This latter tendency is to be seen, for example, in the saying attributed to R. Baruch, the grandson of the Baal Shem Tov, that the simple meaning of the words is higher than the *kavvanot*, e.g. simply, 'Blessed art Thou, O Lord' and no more, though with powerful emotional delight and longing. In the same vein another Hasidic master said that the Yiddish names for God are the main *kavvanot*.[2] R. Samuel of Shinov[3] records that on his first visit to R. Simhah Bunam of Pzhysha (d. 1827) he complained of headaches after his prayers in his efforts to concentrate on them. The Zaddik replied that prayer has nothing to do with the head but with the heart. 'From that time onwards', R. Samuel concludes, 'I never suffered from headaches when I prayed.' Habad would emphatically disagree with the emotional approach. For Habad contemplative prayer is very much a severe intellectual exercise, in which emotional rapture and the like must follow on contemplation but not be a part of it.

To sum up what has been said until now in this chapter and in the previous one on the history of *kavvanah* in prayer, there are

83

six main stages: (1) The Talmudic rules about *kavvanah* in the sense of reflection on the 'plain meaning' of the words of the prayers and an awareness that the worshipper is in God's presence. Belonging to this stage are the rules governing the instances when *kavvanah* is not demanded; (2) The greater stress on *kavvanah* by the medieval thinkers as part of their battle for greater inwardness. At this stage *kavvanah* still retains its original meaning but greater demands are made of the worshipper to attain it; (3) In the Kabbalistic scheme (especially in its Lurianic version) *kavvanah* yields to *kavvanot*. The 'plain meaning' of the words is ignored in favour of concentration on the divine names and their combinations at which the words of the prayers are said to hint; (4) The early Hasidic shift of emphasis from the Lurianic *kavvanot* to 'attachment' (*devekut*) achieved by means of the 'atomisation of the letters'; (5) The reaction of various Hasidic groups to the latter either in favour of a return to the Lurianic *kavvanot* or a return to the 'plain meaning' of the words; (6) The Habad idea of contemplation as reflection on the Kabbalistic scheme in detail but not in relation to the particular words and letters of the prayers.

It so happens that we are in possession of a profound document in which the Habad technique is described in great detail by one of the foremost thinkers and masters of Habad. This is the *Kunteros Ha-Hitbonanut*[4] ('Tract on Contemplation') by R. Dov Baer of Lubavitch (1773–1827). R. Dov Baer, to whom reference has already been made in this book, is known as the 'Middle Rabbi' and was the son and successor of R. Shneor Zalman of Liady, the founder of the Habad system. Though caution must be exercised in assuming too readily that all R. Dov Baer's ideas are necessarily those of his father or of the movement as a whole, it is safe to conclude that we have in the document a reliable account, at least in its general terms, of what is involved in contemplation as understood by Habad. We embark here, therefore, on a detailed description and analysis of the *Kunteros Ha-Hitbonanut*.

R. Dov Baer begins[5] by stating that his aim in the tract is to explain both what constitutes contemplation and its content; in

other words, both the psychological processes involved in the act
of contemplation and the actual topics and themes upon which the
Hasid should reflect. R. Dov Baer first analyses the meaning of
contemplation, which he defines as 'powerful reflection on the
profundity of a subject, pondering over it until it is understood
perfectly in all the details of its various parts'. It is the opposite of
a mere superficial glance at a subject.

Every idea has its 'depth', 'length' and 'breadth' so that contemplation involves reflection on all three. Reflection on the
'breadth' of an idea means that its full implications are uncovered;
it is the 'width' of the river which has far greater extension than
the mere trickle of the brook. Reflection on the 'length' of an
idea means that an attempt is made so to grasp the subject that it
can be conveyed, by means of various illustrations, to one incapable otherwise of grasping it; it is the 'length' of the river flowing
far from its source. Reflection on the 'depth' of an idea means
that an attempt is made to grasp the essential point of the subject;
it is the 'depth' of the river in its underground source. As explained
in greater detail by R. Hillel, R. Dov Baer's disciple,[6] the illustration of the river is applied as follows. The underground source of
the river represents Hokhmah. The idea springs into the mind
spontaneously, from the unconscious, as we would be inclined to
say. The first flow of the river above ground represents Binah, the
beginning of contemplation proper. Although, at this stage, it
is no more than a trickle, it contains within itself the force
provided by the subterranean source and, *in potentia*, the whole
subsequent flow of the river. The idea has erupted into the mind
and its essence is grasped. The breadth of the river refers to the
expansion of the waters *near to their source*, i.e. the idea once
grasped is pondered on so as to uncover all its implications, so as
to understand what it really means in all its details. But if one
really understands an idea, one is able to convey it to others by
adapting the form in which it is expressed to the intellectual
capacity of the recipient. This is the length of the river. The
reference is not so much to the actual teaching of the idea to
others as to the ability to have the idea so clear in one's own mind
as to be able to see how it can be conveyed to others. The Hebrew

for 'contemplation' (*hitbonanut*) has the same root as Binah. But, R. Dov Baer remarks, *hitbonanut* is an intensive form of the verb and this is to indicate that only prolonged and rigorous reflection in depth qualifies as contemplation.

Furthermore, there are two types of contemplation,[7] represented by the Hebrew terms *binah* and *tevunah*. The man who has grasped the idea in all its details, as above, has attained to the stage of *binah* but he does not reach the more elevated stage of *tevunah* until he is able to use his deductive powers in order to grasp those further ideas that are only implicit in the original idea contemplated. For example, the man who has a complete grasp of a subtle legal theory has attained the stage of *binah* so far as his theory is concerned. But he does not attain to the stage of *tevunah* until he is capable of stating with complete conviction, on the basis of his theory, whether A or B would be culpable in law. Or, to give another example,[8] there is a good deal of difference between a man who has merely read widely about architecture and the professional architect whose reading has been supplemented by his practical skills in which he puts his academic knowledge to use. True contemplation has as its aim the attainment of *tevunah*, not of *binah* alone.

There are thus two stages of contemplation in prayer. The first is that of *binah*. This means reflection with deep concentration on the theme that God 'fills all worlds', that all there is has been created by God out of nothing and that it is by His power alone that all things are sustained. It is not sufficient to reflect on the bare idea but to grasp it in all its implications by means of various illustrations and analogies, such as that of the soul giving life to the body or that of the spark emerging from the flame. But it is possible for a man to obtain a theoretical understanding of this idea without being able to 'use' it in prayer. Many Hasidim, remarks R. Dov Baer, have a good knowledge of these tremendous themes in an academic way but fail to see of what relevance they are to the life of prayer. This is because they have never tried adequately to apply the themes of their studies to the life of prayer. They are more abstract religious thinkers than true contemplatives. The stage of *tevunah* is reached when the idea has become so much part of man that he can 'use' it in his prayers in order to induce the love and fear of God.

There are two methods of contemplation:[9] (a) the general method; (b) the detailed method. The general method is to dwell on the general idea of God's immanence, that all is in God. The detailed method is to reflect on the way in which God is immanent in each creature, on the way in which each is in God, on the divine vitality by which each creature is sustained and in which it has its being, as well as upon all the complex details of the Kabbalah. The worshipper, when adopting this detailed method, has in mind the whole system of divine emanation, from the highest point of the Sefirotic realm down through the whole marvellous chain of being to the lowliest creature in this physical universe. Of the two the detailed method is to be preferred, provided always that the details are connected in thought with the general idea of God's unity. (R. Dov Baer states that his father had told him in the name of the Maggid of Meseritch that this method should also be adopted when studying any detailed exposition of the divine mysteries in the Zohar or in the writings of the Lurianic school.) The fullest comprehension of every detail should only serve to fortify the general idea that all is in God. While the detailed method is to be preferred, R. Dov Baer, none the less, advises beginners to adopt, at first, the general method until they have gradually trained themselves to practise the detailed method.

Further, on the detailed method, R. Dov Baer remarks[10] that whenever a man engages in contemplation by this method there are two aspects to his thoughts. In reflecting on each detail he has in mind that the 'somethingness' of creatures stems from the divine Nothingness. This can, however, be of two kinds: (a) the reflection that 'somethingness' comes out of Nothingness; (b) that it is out of Nothingness that 'somethingness' comes. That is to say, in reflection of the type (a) the emphasis is on created things. In reflection of the type (b) the emphasis is rather on the way in which the divine Nothingness has brought them into being. Now the more one engages in reflection of the type (a) the greater the joy in comprehension, since reflection on finite things, albeit in their relation to the divine immanence, is not too difficult for finite man. But reflection of the type (b) is concerned with that which is utterly beyond all human comprehension. That is why the term Nothingness is used. Here the emphasis on the divine Nothingness means that the soul of the contemplative can never be satisfied, so that here the more profound and intense the act of contemplation the greater will be the resulting sense of remoteness and sorrow. When, for instance, man reflects on the myriads of stars in their courses, on the immensity of the space they occupy and on their size in relation to the earth, there is delight in the thought that all these have come into being out of the divine Nothingness. The more man understands the immensity of the miracle of their sheer existence the more he marvels, the greater his sense of wonder that all these came from 'nowhere' and the more intense his comprehension of God's majesty. But when he goes on from there to consider the nature of that divine Nothingness, his mind can only tremble in awe at the overwhelming mystery. Similarly, when a man reflects on the 'somethingness' of creatures he senses that he, too, is something. But when he begins to reflect on the divine Nothingness, his total inability to comprehend reduces him to a state of 'nothingness', and there is, in the standard Hasidic terminology, 'self-annihilation' (*bittul ha-yesh*). These two types of contemplation are, in fact, inseparable. For unless there is joy and wonder in contemplation on the 'somethingness' of things, there is little meaning to the idea that they all came from the divine Nothingness. On the other hand, there is little value in contemplation if the mind remains imprisoned in its reflection on the 'somethingness' of creatures without gazing beyond them to the divine Nothingness which sustains them all.

R. Dov Baer draws certain conclusions from this for the fuller contemplative exercises.[11] There is both joy and pain when lovers part for a time. These emotions, though conflicting, are, in reality, two sides of the same coin. The very poignancy of the pain they experience is the fruit of love, and that love is more intense than ever before because the pain of parting brings to the lovers a full realisation of what their love means to them. Similarly, the deeper a man's delight in his comprehension of the divine, the greater is his sorrow at his remoteness from the divine. For there is no limit to man's comprehension of the Limitless, there are no confines to man's spiritual ambitions. The nearer man comes to God the greater his sense of remoteness. The more intense his delight, the more powerful his longing and the more profound his sadness. The true test of authenticity in contemplation is whether or not the soul laments her remoteness from God. Where there is only joy, where man enjoys God without any sense of remoteness from Him, the act of contemplation is superficial. Hence R. Dov Baer advises his followers to rise at midnight to weep for their sins, which create a barrier between the soul and God. And it is for this reason that the Maggid of Meseritch taught that the 'secrets of the Torah' can only be comprehended by one 'whose heart is constantly anxious within him'.

The rest of the *Tract on Contemplation* contains a detailed description of the whole Kabbalistic scheme. This R. Dov Baer presents as the subject of contemplation. Having analysed the mechanics of contemplation, he gives the detailed topics on which contemplation should feed. It is obviously beyond the scope of this chapter to follow R. Dov Baer further. But the bare outlines of the scheme might be recorded briefly (even though for their interpretation a concentrated study of the Kabbalah is required) so as to convey something of the scope of the Hasid's contemplation as conceived of by R. Dov Baer. We can do no more than refer to the skeleton, adding that, of course, the mystical adept is required by R. Dov Baer to clothe it with the flesh of full meaning and significance.

Before the *tzimtzum* (God's withdrawal 'from Himself into Himself' in order to make 'room' for the world) there was only God as He is in Himself. (It should be noted that the Kabbalists think of all these processes as occurring outside time, so that terms like 'before' and 'after' are not really applicable.) In order for creatures to emerge as the recipients of His bounty, since it is the nature of the All-good to give of His goodness to others, the *tzimtzum* takes place. R. Dov Baer[12] compares it to a profound idea in the mind of a teacher. In order to convey the idea to his pupil, the teacher has to concentrate on the essential point of the matter and has to 'withdraw' from his comprehension of the full depth and breadth of the idea. After the *tzimtzum* a 'residue' of the divine light penetrated the 'empty space' left by the *tzimtzum*. (Again the Kabbalists do not think of 'space' in its literal sense but of the primordial 'space' into which eventually space and time as we know them emerged.) The light of En Sof (again used in a figurative sense) illumines the 'empty space' but no longer fills it. The highest and lowest stages of all the successive degrees by which the light of En Sof is unfolded are called respectively Keter ('Crown') and Malkhut ('Sovereignty'). These are, in fact, the names of the highest and lowest Sefirot but are used, too, at this early stage before the Sefirot have emerged. The 'line' of light from En Sof which penetrates the 'empty space' in order to illumine it and to sustain whatever is to emerge there, is called Malkhut of En Sof and this, in turn, becomes the Keter of the next stage which is known as Adam Kadmon ('Primordial Man'). In the same way the chain of emanation wends its way downwards by degrees. Malkhut of Adam Kadmon becomes Keter of the World of Emanation, the realm of the Sefirot. Malkhut of the World of Emanation becomes Keter of the World of Creation. Malkhut of this world becomes Keter of the World of Formation. Malkhut of this world becomes Keter of the World of Action. Within the whole process there are countless variations and combinations in which the light of En Sof is contracted and expands, illumines this way and that, so as to sustain all worlds. Much is demanded then of the Habad Hasid who wishes to have *kavvanah* in his prayers. His mind must dwell on all these stages with the aim of seeing all of them as in essence only the infinite light of En Sof.

There is a further idea which is behind the whole doctrine of Habad contemplation. This is that the lowest stage of all the 'upper worlds'—Malkhut of the World of Action—reaches back to, and is united with, the highest stage of all—Malkhut of En Sof—and this, in turn, is united with En Sof. Since the actual physical universe is only the lowest and final manifestation of the World of Action, all finite creatures are ultimately united in and embraced by the unity of En Sof. This is the mystical meaning given to the verse: 'I am the first, and I am the last' (Isa. 44: 6), i.e. from the highest stage of all, the first impulse, as it were, in En Sof, to the final manifestation of the divine creative activity, all are included, as the Habad thinkers are fond of saying, in God's simple unity. The Habad contemplative is expected to become thoroughly familiar with all this, so that when he reflects in his prayers on the details of the process there is an automatic compression of them all into the one great principle of unity. It is for this reason, Habad teaches, that there are no references in the Book of Psalms to the 'higher worlds', only to God's majesty as manifested here in the physical universe. For, in reality, there is no 'separation' between the processes of the higher realms and those observed in the physical world. They are all part of the same process and are all embraced by the divine unity. The Hasid, trained in the Kabbalah and using it in his prayers, dwells in his thought on all the complex details of the chain of emanation and, through profound reflection on them, learns to perceive that from beginning to end of all the creative processes there is only the divine unity, by the light of which all separate things are illumined and by which they are given the appearance of reality.

It remains to be said that Habad contemplation takes place especially while the Shema is recited, while during the Eighteen Benedictions more emphasis is placed on petitionary prayer according to the plain sense of those benedictions. This is stated clearly in a number of Hasidic works produced by the Habad thinkers, e.g. in R. Dov Baer's *Imre Binah* (Introduction), where the author also warns against recourse to the Lurianic *kavvanot*. Part of this Introduction should be quoted as an important contribution to the theme of this chapter.

> When a man gives his heart, spirit and soul to God when he says, 'The Lord is One' with self-sacrifice, then spirit attracts spirit and the revelation of the light of En Sof's essence is drawn in actuality, to illumine with a new light during the Eighteen Benedictions, to each person when he offers his prayers and supplication in humility and bitterness of soul, to entreat for great mercy also in connection with material things, children, life and sustenance, and for all things appertaining to man's soul. But if a man's heart does not concentrate on God during the recitation of the Shema then the Will of the Lord does not operate at all during the Eighteen

Benedictions. . . . The wise will increase his knowledge to discover further detailed *kavvanot* by labouring hard in the study of the Zohar and the writings of the Ari. It all really comes to the same thing, namely, the comprehension of the simple unity alone. He should not attempt to climb up on the ladder of *kavvanot*, divine names and their unification, as is the practice of the Kabbalists, for God has no desire for these. All He wants is the single *kavvanah* in which man binds his soul to His true essence, blessed be He, alone. . . . God searches out all hearts. There are some whose sole aim is to achieve deep *kavvanah* and the unification in accordance with the Kabbalah alone so that he can say, 'I know the mystery, I know the mystery'. And his heart is not truly firm and sincere to be directed solely towards His essence, blessed be He, alone.

CHAPTER VIII

Ecstatic Prayer

The two terms used in Hasidic literature for ecstasy in prayer are: *hitlahavut* (from *lahav*, 'flame') i.e. burning enthusiasm; and *hitpaalut* (from *paal*, 'to do', 'to act'), in the intensive and reflexive form used here, to be acted upon, to be affected, hence ecstasy. The first term, and the one most frequently used, *hitlahavut*, denotes chiefly enthusiasm in prayer. The second term, *hitpaalut*, denotes chiefly the effect of prayer on the worshipper, the rapture that is attendant upon contemplative prayer. The term *hitpaalut* is chiefly used by the Habad thinkers in whose school there is considerable discussion on the meaning and value of rapture in prayer. This will be considered later in the chapter. First, we must examine the more frequent term, used by practically all the Hasidim, as well as the general idea of prayer in a spirit of boundless joy, delight and warmth.

To be completely absorbed in prayer, to lose the self and 'strip off one's corporeal nature' (*hitpashtut ha-gashmiyut*), to burn in longing for the divine, these were the aims of Hasidism from the beginnings of the movement. In an early Hasidic text[1] the following advice is given on how the Hasid can avoid thoughts of self and pride during his prayers:

> He should reflect, before he begins to pray, that he is prepared to
> die while he is praying as a result of his concentration. There are,
> in fact, some (Hasidim) whose concentration in prayer is so
> intense that, were nature left to itself, they would die after uttering
> no more than four or five words in God's presence, blessed be He.
> Once he thinks of this he will say to himself: Why should I have
> any ulterior motives when offering this prayer? since he is ready

to die after uttering only a few words. In reality, it is by God's great mercy, blessed be He, that strength is given him to complete his prayer and yet remain alive.

The idea behind this text is that it is dangerous to approach God in prayer (a far cry from the conventional Jewish attitude to prayer!). Man's soul, seeking her Source, is ready, at the time of prayer, to leave the body behind to become absorbed in God. It is only by a special grace of God that the peril is averted. In a report (obviously to be accepted with more than a grain of scepticism since the author lived several decades after the heroes mentioned) by R. Israel of Koznitz (d. 1814) it is even suggested that, were it not for God's grace, man would be so lost to self when he begins to pray that prayer itself, involving bodily processes, would be impossible.[2]

> I have heard it said that the holy Rabbi, our teacher R. Gershom [of Kutov] once said this to our master R. Israel Baal Shem, of blessed memory, 'As long as you are able to recite voluntarily in your prayers the words *Blessed art Thou* you should know that you have not yet attained the ideal of prayer. For when he prays a man must be so stripped [of his corporeal nature—*be-hitpashtut*] that it is impossible for him to find the energy and the intellectual ability to speak the words of the prayers.' This is perfectly true. Yet there is a still higher truth. This is when a man is stripped of all corporeality, of every kind of will, and is bound only to his Creator, so that he no longer knows how to recite his prayers because of the awe he experiences and because of his attachment to God, yet, none the less, he recites his prayers in good order. This is because heaven has pity on him, endowing him with speech and the power to pray, as it is said, 'O Lord, open Thou my lips' [Ps. 51: 17].

A number of the Zaddikim were especially noted for their ecstatic prayers. R. Levi Yitzhak of Berditchev (d. 1809) is the subject of numerous Hasidic tales describing his ardour in prayer, and there is undoubtedly a core of historical truth behind all the legends. Of R. Levi Yitzhak it is said[3] that he used to pray with such awe of God that he was physically incapable of staying in one place and he would move about while praying. His burning enthusiasm (*hitlahavut*) was so infectious that all who were present when he recited his prayers would be brought nearer to God. On the festival of Shavuot, the feast commemorating the giving of the Torah, it is said, R. Levi Yitzhak was engrossed in the morning prayers for no less than twelve hours at a time. After leading the congregation in prayer during the whole of the Day of Atonement, R. Levi Yitzhak used to cry out aloud, 'My heart is on fire'. R. Israel of Koznitz is reported to have learned the art of ecstatic prayer from R. Levi Yitzhak. The Maggid of Koznitz[4] writes that a man must fear God as well as love Him, otherwise the great love a man has for God would lure his soul away from his body and he would die in longing during his prayers. The Maggid's son, R. Moses, states that on more than one occasion his father fainted during his prayers and it was only with difficulty that they were able to revive him.[5] The author of a biography of the Maggid[6] remarks that in his youth he made the acquaintance of an elderly Hasid whose father knew the Maggid well and from whom he heard details concerning the prayer life of the Maggid. Here, too, there is no doubt a core of fact behind the report. The Maggid had a sick, emaciated body. He had to be carried in a chair from his house to the synagogue, but as soon as he entered the house of prayer he would cry out, 'How full of awe is this place!' (Gen. 28: 17). He would then leap to the prayer-desk 'as if he were flying through the air'. The Maggid was so delicate that he was unable to wear shoes and stood, while praying, in his socks on a bearskin. In spite of his ill health, when he recited the verse, 'Sing unto the Lord a new song' (Ps. 149: 1) his weakness would leave him and he would sing in joy 'like a little girl'. He used to say that in all the world there is no greater delight than a prayer recited well.

Another Zaddik renowned for his *hitlahavut* in prayer was R. Aaron of Karlin (1736–72), disciple of the Maggid of Meseritch. In the legends told of R. Aaron *hitlahavut* is a state that is compatible not only with the love of God but also with the fear of God, love and fear being close to one another and complementing one another.[7] There is a Hasidic tradition[8] that R. Shneor Zalman of Liady described R. Aaron's fear of God in this way. It is as if he were tied to a post with a soldier in front of him directing his musket at his heart and he were to see the flash as the soldier fired and the bullet sped towards him. And this was his fear when he was merely in the state of smallness of soul. Hasidic legend has it that when R. Aaron used to recite the Song of Songs a great disturbance would take place in heaven and the ministering angels would cease their praises in order to listen to R. Aaron's holy melody. It used to be said of R. Aaron that he was burned up in his fear of the Creator. To this day the Hasidim of the Karlin dynasty in Jerusalem are known for their extraordinary *hitlahavut* during their prayers. An eye-witness of the prayers in the Karlin conventicle at Brest-Litovsk at the beginning of this century described the astonishing *hitlahavut* of the Karliner Hasidim from the beginning of the prayers to the end as surpassing the warmth of the average rabbinic prayer even at the holiest hour of the Day of Atonement. The rabbi of the town, R. Hayim Soloweitchick, though certainly far from being a Hasid himself, told his visitor that he would send children to pray in the Karliner *stiebel* in order to provide them with enough spiritual fare to last all their lives.[9]

The Zaddikim of the dynasty of Belz in more recent times were renowned for their *hitlahavut* in prayer. On Rosh Ha-Shanah and Yom Kippur at Belz, the Zaddik himself would lead the prayers. When I was a boy I once heard an elderly Belzer Hasid describe the prayerful atmosphere in the large synagogue at Belz at the end of the last century, of which he was a witness. He declared that the mood of elevation when the Zaddik led the Hasidim in prayer was such that if the High Priest himself had returned to earth and offered to lead the prayers the Hasidim would have sent him packing, requiring no substitute for their beloved Zaddik. It is reported that when the second Zaddik of the dynasty shouted out loud the words 'one and one' (*ahat ve-ahat*) in the additional service of Yom Kippur, describing the procedure in Temple times on the holy day, it seemed as if the walls of the great synagogue, in which thousands of Hasidim were assembled, would totter. Of his son the following is reported:

> The Hasidim who gathered under the shade of his son, our holy master, our teacher and mentor, R. Issachar Dov, may the memory of the righteous be for a blessing, of Belza, say that his sensations and *hitlahavut* on the Days of Awe were indescribable. The mood

of elevation reached its peak when he recited 'Out of the depths' (Ps. 130) before the *shofar* was sounded. He would recite one verse while weeping bitterly so that no one present could fail to have his heart melt like water. Immediately afterwards, he would recite the next verse with such joy and exultation that it was hard to believe that only a moment before he was in tears. The pouring out of his soul in prayer like a son longing for his father went straight to the heart of every one of the worshippers who, at that moment, reached a spiritual degree he could never have attained through his own efforts.[10]

R. Baruch, grandson of the Baal Shem Tov, was another Zaddik especially famous for *hitlahavut*. Of this Zaddik (d. 1811) the Hasidim used to say that after the ritual immersion on the eve of the sabbath he would recite the Song of Songs with such *hitlahavut* that those who witnessed it would imagine that fire burned all around him. It is related of R. Zevi Hirsch of Zhydachov that in his youth he visited R. Baruch together with a companion in order to hear the Zaddik recite the Song of Songs. When the Zaddik reached the verse, 'For I am love-sick' (2: 5) R. Zevi Hirsch's companion ran from the room in terror. R. Zevi Hirsch himself bravely stayed on but when the Zaddik reached the verse, 'For love is as strong as death . . . the flashes thereof are flashes of fire, a very flame of the Lord' (8: 6) R. Zevi Hirsch almost lost his reason 'because of the great attachment and longing'.[11]

As we have seen in the chapter on gesture in prayer, the followers of R. Abraham of Kalisk and R. Hayim Haikel of Amdur, disciples of the Maggid of Meseritch, carried their enthusiasm in prayer so far as to turn somersaults while reciting the prayers. In the rules drawn up by R. Hayim Haikel, said to be based on the teachings of his master the Maggid of Meseritch, there are a number of references to *hitlahavut*:[12]

It is also an important rule in prayer that a man should allow his intellect to prevail when he recites the words of the prayers so as to shatter the barrier which separates [him from God] until he cleaves to God, blessed be He. For every letter [of the prayers] is a great world extending upwards *ad infinitum* and with every letter he utters with his mouth he bestirs those worlds up above. Consequently, he should recite the words [of his prayers] with great enthusiasm [*hitlahavut*], with great joy, and with great attachment [*devekut*]. It is another great rule that in whatsoever he does a man should intend only to give satisfaction to the Shekhinah. He should have no thought of self, not even to the slightest degree, for he is vanity and emptiness so why should he do it for his own pleasure? Even if he makes many preparations so as to be able to serve God with attachment, but does this in order to obtain personal delight from his act of worship, then he is only a self-worshipper. The main thing is that all his worship should be for the sake of the Shekhinah and there should be nothing of self in it, not even to the slightest degree. At times a man is like unto a drunkard in the joy he has of the Torah because a great love burns in his heart. At times a man is able to recite his prayers at great speed because the love of God burns so powerfully in his heart and the words emerge from his mouth automatically.

The 'quietistic' view mentioned in these rules, that even delight in worship must be spontaneous but if sought for has too much selfhood in it, is reminiscent of the Habad view we shall consider later on in this chapter. In the same vein R. Abraham of Slonim (1804–84) records[13] that R. Menahem Mendel of Vitebsk is reported as saying that in his prayers he was like a miserable beggar who seeks entrance to the king's palace but is thrown out again and again, yet persists in trying to gain entrance to the king. R. Abraham commented that the 'throwing out' refers to 'the delight and broadening of the mind' that a man may experience in his prayers. R. Menahem Mendel's spiritual state was so high that whenever he became aware of how pleasant it was to pray he looked upon it as if God were casting him away. R. Abraham[14] is also reported to have said to his followers that man's ecstasy in prayer sometimes comes from the liver but he deludes himself into thinking that it comes from the heart! R. Abraham[15] said further that unless a man's heart is pure his burning enthusiasm in prayer is carried over also to the evil in 'the innermost recesses' of his heart.

It was left, however, largely to the Habad school to consider in detail the question of ecstasy (*hitpaalut*) in prayer.[16] Habad, it must be repeated, is a contemplative movement with a strong suspicion of emotional religiosity. R. Shneor Zalman of Liady, the founder of the Habad movement, studied for a time with R. Abraham, the 'Angel', son of the Maggid of Meseritch. A later Habad thinker, R. Hillel of Poritch (d. 1864), describes what seems to be an authentic Habad tradition, according to which R. Shneor Zalman learned a new method of divine worship from the 'Angel'. R. Hillel[17] writes:

I have heard in the name of the holy R. Abraham, son of the Rabbi, the Maggid, his soul is in Eden, that a new method of divine worship was suggested to him by the battles of Frederick [the Great]. This is the matter of 'attackieren'. It appears that they do not array themselves, as in former times, to attack each other but, on the contrary, they fly from the enemy and then surround him until he is compelled to surrender. Similarly, divine worship in former times consisted in a war with evil. Man coerced his traits of character by means of that type of contemplation that leads to ecstasy. But he [the 'Angel'] discovered a new method by means of which man becomes attached to the category of the divine itself. This is achieved by means of contemplation on the profound mysteries of the higher Partzufim ['Configurations'] or the [mystical] reasons for the divine commandments. These have no connection whatever with ecstasy of love and yet the divine light is drawn down from above to surround the evil until it is automatically vanquished. He [the 'Angel'] stated further that there is another difference. According to the earlier methods of divine worship, the battle was joined in one detail at a time. For instance, when a man engaged in contemplation on those matters which concerned ecstasy of love he attained to an ecstasy of love and by this means he transformed evil loves. Similarly, when he engaged in contemplation on those matters which concerned fear he attained to an ecstasy of divine fear and by this means he transformed evil fears. But according to the present method man's attachment to the divine itself, in a general manner, effects both the conquest of evil and its transformation in all details at once. Now although this way is very lofty, it is essential for the lowly souls of this generation who cannot prevail at all over the evil within and who fall into a melancholy state when they desire to search for the 'how' and the 'why' in their innermost heart. And even if they do not search within but simply attach themselves in that form of contemplation which concerns divine love and fear, no love and fear result from it, as is explained fully in the *Tanya* [the classic work of R. Shneor Zalman]. Consequently, our master and teacher, his soul is in Eden, counselled that one should engage in no other form of contemplation than that of the divine itself, in profound reflection, and then, automatically, all the workers of iniquity will be scattered and humbled.

R. Hillel concludes that this is the basis of the whole Habad system.

What R. Hillel is saying in this passage is that, in the older view, contemplation was an attempt to induce ecstasy with the special aim of combating the evil propensities in human nature. If, for example, a man was bothered by love of evil things he would try to dwell in his contemplation on the love of God until he was moved to ecstasy by the thought of this love. The ecstatic love of the divine would then be strong enough to counteract the love of evil in his soul. The Habad method is quite different. Instead of a direct assault on the evil traits in one's character, the far better way is to dwell in contemplation on the divine mysteries. This will have the effect of bringing man's soul nearer to the divine and the evil in his soul will be vanquished automatically.

Here, as in other matters, Habad takes a line of its own. We have seen in the previous chapter how R. Dov Baer, R. Shneor Zalman's son and successor in the leadership of Habad, described in detail the Habad technique of contemplation. The whole Sefirotic scheme, the Partzufim, is surveyed in the mind. It is in the first instance a purely intellectual exercise though, as R. Dov Baer remarks, it is part of the life of prayer and has to be engaged in with warmth and vitality. What precisely is the role of ecstasy (*hitpaalut*) in this scheme? This was a major problem for the Habad thinkers after the death of R. Shneor Zalman.

Soon after the great master's death his son, R. Dov Baer, was obliged to send a letter to the Habad Hasidim urging upon them that *hitpaalut* was an essential ingredient in the life of prayer.[18] Some Hasidim had concluded from R. Shneor Zalman's stress on intellectual comprehension and suspicion of emotion that he rejected ecstasy entirely. R. Dov Baer is at pains to point out how mistaken such a view is. Ecstasy, he remarks, is essential because unless the heart is moved in rapture as the fruit of contemplation, clear evidence is provided that the act of contemplation suffers from complete lack of vitality. It is thinking about the divine mysteries in a purely academic way, whereas the true ideal is for contemplation to be 'used' in order to awaken in the soul the love and fear of God. But R. Dov Baer realises that the question is one of great subtlety and elusiveness with the dangers of self-delusion ever present. Consequently, soon after writing his letter, he sent his *Tract on Ecstasy* as counsel to his followers. This tract is one of the most remarkable compositions in Jewish mystical literature. It is one of the very few attempts by a Jewish mystic to describe the mystical states experienced in prayer. A detailed account of the *Tract on Ecstasy* has been attempted elsewhere.[19] Here we need only point to some of its main features.

R. Dov Baer first[20] calls attention to the new emphasis which his father gave to the question of ecstasy in prayer and explicitly distinguishes between this and the older techniques of the Hasidim.

> Observe, the opening of my words gives light on the general distinction between the older ways of Hasidism and those Hasidic ways which our master and father, our teacher and instructor, of blessed memory, his soul is in Eden, bequeathed to us and illumined for us by the light of his doctrine. For his chief aim from the beginning of his service in holiness (more than once did I hear it from the mouth of his holy spirit, blessed be his memory, that this was his chief aim and the purpose of his efforts with real self-sacrifice on behalf of our fraternity) was only that the revelation of the divine be fixed firmly in their soul. That is to say, the ecstasy of their soul should be only a divine ecstasy and not an ecstasy of the fleshly life, for this is not divine ecstasy at all. This is a fundamental principle and it contains the essence of the matter, for it is the distinction between those who serve the Lord with the soul and those who only serve the Lord with the body. Included in this general principle are many and exceedingly complex details.

For R. Dov Baer, true ecstasy is when man experiences, as a result of his severe and prolonged contemplation, the nearness of God. His soul is moved by the divine. In R. Dov Baer's terminology, this is 'serving the Lord with the soul'. 'Serving the Lord with the body' or 'ecstasy of the fleshly life' is a mere goading of the self into a passion, in which contemplation is used solely as a means to an end, the end being the thrill and excitement experienced. It is basically, according to R. Dov Baer, no different from any other kind of self-titillation. It is material and cheap and not really divine worship at all. This kind of spurious ecstasy is hinted at[21] in the rabbinic saying, 'Do not pray with the blood'. Actually, R. Dov Baer is rather more precise. The state of artificial stimulation is not really called serving God at all. It is sheer delusion. 'Serving the Lord with the body', in its more precise sense, refers to a higher stage in which man does have an experience of God, but when what is moved is the basic, vital bodily force, not the soul. It is not really a spiritual experience but an emotional one. Consequently, R. Dov Baer goes on[22] to describe in acute detail various states of soul, one higher than the other. The essential idea here is that at a high stage of authentic contemplation the divine in man's soul meets God, as it were. The divine meets the divine. But in this there are many stages which R. Dov Baer seeks to delineate. The actual analysis need not be repeated here.

R. Dov Baer's interpretation of his father's ideas did not win universal acceptance. His former friend and the chief disciple of R. Shneor Zalman, R. Aaron of Starosselje (1766–1829), refused to recognise R. Dov Baer's authority and set up eventually a rival court in Starosselje. Habad tradition, which is amply supported by the texts we have, has it that these two Habad teachers differed, among other matters, on the role of ecstasy in the life of prayer. R. Aaron was the author of a comprehensive exposition of R. Shneor Zalman's teaching, published under the title: *Shaare Ha-Yihud Ve-Ha-Emunah*[23] ('The Gates of Unification and Faith'). Although neither R. Dov Baer nor R. Aaron refer to one another directly in their writings, it requires no great insight, in view of the sound Habad tradition, to recognize the marked differences in the approaches of these two masters. In R. Aaron's Introduction he is at pains to reject, as R. Dov Baer does, the purely emotional approach. R. Aaron, too, speaks of the harm done in contemplation by the erection of a barrier of self-awareness between the worshipper and God. But R. Aaron is far less severe on spurious ecstasy than is R. Dov Baer. It appears that for R. Aaron ecstasy is so important that the Hasid is justified in taking the risk of attaining only a sham ecstasy. Furthermore, in R.

Aaron's system, even the less authentic type of ecstasy is not devoid of value. R. Aaron writes:[24]

> Now although I have written above in the name of our teacher, his soul is in Eden, that man's labour in worship should be to purify himself of self-awareness, nevertheless, all his holy words were always to encourage the heart and to validate every type of ecstasy according to each person's capacity. No man's heart should be disturbed because of his realisation that the ideal type of human worship and ecstasy should be one from which all aware-ness of self has been removed and in which there is no admixture of evil. For a man may come to view all ecstasy with suspicion in his fear that it may contain some mixture of self-awareness and that his love is illusory, imperfectly refined and unauthentic. The result may be that he will not allow himself to engage in that type of contemplation which embraces love sensed in the heart. Therefore he [R. Shneor Zalman] would validate every kind of love, and he urged his followers not to be apprehensive about the illusory nature of their love. The whole of his holy work is based on the verse, 'But the word is very nigh unto thee, in thy mouth, and in thy heart, that thou mayest do it' (Deut. 30: 14). And the student of his holy work will see that all his words are intended for the encouragement of the ecstasy of each one, in whatever fashion it may be, and not, God forbid, to reject it.

Habad tradition describes, too, the differences between R. Dov Baer and R. Aaron in their personal religious life, reflecting their different views on ecstasy. R. Aaron, it is said,[25] used to pray with a great shouting so that all who observed him praying were themselves moved to ecstasy. Of R. Dov Baer, on the other hand, it is said[26] that he would stand immobile in prayer for as long as three hours at a time and that at the end of his prayer his hat and shirt would be soaked in perspiration.

At all events the whole debate is peculiar to Habad. Among the other early Hasidic authors it is surprising how little mention is made of ecstasy (*hitpaalut*) at all in the sense of rapture following on profound contemplation. Their emphasis is almost entirely on *hitlahavut*, the burning enthusiasm and emotional warmth in which prayer is undertaken.

CHAPTER IX

The Elevation of 'Strange Thoughts'

A doctrine of much significance in early Hasidism but one that was eventually abandoned by the majority of later teachers is that of elevating 'strange thoughts' (*mahashavot zarot*).[1]

We have noted in the previous chapters how concerned the Hasidim were to avoid thoughts of self during prayer. The ideal for the Hasid was to lose himself in the divine. Yet the Hasid could not help experiencing in his prayers the intrusion not alone of selfhood but of thoughts opposed to the Jewish tradition. These 'strange thoughts' were generally of three kinds.[2] In the literature on the subject in Hasidism there are repeated references to 'strange love', to 'pride' and to 'idolatry'. 'Strange love' refers to thoughts of sexual sin or sexual imaginings. 'Pride' refers to thoughts of how wise and pious the Hasid was. 'Idolatry' refers to thoughts about irreligion, the denial of Judaism or the attraction of Christianity.

What was the Hasid to do? A dialectic developed[3] in early Hasidism between the conscious attempt to reject the 'strange thoughts' by pushing them out of the mind and the attempt to keep them in the mind but to 'elevate' them. Elevation in this context means to trace them in the mind to their source in God (since from Him come all things) and so deprive them of their baneful power. For example, if the Hasid suddenly finds that his devotions are being distracted by thoughts about a woman he knows, he begins to dwell on the fact that her beauty, which is the cause of her attraction, is only a very pale reflection of the source of all beauty on high and this helps him to sense the illusory nature of all physical beauty in comparison with the divine. By having this in mind during his prayers the Hasid has managed to cope with the distraction not by rejecting it but by using it and so redeeming it for the holy. Or if the Hasid finds that his thoughts are turning towards a sense of his own importance, he should dwell on pride as a manifestation here on earth of God's majesty and he will then be led on to elevate the pride to its source in God and so transcend the self in the very process of having his attention drawn to it. Or if he finds himself entertaining idolatrous thoughts during his prayers, he should remind himself that the lure of idolatry is occasioned by the desire in the human breast to worship. Very well then, let it lead to the Being alone worthy of human worship. In these ways the 'strange thoughts' themselves lead man back to God and are 'elevated' rather than rejected. Naturally, this whole doctrine aroused the ire of the Mitnaggedim. Among the Hasidic masters themselves the problem was approached in different ways and various techniques were evolved. These we must now examine.

R. Jacob Joseph of Pulnoye reports:[4]

> As I have heard from my master [the Baal Shem Tov] how to put right the strange thoughts. If it is thoughts of women he should intend to elevate them by attaching them to their root in Hesed ['Lovingkindness'], according to the mystery of, 'And if a man shall take his sister. . . . it is Hesed' [Lev. 20: 17]. And thoughts of idolatry produce a flaw in the Tiferet ['Beauty'] of Israel. And enough has been said.

The reference here is to the Sefirot of Hesed and Tiferet. According to R. Jacob Joseph the word *hesed* (English translation 'shameful thing') in the verse in Leviticus dealing with incest means the Sefirah Hesed. Even illicit love stems ultimately from Hesed but, of course, it must be rejected. When the Hasid is afflicted with illicit sexual thoughts during his prayers he should dwell on the 'mystery' and thus 'attach' the thought to its source in Hesed. The Sefirah Tiferet is especially attacked, as it were, when a man has idolatrous thoughts. A 'flaw' has been produced in that realm since man's thoughts have an effect on high. The beauty and splendour of God's sovereign rule has been given to another. When the Hasid finds himself afflicted with idolatrous thoughts during his prayers he should reflect on this and thus strengthen his allegiance to God. In this way the thought itself has helped him to come nearer to God and has become 'elevated' in the process. In the same passage R. Jacob Joseph observes that since there are so many thoughts which God brings to man in his prayers in order for him to 'put them right' and elevate them, it follows that the 'strange thoughts' differ, and those he has one day are not necessarily those he has the next day.

The theory behind the whole process of elevation is the Lurianic doctrine of the 'holy sparks'. The doctrine runs that at one stage in the process by which God emerged from concealment the 'vessels' of the seven lower Sefirot (*Hesed*, *Gevurah*, *Tiferet*, *Netzah*, *Hod*, *Yesod* and *Malkhut*) were too weak to contain the divine light and, when the light burst into them, they were shattered. Although they were later reconstructed, there was an overspill of the divine light and this proceeded from 'world' to 'world', the overspill of one world forming the sustaining power of the world beneath it, until, eventually, the overspill nourished the 'Other Side', the 'Shells' (*kelipot*), the denizens of evil. This cosmic catastrophe[5] is known as the 'breaking of the vessels' or 'the death of the kings'. As a result of it 'holy sparks' were scattered in all things. By using the things of the world in a spirit of consecration man releases these 'holy sparks' and redeems them for the holy. By thus elevating the 'holy sparks' man provides the Female (the Sefirah Malkhut), the Shekhinah, with the 'female waters' which enable Her to be united with the Male (the Sefirah Tiferet) and so assist the 'sacred marriage' by means of which harmony is promoted in the Sefirotic realm and the divine grace can flow. There are in all 288 'holy sparks', hinted at in the verse, 'And the spirit of God hovered [*merahefet*] over the face of the waters' (Gen. 1: 2). The word *merahefet* represents *met* ('the death of') *rph* (= 288). In the Kabbalah there are references to 'holy sparks' existing in evil, too, but these are to be redeemed not by elevation but by rejection. When man rejects evil to which he is tempted, he thereby releases and redeems the 'holy sparks' therein. In the Sabbatian heresy the 'holy sparks' even in evil can be elevated, hence the Sabbatian notion of 'holy sin'. Hasidism naturally rejects this, but the influence of the Sabbatian doctrine is clearly seen in the new Hasidic idea that the 'holy sparks' in evil can be redeemed through elevation. The Hasid does not, of course, embrace evil in practice in order to redeem the 'holy sparks'. But he does embrace it in thought, i.e. when the 'strange thoughts' come to him in his prayers. The Sefirot are arranged in columns. Those on the right represent Hesed, those on the left Gevurah. Thus, for example, illicit love stems ultimately from the right column while the crime of murder stems ultimately from the left column. After these preliminary remarks we are now in a position to understand the following important observation of R. Jacob Joseph.[6]

It seems to me that the idea of prayer can be explained in accordance with the tradition I have from my teachers and from books that each day a different intention is required in prayer. That is why the Talmud rules that one should introduce something new in each prayer. There is convincing proof of this in the fact that the idea of prayer is to refine the sparks, of the 288 sparks of the broken vessels. This belongs to the mystery of the elevation of the female waters to Malkhut so that husband and wife can become united. The elevation of the sparks is produced by the thoughts which arise in man's mind when he offers his prayers. The wise man with his eyes in his head knows how to refine the inner parts of the strange thoughts, the holy sparks which have entered into the shells to become strange thoughts. For example, if there come to man lustful thoughts about women this derives from Hesed, as it is said, 'If a man takes his sister . . . it is Hesed' [Lev. 20: 17]. He should understand that if he has this desire, merely because of the single holy spark that is there, how much greater will be his delight if he attaches himself to the Source of this delight, for there the delight is altogether limitless and incomparable. The same applies to thoughts of idolatry, God forfend, and the shedding of blood, which is of the left column. To dwell on this theme at length is dangerous and the wise will be silent. Now we know from experience that it is impossible for the same thought to be present each day as on the day before and the day before that. It follows that the prayers in which he introduces something new out of his thoughts must also differ. For this to be achieved a broad mind and great powers of concentration are necessary. As is well known, man's mouth, heart and thoughts must be in perfect accord.

The startling nature of the doctrine is obvious. The Talmud, in its reference to the introduction of something new, means only that a new petition should be introduced each day into the prayers. For R. Jacob Joseph the meaning is that each day a new 'strange thought', which comes automatically into the mind and is sent by God for that purpose, must be elevated. In addition to the three types of 'strange thought' mentioned earlier, R. Jacob Joseph refers, too, in this passage, to murderous thoughts. The destructive urge in man can only have come into being because there is the power of Gevurah on high. R. Jacob Joseph is saying that when such urges intrude even in prayer, they can be 'sublimated' by attaching them to their source in Gevurah, the left column.

In another early Hasidic source, it is acknowledged, however, that not every 'strange thought' can be elevated. After stating that one who does not believe that 'strange thoughts' should be elevated denies God's limitless power, which is in all things including this thought, this author goes on to say:[7]

> However, it sometimes happens that one has to reject [and not elevate] a [strange] thought. You might ask, 'How can I know which thought to reject and which to bring near and elevate? A man should consider the following. If no sooner than the strange thought arrives there immediately comes to mind the means of putting it right and elevating it, then he should bring it near and elevate it. But if the thought of how to put it right does not come into the mind, then it can be assumed that it has come to nullify man's prayer and to confuse his thoughts. He is then permitted to reject that thought, for if one comes to slay you be first to slay him.

The comparison of the 'strange thoughts' to be rejected as justifiable homicide is interesting. Strictly speaking every 'strange thought' should be elevated, but if a man finds himself psychologically incapable of performing the task of elevation and in the meantime the thought may 'slay' his prayer, then, in self-defence, he is allowed to murder that thought.

R. Menahem Mendel of Vitebsk, disciple of the Maggid of Meseritch, develops his own philosophy of the elevation of 'strange thoughts'.[8] There is danger in the whole exercise, remarks this author, so a man must approach it in great trepidation, as if he is a calf being led to the slaughter or a plant, which, the rabbis say, an angel smites, ordering it to grow. The point of these similes is that the calf finds its ultimate perfection, according to the Kabbalah, in being slaughtered in the proper ritual manner and then being eaten by a righteous man. Similarly, the plant was created to grow and is yet reluctant to grow lest it grow to be deformed. The elevation of 'strange thoughts' is a creative process, essential to the perfection of all creation, but it is still fraught with danger and can so easily go wrong. Man should welcome the 'strange thoughts' when they come and seek to elevate them, but should never consciously put himself to the test by introducing 'strange thoughts' into his mind for the sake of elevating them. Moreover, no 'strange thought' would ever fall into a man's mind unless something of it were already there. By seeing God in the 'strange thought' it is elevated to Him.

> The general principle in connection with the subject of elevation is that whatever happens to man he has something of that thing within himself, for better or for worse, and when like meets like it bestirs itself. Consequently, he must immediately bind himself to God after the fashion of that particular thing that happens to him, by thinking to himself, Behold, this is God since there is nothing apart from Him.

A less sophisticated statement of the whole doctrine of elevation is given by R. Mordecai of Tchernobil (d. 1837), son of R. Menahem Nahum of Tchernobil, disciple of the Maggid of Meseritch. This is how R. Mordecai describes the practice of elevation:[9]

> Advice on how a man can bind himself to God alone and with no admixture of strange thoughts. It is well known that in all things the husk precedes the fruit; fruit, for example, cannot be eaten until the peel is first removed. So, too, as it were, when man

comes to speak before God the strange thoughts arrive immediately and it is for his own good. The wise man will have his eyes in his head to know whence the strange thought comes. There are two aspects. The first is to turn from evil. The second is to do good, and is implied in the verse, 'for thereof must we take to serve the Lord our God' [Exod. 10: 26]. The turning from evil involves the rejection of the strange thought so as not to heed it. The second aspect involves taking this very quality and serving the Lord therewith. Behold it is written, 'thou art clothed with glory and majesty' [Ps. 104: 1]. This means that every strange thought is a garment to the supernal mysteries. For example, if there fall into man's thoughts feelings of self-glorification, God forbid, he should take it and use it in order to glorify and exalt God, the Source of all qualities. The main thing is achieved by the fear of heaven, namely, faith. He should believe in perfect faith that the whole world is full of His glory and that no place is empty of Him and that His dominion extends over all, including the 'shells', in the category of, 'And Thou givest life to them all' [Neh. 9: 6]. Then, 'The Lord is nigh unto all them that call upon Him' [Ps. 145: 18]. In truth He is very near. Little by little, as man removes himself from evil, he will see immediately a bright light. As the rabbis say: God says, Open for Me a small aperture no bigger than the eye of a needle and I will open for you an entrance as large as the door of the entrance hall of the Temple.

R. Moses Hayim Ephraim of Sudlikov, grandson of the Baal Shem Tov, reports, in the name of his grandfather, a method of dealing with 'strange thoughts' in reverse, as it were.[10] The usual technique of elevation is to connect the 'strange thought' with its particular source in the Sefirotic realm. But the opposite effect can materialise. Through dwelling in thought during prayer on some aspect of the Sefirotic realm it is possible for a 'strange thought' stemming from that realm to be awakened. The antidote is to give expression to that thought in the practice of religion or, at least, by acting it out in some licit pursuit.

It is well-known, in the name of my grandfather, of blessed memory, that a man must be extremely cautious in what he does after he has prayed, for he is then prone to fall into the trap of anger, God forfend, or other unworthy things. That is to say, if he prays in accordance with the quality of fear he falls from this afterwards into anger, God forbid, and if he prays in accordance with the quality of great love he can sometimes come to have a love he should not have. From this you can draw conclusions with regard to every other quality. The sound counsel to deal with this problem is for him to engage immediately after his prayers in either the study of the Torah or in work. These matters require a lengthy exposition and a profound elaboration since it is not a topic that is allowed to be recorded in writing.

We can see why this author is so circumspect. If 'strange thoughts' can hinder prayer and yet be elevated, a psychological connection between the thought and its elevation has been established. It follows logically that prayer can cause psychological harm. Prayer in the spirit of love awakens the capacity for love in the soul and once this is present it can lure the worshipper into illicit love. A technique of 'sublimation' is therefore recommended.

The Hasidic doctrine of elevating 'strange thoughts' was especially offensive to the Mitnaggedim. In the ethical will of one of Hasidism's chief foes, R. David of Makov, written between the years 1811–14,[11] the writer pours out all his wrath on the doctrine:

> Therefore, who can contain himself and who can fail to cry out in protest against this abomination and heresy in which an idolatrous image is brought into the Temple on high? They [the Hasidim] say that if there enters the mind a strange thought of some Gentile woman whose name is Kashka or Margarita, their unclean names, it is necessary to elevate them to the holy place on high. Woe to them! How can they fail to see that they are allowing themselves to be pushed away from the community of Israel?

The same author, in his *Shever Posheim*,[12] writes of the doctrine, 'Woe to the eyes which see this and woe to the ears which hear it and to anyone who believes in these doctrines which have their origin in playing with foreign children.' The author means that the whole doctrine is a foreign importation into Judaism from pagan philosophies.

The account of R. David of Makov, as an extremely hostile witness, must obviously be taken with more than a grain of salt but he may, none the less, be basing himself on Hasidic practices he has heard about and which he describes so vividly. He is especially incensed at the words of R. Jacob Joseph of Pulnoye quoted earlier in this chapter regarding the elevation of lustful thoughts of women to the Sefirah of Hesed. It will be recalled that R. Jacob Joseph refers to the 'mystery' of, 'If a man take his sister. . .' On this R. David writes:[13]

> Woe is to me, woe is to me! For the mystery they have invented is one that God did not order. And Aha to them, how can they dare to bring filthy strange thoughts into the innermost precincts and 'The spider thou canst take with the hands, yet sits in the king's palace' [Prov. 30: 28]. God forbid! No such way of putting right strange thoughts is found in any of the sources or in any of the *tikkunim* ['perfections', 'means of putting right'] of the Ari of blessed memory, or in any other of the authentic early works. Consequently, their prayer is like a dream in which a man only sees that which he thinks about. When they wish to push the strange thought away they begin to cry out aloud and with many shoutings, to say nothing of peculiar words in the middle of the Eighteen Benedictions, such as 'Bam, bam, bam', 'Ee, ee, ee', 'Nu, nu, nu', 'Geh, geh, geh', 'Um, um, um', reaching to the very heavens, attended by gestures and the smiting of their elbows against their bodies and with their knees knocking together, all in order to show that by means of fear they are pushing the strange thought aside. After the thought of fornication and so forth has departed from him, he [the Hasid] then intends to become elevated through [the thought of] this fornication to [the Sefirah of] Hesed. He then cries out 'Nu, nu, nu', to hint that he is journeying and flying aloft and that he is raising his thought from the depths of the earth to the high heavens. And once he imagines that he has reached to the place he is obliged to reach he begins to sing and to hum melodies of the house of feasting, the songs of profane love. They [the Hasidim] smite their hands together and sometimes they do this until the ears tingle for about half an hour in the middle of the Eighteen Benedictions because of their joy that their prayers have ascended through the strange thought and its nullification, as that unclean book remarks.

Eventually, and no doubt partly, at least, under the influence of the attacks of the Mitnaggedim, the later Hasidic teachers dropped the whole doctrine of elevating 'strange thoughts', justifying their departure on various grounds. Even R. Shneor Zalman of Liady, a disciple of the Maggid of Meseritch, can remark:[14]

> Even if lustful imaginings and other strange thoughts enter his mind at the time of his worship, in the study of the Torah or in prayer, he should take no notice of them but should straight away

disregard them. He should not be so stupid as to engage in elevating the quality of the strange thought, as is well known, for those matters apply only to the Zaddikim into whose mind there fall not their own strange thoughts but those of other people. But as for a person into whose mind there enter his own strange thoughts, stemming from the evil in his heart and situated in the left ventricle, how can he elevate them if he himself is securely fastened there down below?

Similarly, R. Nahman of Bratzlav, great-grandson of the Baal Shem Tov, writes:[15]

When strange thoughts and imaginings attack a man but he strengthens himself to prevail over them, then the Holy One, blessed be He, has great delight from it and it is very precious in His eyes. To quote a parable: it sometimes happens that kings on a carnival day arrange for contests between different wild beasts. The kings stand by and witness it and have great pleasure from the contest. In the same way, thought comes from the category of man's vitality [hiyut] and holy things are in the category of clean beasts [hayot] while evil thoughts are in the category of unclean beasts [hayot]. From above these are allowed to struggle with one another and the Holy One, blessed be He, has great delight when man prevails over the unclean beasts and conquers them. The general principle is this: it is quite impossible for a man to have different thoughts in his mind at the same time. Consequently, he can easily drive out evil thoughts simply by doing nothing, that is to say by refusing to think that thought but to think of something else, of the Torah or of worship or even of business. For it is quite impossible for two thoughts to be together in any circumstances. I have already explained that one has no need to engage in battle and wave the head backwards and forwards in order to drive the evil thoughts away, for this has no effect whatsoever. On the contrary, by this means the evil thoughts become stronger. He should rather ignore them completely and simply carry on what he is doing at that time, whether it be studying the Torah or offering his prayers or engaging in business and he should not look behind him at all. The result will be that the strange thoughts will vanish automatically.

But with regard to both these teachers, R. Shneor Zalman and R. Nahman of Bratzlav, the matter is more complicated than appears on the surface, as Tishby and Dan have demonstrated.[16] In connection with R. Shneor Zalman's views it is important to appreciate that his work, the *Tanya*, contains the advice he gave to the Hasidim but, it has been claimed with some justice, the Habad philosophy which he held has an esoteric side as well, and that in this the doctrine of elevation does play a part. Indeed, in the sections of the *Tanya* that were added from R. Shneor Zalman's writings, after his death, it is stated that man's chief task in worship is to elevate the 'holy sparks'.[17] However, in view of the firm statement in the *Tanya* quoted above, I am not at all convinced that Tishby and Dan are correct in drawing the conclusion that in its esoteric view Habad does favour the doctrine of the elevation of 'strange thoughts'. Certainly in the Habad sources quoted by Tishby and Dan the redemption of the 'holy sparks' either does not refer to prayer at all or, where it does, it seems to mean that the 'divine soul' must struggle with the 'animal soul' and with the latter's 'strange thoughts'. Nothing is said in any of these sources of the conscious reflection on the 'strange thoughts' in order to raise them to their source as in the earliest Hasidic teachings.

So far as R. Nahman of Bratzlav is concerned, Tishby and Dan are right to call attention to other passages in his works which suggest that the total rejection of 'strange thoughts' is a doctrine for the ordinary Hasid not for the Zaddik, who is obliged to engage in the task of elevation. Thus R. Nahman remarks:[18]

From the time of the breaking [of the vessels] the sparks fell into all the worlds and they are elevated little by little from one stage to another through the prayers of the Zaddik. When the Zaddik prays and thus attaches himself to that [divine] attribute to which his current spiritual stage corresponds, a strange thought comes into his mind of the same nature as that attribute. When the Zaddik ascends still higher there comes into his mind a strange thought from that higher attribute. The Zaddik must know from which attribute and from which world the strange thought comes and he must know how to elevate it to that attribute and to that world which corresponds to the stage in which he now finds himself. It can happen, however, that the Zaddik desires to elevate it but is incapable of so doing. The reason for this is that the strange thought that comes into his mind belongs to a higher stage than that in which he finds himself at present. Consequently, it is impossible for him to elevate it for there exists for him a lower stage, namely, that in which he finds himself at present.

In reality, as J. G. Weiss has shown,[19] there is already in the anthology *Likkute Yekarim*, published in Lemberg in 1792, a definite protest against the doctrine of elevating 'strange thoughts', achieved by a careful selectivity in the use of earlier Hasidic material. The work is attributed to R. Meshullam Phoebus of Zbaraz, a disciple of the Maggid of Meseritch. No passages regarding the elevation of 'strange thoughts' are quoted at all in the *Likkute Yekarim* and it is clear that the compiler is at variance in this matter with early Hasidism, including the view of his own master, at least so far as the masses are concerned. This means that quite early on in the history of Hasidism an idea which loomed very large in the philosophy of the movement was at first quietly played down and later dropped altogether.

However, from the little work *Derekh Emet* by R. Meshullam Phoebus[20] we learn that he did not reject entirely the doctrine of elevation, but limited it to the saints who had trained themselves in separation from the world. R. Meshullam Phoebus writes:

This should be your rule. To be sure, you know it yourself, but the writings of the holy master R. Dov Baer [the Maggid of Meseritch], of blessed memory, have been revealed to many people, few of whom are able to compare themselves to him to do as he did even in the slightest way. They observe that in these writings there occurs something like the following: 'From an evil love which comes to a man he is able to grasp the love of the Creator. For he is able to advance an argument from the minor to the major. If he has a desire to love this stupidity, which is only the waste that has fallen at the breaking [of the vessels], then how much more should he love the Creator from whom this love stems. The same applies to an evil fear and to base pride and to the desire to score off others.' Now those who are lacking in intelligence imagine, when they read this kind of thing, that it is quite an easy matter to argue from the minor to the major, just as one argues from the minor to the major when one studies the Talmud. But there in the Talmud it is an academic exercise whereas here practice is involved. Only one who is stripped of materialism is capable of using here the argument from the minor to the major. For if a man is still attached to materialism and lusts, and volitionally obtains pleasure from them, he certainly knows nothing of the love of the Creator, His fear and His glory, for he has never tasted them, and Scripture says, 'Taste ye and see that the Lord is good' [Ps. 34: 9]. Such a man will fall, God forbid, into a deep pit unless he takes the greatest possible care. He can argue from the minor to the major and bestir himself as a result to have an even greater love and fear of the Creator.

The summary of the whole matter given by the Hasidic master R. Zevi Elimelech Spira of Dinov[21] (d. 1841) is worth quoting in full for the light it throws on the way in which the doctrine of elevating 'strange thoughts' was finally rejected but with certain qualifications. R. Zevi Elimelech writes:

After these matters I want to remind myself and people like me of a certain detail found in the writings of the disciples of the Baal Shem Tov, may the memory of the righteous be for the life of the world to come. They say that when at the time of Torah study or of worship there falls a strange thought or imagining into man's mind, he should not push it away from his mind but should raise it to its root. That is to say, if it is a thought of fornication and so forth, which belongs in the category of love, he should raise it to its root, to the quality of true love, which is the quality of Hesed. The same applies to a thought of fear. He should raise this to the quality of Gevurah, and so with regard to Tiferet. For these thoughts come from the sparks which fell when the breaking [of the vessels] took place and they come to man so that he might elevate them. It would follow from this that a man ought not to push the thought out of his mind. On the contrary, he should dwell on it at length until he succeeds in elevating it to its root by means of the various techniques known to the enlightened. Know, my friend, that these matters are not to be taken literally as the practice for everyone. For if you will say thus then, God forbid, the negative precept of, 'That ye go not about after your own heart' [Num. 15: 39], which we have been commanded, will fall to the ground. Rather, you should know that these matters affect only the perfect Zaddikim, whose heart are slain within them, and who know for certain that desire and lust are non-existent so far as they are concerned.[22] For such men, where did the strange thought come from? It certainly cannot have come from their evil inclination for this they have converted into the good and the sweet. It can only be that this thought comes from the sparks of the breaking [of the vessels] so that they can be elevated. It is otherwise with regard to one in whom the evil inclination still burns and who lusts after his desires. Even though he does not actually do anything [evil] lust lurks hidden within him to desire both that which is permitted and that which is forbidden, the lusts of the flesh. How, then, can you say that he can succeed in elevating it since this lust is part of the evil and the material that is within him? Consequently, for such a person no alternative is available except to fulfil the command, 'That ye go not about', to push aside the thought as soon as he notices it. (For all this see the work *Tanya* of the Hasid, the Gaon, our master Rabbi Shneor Zalman, may the memory of the righteous be for a blessing). In my opinion this is the meaning of the verse, 'That ye go not about after your own heart and your own eyes, *after which ye go astray*' [Num. 15: 39]. This means: When I command you not to go about, that is, to push aside the evil thought the moment you think of it, this applies only if that thought belongs to the kind of thoughts after which you still go astray. You still have within you desire and lust for that particular thing that enters your mind. Therefore, this thought stems from animal lusts. It is otherwise if it is the kind of thought after which you no longer go astray, for the inclination for that particular thing has ceased so far as you are concerned. Then there is the better counsel that you raise it to the Lord since, then, the thought is from the sparks of the breaking [of the vessels] and has come to you in order for you to elevate it. If this is correct, then it might be inferred, even in the case of one who is not a perfect Zaddik but who knows for certain that he has no desire for that particular thing, the thought of which falls into his mind, that the thought is also from the sparks of the breaking [of the vessels] and that, therefore, it is proper for the enlightened to engage in the need to elevate the thought in accordance with his intellect and understanding.

It will be seen from the above that R. Zevi Elimelech's rejection of the doctrine is less complete than that of R. Shneor Zalman, whom he quotes. R. Shneor Zalman limits the doctrine to the Zaddikim and implies that these are no longer in the land of the living, so that 'nowadays' the whole doctrine has lost its relevance. R. Zevi Elimelech, on the other hand, seems to leave room for the practice even for those who are not Zaddikim, provided the thought is not one of a lust to which the worshipper is himself prone. Not only does R. Zevi Elimelech advocate the practice for this kind of person even 'nowadays' but, in the continuation and conclusion of the passage quoted, he goes on to permit a strictly qualified form of the practice for all the Hasidim. There he remarks that once the evil thought has been rejected the Hasid should have in mind the particular divine name which, according to the Kabbalah, represents that Sefirah to the category of which the 'strange thought' belongs. Thus, for example, if the Hasid has a 'strange thought' about women in the middle of his prayers he should not endeavour to elevate it and yet, after he has rejected it, he should allow his mind to dwell on the divine name El, which, in the Kabbalah, represents the Sefirah Hesed. R. Zevi Elimelech concludes:[23]

> From the above it follows that in the main the occupation of elevating thoughts is only for the remnant called by the Lord, but so far as the masses are concerned the evil thought must be rejected so as to fulfil the command, 'That ye go not about'. Nevertheless, after he has pushed it aside it is proper for him to have in mind and to depict to himself those divine names which are required for the thoughts to be elevated, each one according to its respective category. For instance, when he has a thought of love he should depict the name El and the Tetragrammaton pointed with the vowel *segol*. When he has a thought of fear he should depict the name Elohim and the Tetragrammaton pointed with the vowel *sheva*, and so forth. There is no need to deal with this matter at any greater length. In manuscript we have profound expositions of this topic. But for the present this is sufficient for the enlightened. May the Lord our God be with us.

The approach of R. Zevi Elimelech is undoubtedly less uncompromising than that of R. Shneor Zalman who refers, as above, to the whole doctrine, so far as the Hasidim 'nowadays' are concerned, as 'stupidity'.

For all that has been said, there was still to be found in the second half of the nineteenth century a Hasidic master, R. Yitzhak Eisik Judah Jehiel of Komarno (d. 1874), who advocates uncompromisingly the old doctrine of elevating the 'strange thoughts'. R. Yitzhak Eisik is certainly aware of the strong opposition to the doctrine that developed even among the Hasidim yet, as the following quotations from his works[24] show, he is insistent that the practice be retained and even for the ordinary Hasid. He writes:[25]

> When some evil and strange thought comes into the mind of any Jew, whether he be great or small, whether he be of those of little

worth or of the great ones in Israel, it comes to him so that he can put it right and elevate it. This applies to every man, not, as some would have it, contrariwise. Such an opinion is nonsense for to God small and great are the same. For if a man does not believe in this he does not accept upon himself the yoke of the kingdom of heaven.

Further, R. Yitzhak Eisik writes:[26]

The being of God is present even in a strange thought and such a thought comes to man in order for him to put it right and to elevate it to the good and broad land, the land of life. If a man does not believe in this he places limits on God's being. It is not as the fools say that the idea of elevating [strange] thoughts applies only to the holy and pure in heart. This is nonsense and such an opinion comes close to disbelief that the being of God is present in every movement and every thought. But all Israel are holy and if one says, 'Hear, O Israel' twice [he has to be silenced[27] and he] places limitations on the belief that God is present in every movement. For if he really believed he would not repeat, 'Hear, O Israel'. If a man pushes the thought away it is as if he had slain a whole configuration [komah]. However, it sometimes happens that the evil in forbidden thoughts becomes too strong and then such thoughts have to be rejected.

Again R. Yitzhak Eisik writes:[28]

It is well known from [the teachings of] our master [the Baal Shem Tov] that one has to elevate thoughts to their root. . . . When a man studies the Torah or when he offers his prayers or, for that matter, at any time of the day, and some strange and evil thought enters his mind, the truth is that it comes to man that he might put it right and elevate it and, in the process, he himself will be elevated to a higher stage in the service of God. If he does not believe in this, or if he says that this idea is only for the great ones of the world, as those who use their own reason imagine, then this is not a complete acceptance of the kingdom of heaven since he places limits, God forbid, on God's being.

On the other hand, R. Israel of Ruzhyn (d. 1850), great-grandson of the Maggid of Meseritch, cannot believe that, at least so far as the ordinary Hasid is concerned, prayer can be free of 'strange thoughts'. That is why he is said to have defended the Hasidic practice of drinking alcohol after their prayers and engaging in gossip. In the process of these activities they wish one another well, drinking a toast to one another. This latter is, in fact, a prayer, since prayer can be recited in any language, and in this prayer the evil inclination has no part since on the face of it it all appears to be a purely secular pursuit.[29] Conscious attempt at prayer is bound to be tainted. Only when something other than prayer appears to be taking place can purity of intention in prayer be achieved in a kind of automatic way.

Judging by the absence of references to the doctrine in later Hasidic literature, it would seem that R. Yitzhak Eisik of Komarno's voice was quite untypical even in his own day. To all intents and purposes the doctrine of elevating 'strange thoughts', once so important a theme in Hasidic theory and practice, dropped entirely from view. Traces of it might still be found here and there, but the doctrine is now only a memory for the Hasidim and occupies no place at all in the Hasidic approach to prayer.

CHAPTER X

Prayer as Inspiration

The phenomenon that words proceed automatically from the mouths of men who are unconscious, or appear to be unconscious, of what they are saying, and the acceptance by believers of such words as being inspired, is not unusual in the history of ecstatic sects.[1] A question here to be considered is whether anything like this is found among the Hasidim with respect to prayer.

An oft-quoted allegedly rabbinic saying—'The Shekhinah spoke out of the throat of Moses'—is not, in fact, found anywhere in the Talmud or in other Rabbinic works.[2] It is used, however, in Hasidic literature in the form, 'The Shekhinah speaks out of their [the Zaddikim's] throat' to denote either the inspired utterances of the Zaddikim when they 'say Torah' or the automatic expression by them of words of prayer.[3] In his famous description of the Maggid of Meseritch at his court, Solomon Maimon tells of the Maggid placing his hand on his forehead at the sabbath table in order to receive inspiration when he 'said Torah'.[4] R. Kalonymus Kalman of Cracow writes:[5]

> This is well known and I have myself seen it of great Zaddikim that when they attach themselves to the worlds on high and they have stripped off the garments of the body, the Shekhinah rests upon them and speaks out of their throat so that their mouth gives voice to prophecy and foretells the future. These Zaddikim are themselves unconscious afterwards of what they have said for they were attached to the worlds on high and the Shekhinah spoke out of their throat.

An extraordinary (in every sense of the word) account of

spontaneous inspired prayer is given by a disciple of the Maggid of Meseritch, R. Uziel Meisels (d. 1786).[6]

It is known of Moses our teacher, on whom be peace, that the Shekhinah used to speak out of his throat. Although no prophet has arisen like unto Moses, nevertheless, with regard to this stage, there are many who have the merit that the power of His Shekhinah, blessed be He, offers praises out of their throat. It is possible that the rabbis, of blessed memory, had this in mind when they said that God Himself prays.[7] This is called 'High praises of God are in their throat' [Ps. 149: 6]. This means: When the exalted presence of the Shekhinah is in their throats, when the power of His Shekhinah speaks, as it were, from out of the throats of the Zaddikim, then 'a two-edged sword is in their hand' [Ps. 149: 6]. . . . And this is the meaning of, 'My mouth shall speak the praise of the Lord' [Ps. 145: 21] since my mouth only produces the words of the Shekhinah, as it were.[8] The God-fearing man does no more than make ready the will to pray but the praise [he utters] itself is not his [but God's] as we have said. This is the meaning of, 'Those who fear Him make ready their will' [paraphrase and reinterpretation of Ps. 145: 19]. The God-fearing man only makes his will ready but 'My mouth shall speak the praise of the Lord'. And this is the meaning of, 'O Lord, open Thou my lips; and my mouth shall declare Thy praise' [Ps. 51: 17]. For one who has reached this stage is a man who is no more than a channel through which the words of the Most High flow and man does no more than open his mouth . . . Praising God means, in the main, that man should be clean of all dross so that the voice from above should not be made corporeal through [coming into contact with] his voice. . . . It is because of this [that the Shekhinah speaks from out of their throat] that we find in Scripture and in the Talmud that the saints sing and dance with great burning enthusiasm [hitlahavut].[9]

In this connection it is relevant to point to the letter attributed to R. Eleazar, son of R. Elimelech of Lizensk, that we have referred to in the chapter on gesture and melody in prayer.[10] Speaking of the spiritual elevation of the Zaddikim, R. Eleazar remarks in his father's name that some of the Zaddikim are not gifted with tuneful voices, yet when they offer their prayers the melody is pleasant and sweeter than honey.

From the above the interesting fact emerges that while the Torah of the Zaddikim was held to be inspired and while, in some sources, the words they utter in prayer are said to be not theirs but God's, there are no references in these sources to spontaneous prayers composed under the influence of the holy spirit. This is not so surprising when we recall that the Hasidim believed strongly that the traditional Prayer Book was composed by inspired men[11] and they were consequently averse to making any additions to the prayers.[12] The only instance I have been able to discover of inspired new prayers under the influence of the holy spirit is in the works of the great-grandson of the Baal Shem Tov, R. Nahman of Bratzlav, a Hasidic master who was, in any event, very unconventional, even from the Hasidic point of view. In R. Nahman's *Likkute Maharan* we find:[13]

'Create me a clean heart, O God' [Ps. 51: 12]. That which a man speaks in private to his Creator is in the category of the holy spirit. King David, on whom be peace, whose stage was most elevated, composed the Book of Psalms by this method. And so it is with regard to everyone. It is in the category of the holy spirit, but according to his own particular category. As it is said, 'In Thy behalf my heart has said' [Ps. 27: 8] and as Rashi explains this to mean, 'In Thy behalf and as Thine agent my heart has said to me'. This means that all the words said by the heart are the very words of God, blessed be He, and this is the category of the holy spirit. It is therefore necessary to introduce something new [into the prayers] all the time, to offer each time new supplications and new entreaties. But in order to reach this [stage] purity of heart is essential. Purity of heart is attained through having the heart on fire and burning for God, blessed be He. Through this is the heart purified. For if a man is to counteract his burning and glowing in sin or in evil lusts, God forbid, through which his heart becomes unclean, he must set his heart on fire to burn for God, blessed be He. As it is said, 'Everything that has been through fire, ye shall make to go through fire' [Num. 31: 23]. When a man has a pure heart he then has the merit of speaking new things each time, and this is in the category of the holy spirit. This is the meaning of, 'Create me a clean heart, O God' and then, 'Renew a steadfast spirit within me' [Ps. 51: 12], that is, to merit the invention of new words which belongs in the category of the holy spirit.

R. Nahman himself composed a number of prayers and he no doubt believed that these were inspired, as his doctrine suggests. Otherwise, further investigation is required to see whether R.

Nahman's is a lone voice in this matter or whether any other Zaddikim have followed the same line of thought. As we have proposed, the first suggestion seems the more plausible, unless new evidence is forthcoming in support of the second.

However, there is a remarkable account of the psychological processes alleged to have taken place when R. Menahem Mendel of Kotzk (d. 1859) prayed, so that it is not irrelevant to quote it in consideration of the theme of prayer as inspiration. A disciple of R. Mendel, R. Samuel of Shinov writes:[14]

> He used to say of himself and his prayers that he goes from below to above and from above to below like the captain of a ship who runs up the rope ladders to the mast in the middle of the ship so as to be able to navigate the ship. So were his prayers. And he recounted the various stages of prayer attained by his disciples. It is well known that he had no efforts, in his prayers but he used to pray as a man converses with his friend, without effort, without raising his voice, yet not in silence either. All the benedictions, too, were not recited silently but with the kind of articulation used when men converse with one another, with the exception of the Eighteen Benedictions [which have to be recited silently]. On week-days his prayers took no more than half an hour but on sabbaths and festivals they took longer. After his prayers he became a different person. It was as if he had arrived from another planet, so much so that he was unable to recognise properly the men of our fraternity and his retainers until his mind had rested completely from his prayers. . . . It is possible that the rabbis were hinting at this when they compared prayer to speech [sihah], as it is said, 'And Isaac went out to meditate [la-suah] in the field' [Gen. 24: 62]. It seems to me that this idea can be made a little more explicit when we consider that speech comes from man's soul unintentionally. For example, when a man is totally absorbed in some profound matter, he speaks words to himself unintentionally and he is himself unaware of what he is saying. All this is because it comes from the root of his soul. The whole of his soul is wrapped around by the words which proceed in complete unity. There is neither labour nor effort involved in this kind of speech which emerges automatically. This is called sihah . . . But dibbur ['talking'] denotes a much harder form of speech, namely, the mind compels the vocal organs to do their work, and here effort is involved . . . This is known to all. Now our father Isaac, who was a perfect burnt-offering, who became sanctified on

Mount Moriah, and whose body and material nature become most elevated, even in this world, his prayer belonged to the stage of *sihah*. That is why in connection with his prayer the expression *sihah* is used. Since it does not say in Scripture with whom he engaged in *sihah*, and since no intelligent person goes out to a secluded place simply in order to talk to himself, the rabbis understood it as prayer. This is a stage of prayer that is very very high and it is impossible to explain it in any greater detail. It is with reference to this that it is said that prayer involves a virtual stripping away of man's corporeal nature. Of Isaac our father even more than this was true, for his body was as holy as his soul. . . . But when a man consciously forces himself to speak, what he then says is not so much the fruit of his soul, and it can even be that he says that which he does not really mean. But *sihah* comes from the essence of the soul. See the remarks of the *Or Ha-Hayim* on the verse, 'And the Lord put a word in Balaam's mouth' [Num. 23: 5]. And it is certainly the fruit of the soul. That is why *sihah* is called 'light' [i.e. 'light speech'] because it comes from the soul automatically without the speaker being conscious of it . . . It is certain that this is a most elevated stage which only the very few can reach.

The work *Or Ha-Hayim* by R. Hayim Ibn Attar (d. 1743) was very popular among the Hasidim. The reference to this author's comment on the verse in Numbers in the context of automatic speech is very revealing. The *Or Ha-Hayim* remarks that God had to 'put the words' in Balaam's mouth because the holy inspired words could not pass through Balaam's unclean psyche. God put the words directly into Balaam's *mouth* which became a separate vehicle for the transmission of the inspired words.

CHAPTER XI

The Prayers of the Zaddik

Hasidism is hardly intelligible without the doctrine of the Zaddik, the spiritual superman whose holy living not only provides his followers with inspiration for their lives but who raises them aloft with him through the spiritual powers that are his. Our concern in this chapter is not with the general doctrine of the Zaddik in all its ramifications, only with its significance for the Hasidic approach to prayer.

The central idea in this connection is that the Zaddik's prayers on behalf of his followers can achieve results far beyond the scope of their own puny efforts at prayer. The term Zaddik in the rabbinic literature means, with few exceptions, no more than 'a good man'. In that literature the superior term Hasid is used for the man of exceptional piety and saintliness. But since all the members of the Hasidic movement were called Hasidim, the term Zaddik was applied to the 'saint' and the roles were thus reversed.[1] The result was that rabbinic passages which speak of the simple good man were now interpreted by the Hasidic masters as referring to the Zaddik in its Hasidic connotation. Such was the fate of a key passage in the Talmud used by the Hasidim for their doctrine of Zaddikism. This is the rabbinic saying that God decrees but the Zaddik nullifies the decree.[2] The original meaning of the saying is simply that a good man can avert God's decree of judgement. In Hasidic thought it comes to mean that the Zaddik is endowed with miraculous powers and that God has delivered into his hands the means whereby the flow of divine grace can either be arrested or encouraged to flow. All depends on the

Zaddik. He has the means of coercing the flow of the divine blessing. It follows that his prayers can produce results that the prayers of his followers could never have produced unaided.

The special efficacy of the Zaddik's prayer is a prominent theme in early Hasidism. Of the Baal Shem Tov himself tales are told of his prayers achieving miraculous results. One such tale[3] tells of how the people needed rain badly. The Gentiles brought out their icons 'as is their custom' but all to no avail. The Baal Shem Tov gathered the Jews of the district together and he himself led them in their prayers for rain. A Gentile scoffed at their efforts, arguing that if the parade of the icons had been ineffective of what use could the prayers of the Jews be? The Baal Shem Tov then declared that rain would fall on that very day. 'And so it was'. The apologetic motif in the legend is very pronounced. The efficacy of the Zaddik's prayer was Judaism's reply to the Christian claim that Christianity was superior to Judaism.

Among many Hasidim the Zaddik acted, as did the Baal Shem Tov in the above tale, as the prayer leader, so that his prayers could assist the prayers of the whole congregation to speed their way to God. The whole doctrine is based on the idea that in the Kabbalah the term Zaddik refers to the Sefirah Yesod ('Foundation') which, in the anthropomorphic symbolism favoured by the Kabbalah, is represented in the human body by the organ of generation. It is through Yesod that the unification of Tiferet and Malkhut takes place. Consequently, the Zaddik on earth, as he offers his prayers, and especially as he leads the congregation in prayer, represents this special aspect of the divine flow of grace, the flow into the Shekhinah (= Malkhut) from Tiferet. R. Zeev Wolf of Zhitomer remarks:[4]

It is known that the prayer leader represents the mystery of 'the Zaddik who is the Foundation of the World' since he brings the flow of the whole congregation's prayers to the Shekhinah. 'From my own flesh I behold God.'[5] At the time of copulation Yesod represents the means by which the limbs of the body as a whole bring their flow to the female. Even when the flow from the extremities of the body has come to an end yet there is still no cessation in the category of Yesod and it still continues to flow. It can be compared to a funnel, wide at the top but becoming increasingly narrow at the bottom where the aperture is. We observe that even when there is no more liquid in the wide part there is still some liquid in the small aperture at the lower end and this continues to drip until there is nothing left. From this one who leads the congregation in prayer should take a wise hint to know how to conduct himself in relation to the congregation. Even when the impression made by the congregation has come to an end and is no more, he should still strengthen himself to the utmost of his capacity and with great awakening, in order to bring the flow of the whole congregation's prayers to the Shekhinah. I have heard it said in the name of the Baal Shem Tov, may his memory be for the life of the world to come, that the congregation commits a great sin when the prayer leader cuts short his melody and wishes to complete a portion of his prayers while they prolong their prayers and thus prevent him from bringing down the flow of grace. If he has to wait until the congregation have finished their prayers his intellectual powers become weak in the meantime and he no longer has the intellectual powers he needs if he is to succeed in bringing the flow to the Shekhinah. Since this is so, how careful must the congregation be in avoiding such a situation, God forbid, for otherwise they will lose much good. And since this is so, then see what great effort and how much toil for the two of them, the prayer leader and the congregation, to work together so as to know how to conduct themselves in prayer, and it is especially onerous for the prayer leader.

It is hard to see how much further traditional and Orthodox Jews could go than the above in the direction of mythological expression in prayer. The process begun by the Kabbalah[6] of seeing Judaism as a mystery religion is here taken to its extreme. The Zaddik, as he leads the congregation in prayer, is re-enacting the supernal mysteries and he must be circumspect if he is to help the congregation achieve its magical purposes. Small wonder that the defenders of the tradition could find some of the Hasidic teachings dangerous to the pure spirit of Judaism as they saw it.

The mechanics of the Zaddik's intervention are described by R. Menahem Mendel of Vitebsk, disciple of the Maggid of Meseritch,[7] as the annihilation of the Zaddik's self so as to reach the highest realm of the Sefirot, at which stage there is neither multiplicity nor division. The Zaddik, who wants nothing for himself, is able to reach in his prayers the divine Nothingness and thus bring down the flow of the divine grace from that region where all is grace. By reaching to the divine Nothingness he 'brings it down' to the lower Sefirot and thus sets the whole process in motion.

Earlier in this book we saw how the Hasidic teachers grappled with the problem of petitionary prayer as in apparent opposition to the Hasidic ideal of self-annihilation in prayer. Since the Hasid was to lose himself in God how could he, at the same time, bring his own needs, material or spiritual, to God in prayer? The general reply is, as we have seen, that prayer is for the 'sake of the Shekhinah', for the divine grace to flow, for God's need to be benevolent to His creatures to be satisfied. This reply would obviously apply *a fortiori* to the prayers of the Zaddik on behalf of all God's creatures. There is nothing of self in such prayers. Yet even here R. Levi Yitzhak of Berditchev can say[8] that some Zaddikim are so lost to the world when they come before God in prayer that they forget all about worldly needs, including the need the world has for the divine grace to flow and which only the Zaddik can accomplish adequately. Thus we have the paradox, R. Levi Yitzhak observes, that the prayers of a Zaddik of lesser degree are answered while those of a Zaddik of a higher degree are not. The former is still sufficiently remote from God to offer the prayers while the latter is so near to God when he prays that he forgets all about his mission.

It is in the Hasidic work devoted more than any other to the doctrine of the Zaddik, the *Noam Elimelekh* of R. Elimelekh of Lizensk (1717–87), that, naturally, we find the greatest emphasis on the prayers of the Zaddik. R. Elimelech remarks that the Zaddik is the channel[9] through which the divine grace flows. The Zaddik, who burns in his ardour for God, who studies the Torah and practices lovingkindness, leaves no work for God to do. It is now the Zaddik's responsibility to bring down the flow of divine grace and God is *absolved* from this responsibility! The Zaddik's prayers for 'life, children and sustenance' help others to attain these.[10] Through the prayers of the Zaddik the sick are healed, the people of Israel are saved from persecution and oppression, they are able to earn their daily bread, and are blessed with worthy sons and daughters. The Zaddik's supporters assist him by giving him of their worldly goods and in this way become attached to him through his dependence on them.[11] Their welfare thus becomes his welfare and his prayers on their behalf can the more readily be answered. At times the Zaddik will curiously indulge in fulsome self-praise, telling his followers of his great worth. But there is no pride in this. It is no more than a clever device by means of which he asserts his right to pray on behalf of others, especially necessary in view of Satan's determined efforts to denigrate the Zaddik and thus prevent him from achieving what is required in the upper worlds.[12]

Again and again R. Elimelech returns to the theological difficulties in the idea of the Zaddik's intervention. God does not change his mind. How, then, can the prayers of the Zaddik bring about a change in the fortunes of those on whose behalf he prays? R. Elimelech gives various replies. The soul of the Zaddik soars so high that it reaches to those worlds where there had never been any decree of suffering and death because there only mercy reigns.[13] Through his prayers for the sick and the unfortunate, he attaches them to those worlds of mercy and the decree is automatically set at naught. In another version, the Zaddik creates new heavenly worlds by the power of his prayers and deeds, and in these new worlds there has been no decree of suffering.[14] Still another solution is that God's decree in the first instance was that the person concerned should only suffer if the Zaddik fails to pray for him.[15] If it be asked why God should make the cure dependent on the prayers of the Zaddik, the answer is that God so desires the prayers of the righteous[16] that he is ready, as it were, to provide any excuse to obtain these. Yet another solution is that good is denied to the sufferer because of his sins but the pure Zaddik, by his prayers, takes the sinner into his domain where there is no sin, so that the cure is brought about automatically.[16a] Yet another solution is that in Heaven only the letters which form the words of the evil decree are created and the Zaddik, by his prayers, succeeds in putting these letters together in a different order so as to form words of blessing rather than of curse. But these Hebrew letters are the letters in which the Torah is written and the Torah is given in love. Consequently, only great love, of a kind beyond the grasp of the majority of men, can succeed in putting the letters together in their right order so as to change the decree for good. The Zaddik has this great love for God and for all men, Gentile as well as Jew, R. Elimelech is at pains to point out.[17]

But how can the Zaddik have these supernatural powers so reminiscent of the great prophets? R. Elimelech replies[18] by quoting a parable of his master, the Maggid of Meseritch.[19] When the king is in his palace he will only leave it to stay for a while in a splendid mansion where full regal honours can be paid to him. But when the king is on his travels he is prepared to enter the most humble dwelling in which hospitality is offered to him, provided it is clean. In this way the early Hasidic teachers invented a rationale for their insistence that miracle-working saints could exist even in their day without abandoning what had become a dogma of their times, the deterioration of the generations. Nowadays, when the Shekhinah is in exile, God dwells in every pure soul free from sin.

In his zeal for Zaddikism R. Elimelech at times borders on the blasphemous. The rabbinic saying[20] that there are three partners to man's creation: God, his father and his mother, is interpreted by R. Elimelech as referring to the Zaddik's role in his prayers of turning God's judgement into mercy. The 'mother' referred to is the Shekhinah, the source of the divine compassion, while the 'father' referred to is none other than the Zaddik to whose intercession man owes his very life.[21]

There is no doubt that R. Elimelech's teachings in the *Noam Elimelekh*, a book which became extremely popular among the Hasidim, set the pattern for the Zaddik as intercessor on behalf of his followers. But in early Hasidism the stress is rather on the role of the Zaddik in prayer as one who aids his followers in their devotional life, raising their prayers aloft by the power of his. The following quotation from the writings of R. Jacob Joseph of Pulnoye[22] is typical of the earlier approach:

The intention of prayers[23] are applicable only to the chosen few, the elevated ones who are few in number, and not to the masses as a whole. For these latter are drunk through the troubles of the exile and are like a drunkard who casts off the yoke of the Torah and accepts the yoke of the world and of business activity. Not so the chosen ones who accept upon themselves the yoke of the Torah. These are called free men, free from the drunkenness of exile. Consequently, it is to them that the intentions and the soul of the prayers are given. It is otherwise with one who engages in business. He is truly called a drunkard as we see with our own eyes and as we know from experience . . . Now God in His mercy, because He desires lovingkindness, gave us the counsel of the 613 precepts of the Torah, known as 613 counsels. And, in any event, the meaning of the word Torah is to show those who keep it the way in which they should walk. Consequently, these two precepts were placed in juxtaposition: 'Him shalt thou serve' [Deut. 10: 20], this refers to prayer; 'And to Him thou shalt cleave' [Deut. 10: 20], which means, cleave to scholars.[24] The Torah hints here at a great principle. This is that the body has no vitality unless it is attached to the soul and then the soul vivifies the body. Not so when the body is separate from the soul, which is separation of the masses from the chosen few in each generation. It is in accordance with this mystery that the Ari, of blessed memory, ordained that before he prays a man should take upon himself the obligation to love his neighbour as himself, to love in his heart every one of Israel, so that his prayer can be included in the prayers of the faithful believers in Israel who know the intentions of the prayers. This is easy to understand.

Thus the relationship between the Zaddik and his followers is that of soul to body. The Zaddik alone knows the soul of the prayers, the right intentions to be contemplated when praying. But, since the masses have an association with the Zaddik, his prayers are accounted as if the masses had recited them, since the soul of the masses and the soul of the Zaddik are as one.

In any event the institution of Zaddikism in its later development did mean that the Zaddik became an intermediary between God and man. The Hasidim, of course, prayed to God themselves but they brought their special petitions to the Zaddik so that he could pray on their behalf. In this connection we must refer to the practice of the Hasidim of presenting to the Zaddik, whenever they paid him a visit or when he visited them, the *kvittel* ('scrap of paper') and *pidyon nefesh* ('redemption of soul').[25] The *kvittel* is a written statement by the Hasid, containing his name and that of his mother, of his more pressing needs, material or spiritual. This is normally presented to an official at the 'court' of the Zaddik together with a sum of money for the upkeep of the 'court' and for general charitable purposes. The Zaddik reads the petition and prays that the particular needs of the Hasid recorded therein should be satisfied. Wertheim[26] rightly refers to the parallel between this and the practice in Biblical times.

And he said unto him, 'Behold now, there is in this city a man or God, and he is a man that is held in honour; all that he saith cometh surely to pass; now let us go thither; peradventure he can tell us concerning our journey whereon we go.' Then said Saul to his servant, 'But behold, if we go, what shall we bring the man? for the bread is spent in our vessels, and there is not a present to bring to the man of God; what have we?' And the servant answered Saul again, and said, 'Behold, I have in my hand the fourth part of a shekel of silver, that will I give to the man of God, to tell us our way' [1 Sam. 9: 6–8].

But the whole institution of the *kvittel* is a Hasidic innovation.[27] It should also be noted that in many later Hasidic circles the Hasid would place a *kvittel* on the grave of a Zaddik so that the Zaddik in heaven should pray there on his behalf.

The Mitnaggedim poured out their scorn on the claims made by the Hasidim for the prayers of the Zaddik, declaring that this was a reversion to an old idolatrous form of worship with the Zaddik as a 'false prophet'. R. David of Makov writes:[28]

Who is a Hasid? One who keeps the rules concerning blessings. Behold, the fools and idiots believe in the waters of presumption, in heretics of various shades [*minim mi-minim shonim*]. They give away their money for 'rectification' and their own household is made bare so that not a penny remains. And they spend their money on the expenses of the journey [to the court of the Zaddik]. On the way he [the Hasid] is afflicted with hunger for he has no money left. He hungers for bread and thirsts for water and no unclean word [i.e. of the Zaddik's prayers] can succeed in bringing down manna from Heaven, Since he has nothing to eat himself he has nothing with which to feed his animals, so that he is obliged to sell his horse in order to revive his unfortunate soul. Then he cries out, 'Woe is me! How abject have I become! I have spent my strength on falsehood and vanity. The support of my family depended on this horse. Whereas the prayer of the rabbi, the Hasid, is of doubtful value, and he will let me down, this horse would have been of certain help. This woman [the Hasid's wife who admires the Zaddik] has enticed me with her smooth words and I did not realise that her paths were ill-directed.' Would that it were engraved with an iron pen and with lead, that, for our sins, the truth has departed. And now O brethren of the house of Israel! For how long will this be to you for a snare and a stumbling-block? That you follow the counsel of the false prophets who steal words from one another in their falsehood and irresponsibility. These men belong to falsehood and vanity. They are hypocrites, silver with dross in it, accustomed to do evil. Behold, it was this sin which destroyed our House, burnt our Temple, and exiled us from our land, as is well known. And yet Satan still dances among us, with the result that exile is prolonged and there is no day whose curse is not worse than the previous one. Where is your wisdom and understanding in the sight of the peoples? And what will the nations say? They will declare that Israel is like all other nations who listen to soothsayers and magicians and inquire of the dead. 'Hath a nation changed its gods, which yet are no gods? But My people hath changed its glory for that which does not profit' [Jer. 2: 11]. Was there ever such a thing in your days or in the days of your fathers? Was there ever to be found a man like this in whom was the spirit of God and who had the power to heal the sick, to enable the barren to have children, to find lost articles, to have powers over life and death? And he turns about in his machinations, whether for punishment or for kindness, like clay in the hand of the potter. As these foolish Hasidim say, three keys are delivered into their [the Zaddikim's] hands[29] and they are little lower than God in their knowledge of good and evil. There can be no real cause for complaint against the little men, weak in knowledge, for they cannot discern between their right hand and their left, to test the matter adequately and to weigh it in the balance so as to know where the truth lies. But there can be complaint against the great men, who know the heart. Why do these step backwards and fail to remove this stumbling-block from Israel, to attack them [the Hasidim] with sticks and to drive them out of all the communities of Israel so that their voice will no longer be heard to cause the public to stumble? And for how long will they be silent, refusing to inform the public of the great confusion, so that the sheep should not be without a shepherd and each man do that which is right in his own eyes, in order to breach the eternal fence which the mighty shepherds have erected for us? Young foxes despoil the vineyards. Wherefore this silence?

In spite of all the opposition to which it gave rise, the doctrine that the Zaddik's prayers are especially effective continued unabated in Hasidism and has so continued down to the present. The late Hasidic master R. Solomon of Radomsk (d. 1866), for example, defends an uncompromising acceptance of the doctrine. He is not unaware of the startling claims made for the Zaddik's prayers and that the Mitnaggedim considered these to be preposterous; yet he still holds fast to the idea. True, R. Solomon remarks,[30] there are no longer to be found the great Zaddikim as in former times but lesser Zaddikim are still to be found and they, too, can succeed in bringing down the divine flow of blessing.

Behold, there are two types of Zaddikim called 'great lights', each of them great in his generation. It is true that in the generation which preceded ours there were great Zaddikim who illumined the world in their righteousness, such as the Zaddikim and the early prophets of ancient times. To them dominion was given and the power in heaven and earth to issue decrees, and it came to pass, light being shed on all their ways. Nowadays, in these generations, although the Zaddikim are not comparable to the earlier ones, yet a man must not despair to declare that, God forbid, we must now grope about like a blind man in the dark. He must rather know that these Zaddikim in their area are also called 'lights'. For, nowadays, in the era of the 'heels of the Messiah', they cannot be expected to have the same elevated stage as those of former times. All is provided for through their efforts and to them alone is the earth delivered. A man must embrace the dust of the feet of the Zaddik who is in his generation or else, God forbid, he will perish . . . This is why Scripture says, 'And God made the two great lights' [Gen. 1: 16], hinting at the two types of Zaddikim, those of earlier times and those of later. 'The greater light to rule the day.' These are the Zaddikim of former generations who had the power to nullify all decrees against the children of Israel. 'And the lesser light', referring to the Zaddik of this generation, 'to rule the night', in the bitter exile which is like night. He, too, has the power of prayer as in former ages. God speaks well both of the early ones and the later ones, for He has eternal paths reaching from heaven by means of which He can be seen on earth.

The Zaddik might imagine that it is positively impious for him to try to nullify the divine decree by means of his prayers. Not so, observes R. Solomon.[31] Noah was of little faith not because he lacked belief in God. On the contrary, he had so much faith in God that he lacked faith in the powers that had been given to him, the Zaddik, to annul the evil decree. But in reality God wished him to pray even for his corrupt generation, just as Abraham and Moses pleaded with God. It is, moreover, not only the duty of the Zaddik to pray that sinners be saved from sin but even when they have sinned he should use his holy powers to release the 'holy sparks' from the 'shells' and restore the lost souls of the sinners, just as Abraham prayed for the doomed of Sodom.[32]

In our own day, a Zaddik like R. Aaron Rokeah of Belz (d. 1957) was believed by his many thousands of followers to have miraculous powers so that his prayers on behalf of others were effective. R. Aaron lived towards the end of his life in Israel. He would invent various excuses to have doctors, expert in different branches of medicine, visit him so that he could bless them, that all their efforts to heal the sick would be crowned with success. Many miraculous tales are told of this Zaddik's power in prayer.[33]

This chapter can fittingly conclude with two prayers of a Zaddik: first the famous prayer, for recitation before praying, of R. Elimelech of Lizensk,[34] and then the Yiddish prayer of R. Levi Yitzhak of Berditchev.

> May it be Thy will, O Lord our God and God of our fathers, Who hears the sound of supplication's cry and Who hearkens to the prayer of Thy people Israel in Thy mercy, to make our heart ready and our thought prepared. Send our prayers into our mouths and let Thine ears hearken to the voice of Thy servants' prayer, as they entreat Thee with the voice of supplication and with a broken heart. And Thou, O God of mercy, in Thy many mercies and in Thy great love, pardon, forgive and grant remission to us and to all who are associated with us and to all Thy people Israel, for all that we have sinned, transgressed, have done wickedly and have rebelled before Thee. For Thou knowest that, perish the thought, it is not in rebellion and with trespass that we have disobeyed Thy commands and the words of Thy Torah and precepts but only because of the power[35] of the evil inclination which burns inside us all the time. It knows no rest and ceases not

until it has brought us into the lusts of this lowly world and into
its vanities. All the time it confuses our thoughts so that even
when we stand to pray before Thee and to entreat for our lives it
confuses our thoughts continually with its tricks. We are incapable
of offering resistance to it for our minds and intellect have become
so weak and we have lost the power to bear it as a result of our
worries and lusts and because of the numerous adversities we meet
in our times. Therefore, O merciful and compassionate God, do
Thou with us as Thou hast promised through the faithful of Thine
house, 'I will be gracious to whom I will be gracious, and will
show mercy on whom I will show mercy', upon which our
rabbis comment, 'Even if he is unworthy', for that is Thy way to
do good both to the bad and to the good. For Thou knowest our
cry, our pain and our sighing so that we are incapable of bringing
ourselves near to Thy worship and to make our souls cleave to
Thee in truth and uprightness. Woe to our souls! Woe, woe to us,
our Father in heaven![36] So now let Thy great compassion and
Thy great and numerous mercies be awakened on our behalf, to
drive away and consume the evil inclination in our midst. Rebuke
it, that it turn away and depart from us and let it not entice us so
as to push us away from worshipping Thee, far be it from such a
thing. Let not any evil thought enter our mind, whether when we
are awake or when we dream, far be it from such a thing.
Especially when we stand before Thee in prayer and when we
study Thy Torah and when we keep Thy precepts, let our thought
be pure, clear and refined, and strong in truth and uprightness,
because[37] of Thy benevolent will towards us. Awaken our heart
and the hearts of all our associates and the hearts of all who desire
our company and the hearts of all Thy people Israel, to declare
Thy unification in truth and in love, to serve Thee with the perfect
service acceptable before the Throne of Thy Glory. Fix firmly in
our heart our faith in Thee, at all times without cessation. Let
faith in Thee be bound up in our heart like a peg hammered in so
that it can never be removed. Banish all the barriers which
separate us from Thee our Father in heaven, and save us from
every cause of stumbling and error. Forsake us not, leave us not,
put us not to shame. Be Thou with our mouth when we speak
and with our hands when we toil and with our heart when we
engage in contemplation. Father in heaven! God of compassion!
Grant us the merit of uniting our heart, thought and action and
all our movements, whether conscious or unconscious, whether
revealed or hidden, that all be united to Thee in truth and
uprightness, without any objectionable thought. Purify our heart

137

and sanctify us. Sprinkle clean water upon us and cleanse us in thy love and compassion. Plant in our heart always the love and fear of Thee unceasingly. And wherever and whenever we go and when we lie down and when we rise up again let Thy Holy spirit burn within us.[38] Let us rely always on Thee, on Thy greatness and love and fear, and on Thy Torah, both Written and Oral, both revealed and secret, and on Thy commandments, that we may unite Thy great and terrible name. Guard us from ulterior motives, from pride, and from anger, petulance, melancholia, tale-bearing and from all other evil traits and from everything that interferes with Thy holy and pure worship which we love. Allow the grace of Thy holy spirit to flow into us that we may cleave to thee and that we may long always more and more for Thee. Elevate us from stage to stage that we may have the merit of reaching the degree of our holy forefathers, Abraham, Isaac and Jacob. Let their merit support us that Thou mayest hear the voice of our prayers that we may always be answered when we pray to Thee either on our own behalf or on behalf of any one of Israel, whether on behalf of an individual or of the community. Rejoice in us and be proud of us and let us produce fruit above and a root beneath. Remember not our sins, especially the sins of our youth, as King David, on whom be peace, said, 'Remember not the sins of my youth and my transgression'. Turn our sins and iniquities into merit and let there flow always to us from the world of repentance the thought of turning to Thee with a perfect heart and of putting right the flaws we have made in Thy Holy and pure names. Save us from being envious of one another and let not the thought of envying others enter our minds nor envy of us their minds. On the contrary, put it into our hearts that each of us sees the virtue of our neighbours and not their fault and that each one behaves to his neighbour in the way that is upright and acceptable to Thee. And let not, far be it that such a thing should happen, any hatred of one another enter our hearts. Strengthen our bonds to Thee in love since it is known to Thee that all we do is satisfying to Thee for this is our main intention. If we have insufficient sense to direct our heart to Thee, do Thou teach us to know in truth Thy good will. And more than all this we offer our supplications to Thee, O God full of compassion, to accept our prayers in compassion. Amen. So may it be Thy Will.[39]

The famous Yiddish prayer recited by R. Levi Yitzhak of Berditchev at the departure of the sabbath and adopted by many of the Hasidim is, in reality, an old Yiddish prayer which the Zaddik adapted in order to give expression to some of the main Hasidic ideas.⁴⁰ A translation from the Yiddish is given here:

God of Abraham, of Isaac, and of Jacob! Guard Thy people Israel from all evil for the sake of Thy praise. As the beloved, holy sabbath departs, we pray that in the coming week we should attain to perfect faith, to faith in the sages, to love of our fellows, to attachment [devekut] to the Creator, blessed be He. May we believe in Thy thirteen principles of the faith and in the redemption, may it come speedily in our day, and in the resurrection of the dead, and in the prophecy of Moses our teacher, on whom be peace. Sovereign of the universe! Thou art He who gives the weary strength! Give, then, also to Thy dear Jewish children⁴¹ the strength to love Thee and to serve Thee alone. And may the week bring with it good health, good fortune, happiness, blessing, mercy, and children, and life, and sustenance, for us and for all Israel, and let us say, Amen.

CHAPTER XII

The Polemic on the Recital
of Le-Shem Yihud

At the height of the fierce controversy between the rabbinic defenders of the *status quo* and the Hasidic innovators in the late eighteenth century, R. Ezekiel Landau (1713–93), Rabbi of the ancient Jewish community of Prague, issued his famous broadside against the recital, before carrying out the precepts, of the mystical formula, 'For the sake of the unification [*le-shem yihud*] of the Holy One, blessed be He, and His Shekhinah', which the Hasidim had adopted from the Kabbalists. The attack appears in Landau's Responsa collection, *Noda Biyudah*, printed soon after the polemical letter in question had been sent.[1] Landau's correspondent had asked him a number of questions, one of which concerned the *le-shem yihud* formula. Landau is very emphatic that the formula should not be recited and he attacks the Hasidim both for reciting it and for their general attitudes. The debate raises a number of important isuues and it had wide repercussions. It is certainly relevant to any consideration of Hasidic prayer.

As we have noted earlier, in the Zohar 'The Holy One, blessed be He' is the name given to Tiferet ('Beauty'), one of the Sefirot. Man, created in God's image, is mirrored after the pattern of those potencies that are the Sefirot, all of them being found in his psyche in miniature. He can consequently influence them and his deeds have a cosmic significance. Man is at the end of a great chain of being reaching upwards to the Sefirotic realm. If he is virtuous, he helps to promote harmony among the Sefirot, with the result that the channels of grace are opened and goodness and blessing flow through all creation. If he sins, disharmony is produced in the Sefirotic realm and the flow of divine grace is impeded. Harmony and disharmony among the Sefirot are frequently described in the boldest sexual imagery. Thus the Sefirah Tiferet is the male principle which acts upon the female principle, the Shekhinah, the Sefirah Malkhut ('Sovereignty'). The harmony in the Sefirotic realm depends ultimately on the union of these two Sefirot; on the mystical marriage of the male and female principles: 'The Holy One, blessed be He' and His Shekhinah. The rabbinic doctrine of the 'exile of the Shekhinah' is understood by the Kabbalists to mean that part of God is, as it were, exiled from God until the restoration is complete, until all the 'holy sparks' will be reclaimed for the holy from the domain of the denizens of evil—the 'shells' (*kelipot*)—into which they have fallen. These 'holy sparks' are released when man performs any deed in a spirit of dedication to God. In the Lurianic Kabbalah generally, as we have seen, the mythological elements are especially pronounced. Here it is said that the unification of Male and Female is achieved when first the Female sends the 'female waters' to the male in order to awaken His love, from which, in turn, the 'male waters' flow to the Female. The 'female waters' are provided by the 'holy sparks' which are released by the deeds of man. Thus by providing the 'female waters' every good deed of man assists in the unification process. Since every good deed assists the unification in this way it is appropriate, the Lurianic school teaches, that this should be expressed verbally before any good deed is carried out, hence the formula: 'For the sake of the unification of the Holy One, blessed be He, and His Shekhinah'.[2]

The actual formula is not found earlier than the sixteenth century. The source in the Zohar given by some later writers[3] does not, in fact, speak of the Shekhinah at all, though the Zoharic doctrine is undoubtedly based on the theme of the unification of Tiferet and Malkhut.[4] The particular Zoharic passage quoted reads:

R. Eleazar said: All man's deeds should be carried out for the sake of the holy name. What does for the sake of the holy name mean? Man should give verbal expression to the holy name whenever he performs any act so that it is done only for His service and then the Other Side will not rest upon it. For the Other Side lies constantly in wait for man in order to rest upon his deeds.

The meaning is clear. The denizens of the Other Side, the demonic side of existence, wish to stake their claim on man's deeds. He can only drive them away by uttering God's holy name before carrying out any of his deeds.

The earliest references to the formula are in Hayim Vital's *Shaar Ha-Mitzvot*[5] and in the sixteenth century Kabbalistic work by Elijah de Vidas entitled: *Reshit Hokhmah* (*Shaar Ha-Ahavah*, Chapter 9). De Vidas remarks that in order to carry out the unification a man should say that he performs every deed he does in order to unite the Holy One, blessed be He, and His Shekhinah and he should depict to himself the two divine names in combination, namely, the Tetragrammaton (representing 'The Holy one, blessed be He') and Adonay (representing the Shekhinah), i.e. in the form *yod, alef, he, dalet, vav, nun, he, yod*, and he should have the intention that through his deed the Shekhinah will arise from Her exile. De Vidas is followed by later Kabbalists who express the idea in almost identical terms.[6] The earliest reference to *leshem yihud* as a standard formula is in the collection of mystical prayers *Shaare Tzion* by Nathan of Hanover[7] which first appeared in Prague (Landau's city!) in 1662. From here it was evidently adopted by the compilers of Prayer Books. Landau refers to its introduction into the Prayer Books as a recent innovation.

The formula appears to have been added to from time to time. In de Vidas there is only reference to the unification of the Holy One, blessed be He, and His Shekhinah. In later versions, as used by the Hasidim,[8] the full formula is 'For the sake of the unification of the Holy One, blessed be He, and His Shekhinah, behold I perform this *mitzvah*, in fear and love, love and fear, through that Hidden and Concealed One, in the name of all Israel, and in order to give satisfaction to my Creator and Maker'. Some versions add, 'and in order to raise the Shekhinah from the dust'.

This latter is found in the *Shaare Tzion* but there is no reference there to 'the Hidden and Concealed One', which appears to be an even later addition.[9] The meaning of this phrase is that the unification is performed through En Sof, 'the Hidden and Concealed One' (God as He is in Himself). The Sefirot do not enjoy any independent existence apart from En Sof and the unification is performed in and through En Sof.[10] In the *Shaare Tzion* and in many later versions there is added, after the words 'love and fear': 'to unite the name *yod he* with *vav he* in complete unification'. The meaning of this is that in the Kabbalistic scheme the four letters of the Tetragrammaton stand for the Sefirot. Thus the *yod* represents Hokhmah and the *he* Binah. These two 'higher' Sefirot play their part in the unification process so that when Tiferet is united with Malkhut there takes place, too, the unification of the Sefirot. The last two letters of the Tetragrammaton, *vav* and *he*, represent respectively the Sefirot Tiferet and Malkhut. Hence the formula: 'to unite the name *yod he* [= Hokhmah and Binah] with *vav he*' [= Tiferet and Malkhut].

A number of early Hasidic writers refer to the formula in its simple form, e.g. R. Jacob Joseph of Pulnoye;[11] R. Elimelekh of Lizensk;[12] R. Levi Yitzhak of Berditchev;[13] and R. Shneor Zalman of Liady.[14]

Landau's Responsum is addressed to 'Rabbi Baer, head of the holy communion of Goitein' (= Kojetein in Moravia). The first part reads,

With regard to the fourth question you have asked regarding the formula *le-shem yihud*, which has only very recently become popular and has been printed in the Prayer Books, behold, in this connection I reply: Rather than ask me the correct formula to be recited, you should have asked whether it should be recited at all. In my opinion this is the grievous evil of our generation. To the generations before ours, who did not know of this formula and never recited it but laboured all their days in the Torah and the precepts, all in accordance with the Talmud and the Codes whose words flow from the spring of living waters, the verse can be applied, 'The integrity of the upright shall guide them' [Prov. 11:3]. They are the ones who produced fruit on high and whose love was higher than the heavens. But in this generation they have forsaken the spring of living waters, namely, the two Talmuds, Babylonian and Palestinian, to hew out for themselves broken cisterns. They exalt themselves in their arrogant hearts, each one saying, 'I am the seer. To me are the gates of heaven open. Through my merit does the world endure.' These are the destroyers of the generation. To this orphaned generation I apply the verse, 'The ways of the Lord are right, and the just do walk in them; but the Hasidim do stumble therein' [Hos. 14: 10]. There is much for me to say in this connection but just as it is a duty to speak when people will listen it is a duty not to speak when people will not listen.[15] May God have mercy on us.

The verse, 'The ways of the Lord . . .' speaks of 'transgressors' (*posheim*) for which Landau has substituted the word Hasidim. It is rumoured that for the second printing of the *Noda Biyudah* the Hasidim bribed the printers to restore the original wording. When Landau heard of it he is reported to have said, 'I turned the transgressors into Hasidim while they have turned the Hasidim into trangressors'[16] though it is extremely unlikely that this actually happened.

Landau then takes up the legal question of whether any express formula is required before the performance of a *mitzvah*. The questioner had argued that 'it is essential to express verbally that one has the "secret intention" ' (i.e. that the *miztvah* is being carried out with the Kabbalistic motive of unification). His proof is from the Talmudic passage[17] in which it is stated that when a man divorces his wife he must state verbally that the bill of divorce (the *get*) is being written for this particular woman (*lishmah*). Similarly, the questioner argues, when a vow is made it is only binding if expressed verbally. Landau replies that on the contrary the Talmudic passage quoted suggests the exact opposite. In that passage a distinction is made between a *get* and a sacrifice offered on the altar, which must also be done with that particular sacrifice in mind (*lishmah*), i.e. a sin-offering must be offered as a sin-offering, not as a burnt-offering or a peace-offering. Now the Talmud there states that while the intention of offering a sin-offering as a burnt-offering or a peace-offering invalidates the act, there need be no express intention or any verbal declaration that the sin-offering is being offered as such, unlike in the case of the *get* where an explicit declaration is required. Thus in both cases the opposite intention (*shelo lishmah*) invalidates the act (e.g. when a sin-offering is offered as a burnt-offering or a *get* is written for another woman with the same name). But where there was intention neither for nor against, but the act was carried out without any intention at all (*setama*), then it is valid in the case of the sacrifice but invalid in the case of the *get*. The distinction is this. A sacrifice is set aside for that particular purpose and it can therefore be assumed that even without any special intention it is offered for that purpose, whereas a wife is not normally divorced so that an explicit declaration is required if her status is to be changed. It follows from all this, argues Landau, that a *mitzvah* does not require any explicit declaration since a *mitzvah*, set aside as it is by God who commanded it, should surely be compared to the case of the sacrifice rather than to the case of the *get*. As for the questioner's attempted proof from vows, surely this only means that the bare thought of taking a vow unattended by any verbal declaration has no binding force, but not that an *act*, such as the performance of a *mitzvah*, requires a verbal declaration to be effective.

In reality, Landau continues, the law in the case of sacrifices is not only that no express declaration is required but that no such declaration should, in fact, be made, nor should there be any express intention in the mind that the sin-offering is being offered as a sin-offering.[18] The reason given for this curious ruling is that it is in order to avoid confusion, i.e. if there is allowed or advocated an explicit declaration of intent, or even the thought of such, this can easily lead to thought or declaration of the opposite and so invalidate the sacrifice. The priest offering the sin-offering should simply offer it without any intention because, once his mind is directed to the explicit declaration, it is only too easy for him to become confused and so say or think that he is offering the sin-offering as a burnt-offering or a peace-offering. If, then, such confusion is feared by the rabbis in the case of sacrifices, where the risk is minimal, then in the case of the *mitzvah* one can argue *a fortiori* that it is far better not to have any Kabbalistic intention in mind, since here the risk (of entertaining heretical thoughts) is great, 'as we have seen clearly demonstrated'. This remark obviously refers to the mystical heresies of the pseudo-Messiah Sabbatai Zevi, against whose crypto-followers there was a determined inquisition in Prague in Landau's day.

In the latter part of the Responsum, Landau deals with another legal problem raised by the questioner. Is not the formula an offence against pronouncing the divine name? Landau observes that in his youth he had heard people reciting the formula and they used the expression 'the name *yod he*'. While it might be argued that the name *yah*, formed from these two letters, should not be pronounced, and this is by no means certain, there can be no objection to pronouncing the individual letters, *yod, he*, in full. On these grounds there can be no objection but, as he has stated, there are weightier objections to the formula.

This latter part of the Responsum reads:

> Your honour writes that it is good to have the knot firmly tied between word, thought and deed. But the Men of the Great Synagogue arranged for us the prayers and benedictions and there is nothing that is not hinted at in the forms of these prayers and benedictions. The benediction is the awakening of speech and thought. Where a benediction has been ordained before the performance of a *mitzvah* it is unnecessary to say anything other than the benediction before the performance of that *mitzvah*. Where no benediction has been ordained it is my habit to state verbally, 'Behold, I am about to do this in order to fulfil the command of my Creator'. This is sufficient. Nothing more is required. As for 'intention', this refers only to the meaning of the words of the prayers. All the *tikkunim* ['perfections'] on high follow automatically on the deeds. However, in connection with your honour's casuistic discussion regarding the formula 'to unite the name *yod he* with *vav he*', whether this falls under the heading of pronouncing the divine name, and you refer to the discussion by the Tosafists as to whether this embraces the pronunciation of the first two letters of the name, so far as I can recall from my youth, I heard these people saying, '*yod he* with *vav he*', each letter in full, and this does not offend against pronouncing the divine name. But I have already revealed my opinion that silence is to be preferred and that the thing should sink into oblivion. Even in the mind there should only be the thought of the meaning of the words [of the prayers and benedictions, that is, and

not the Kabbalistic mysteries]. In this way you will walk in safety
and not stumble in anything. More than this one should not
elaborate on these matters, and I must be brief because of my
heavy schedule. With kind regards, Ezekiel Landau.

The Hasidic reply was not long in forthcoming, in the work
Shaar Ha-Tefillah ('Gate of Prayer')[19] by R. Hayim b. Solomon
of Czernowitz and Mohilev (d. 1813). The reply is worded in
such a way that it indicates that Landau was still alive when it was
written. It is a not unexpected blend of deference to a great
rabbinic authority and Hasidic defiance of opponents of the movement. (It should, however, be noted that R. Hayim's reply is not
in any way an 'official' or 'authorised' statement. He was, to some
extent, somewhat apart from the mainstream of Hasidism.[20])
R. Hayim begins:

I opened my eyes to see the lengthy statement in the work of the
great and famous Gaon, righteous and upright is he, Our Master,
Rabbi Ezekiel Segal Landau, head of the Court and principal of
the Yeshivah in the holy community of Prague. His heart was
lifted up to speak proudly, arrogance proceeding from his mouth,
to touch the anointed of the Lord, engaging in contention with
the Zaddikim of our generation. Generalising, he turned them all
into transgressors, applying to them the verse, 'The just do walk
in them; but the Hasidim do stumble in them'. The true prophet
had already foretold this, that they would say such things of the
righteous Messiah, when he said, 'He was numbered with the
transgressors' [Isa. 53: 12]. But the prophet goes on to say, 'Yet he
bore the sin of many, and made intercession for the transgressors'.
Reading between the lines of his letter it is clear that his sole
intention was to chide. For it is his sound method in all his Responsa
to investigate the source of every law in the Talmud and among the
early Codifiers. Yet here he did not penetrate to the depths of the
law and he fell into error because he allowed his temper to get the
better of him so that on this question he overlooked the simple
meaning of the Talmudic discussion and the law as laid down
explicitly by the early and later Codifiers, as I shall explain.

First, R. Hayim observes that the ruling is that 'the precepts
require intention' *(kavvanah)*.[21] This means that before carrying
out a *mitzvah* one should be aware that one is so doing. It would
seem, therefore, that the case of the *mitzvah* is to be compared to

that of the *get* not, as Landau has argued, to that of the sacrifice. On this point Landau is closer to the correct legal opinion. There is no mention anywhere in the Talmud or Codes that a verbal declaration (other than the benediction where this is ordained) is required before carrying out a *mitzvah*. (It might incidentally be mentioned that both authors appear to have confused 'intention', *kavvanah*, with the very different concept of *lishmah*, a perhaps inevitable consequence of trying to apply Halakhic categories in attacking or defending Hasidic innovations.[22] In the case of the *get* and the sacrifice the discussion concerns an act performed for a specific purpose, i.e. the *get* for this particular woman, not for any other, the sacrifice as this particular offering, not any other. But in the case of *kavvanah* in connection with a *mitzvah* the meaning is whether *mitzvot* in general required to be carried out with the the express intention of serving God.) R. Hayim[23] refers also to another type of 'intention', that of the *meaning* of the particular *mitzvah*, e.g. as in the case of *tefillin*[24] and *tzitzit*.[25] Since we now have the Kabbalah, R. Hayim continues, why should we not have in mind as much of the Kabbalistic reasons for the *mitzvot* as we can when we carry them out?

When the two Responsa are set side by side it becomes clear that the basic issue between Landau and R. Hayim is not the purely legal one but the meaning of 'intention' *(kavvanah)*. For a trad-itional rabbinic scholar like Landau, all the 'perfections' on high follow automatically from the performance of the *mitzvot*. (Many of the early Hasidic leaders themselves did not practise the Lurianic *kavvanot*.[26]) Landau, it must be noted, does not deny the truth of the Kabbalistic scheme. He admits that there are 'perfections' on high produced by man's deeds. But he cannot find any warrant for the view that these have to be in the mind of the worshipper for the worship to be effective.[27] R. Hayim, on the other hand, as an orthodox Kabbalist, wishes the older concept of *kavvanah* to embrace deep reflection on the Kabbalistic scheme. He quotes a well-known passage in the Zohar[28] that the Torah has a body and a soul, the soul of the *mitzvot* being their significance in the Kabbalistic scheme. R. Hayim admits that the revelation of these mysteries is comparatively recent but, he argues, once they have been revealed, man must avail himself of them if his worship is to be complete. In R. Hayim's own words:[29]

> With regard to what he writes there, that the generations prior to ours, who did not know of these matters, labouring all their days in the Torah, were better than ours, I read, 'Say not that the former days were better than these, for it is not out of wisdom[30] that thou inquirest concerning this' [Eccles. 7: 10]. These matters have been throughly investigated before now in an intelligent and convincing manner, with the greatest clarity and with one refinement after another, that the main purpose of the Torah and *mitzvot* is their inner meaning and their spiritual aspect and the names of the Holy One, blessed be He, concealed in them. All the holy books are full of this, headed by the expert Gaon, author of the Holy Shelah. They have elaborated on this theme, producing clear proofs that there is a vast difference, of an infinitely higher degree, between one who studies the Torah and performs the *mitzvot* according to the simple meaning alone and one who gazes at the spiritual light and the names of the Holy One, blessed be He, concealed in them. Apart from all these advantages, behold, by this means man acquires a great additional love and fear of God when he keeps the *mitzvot* and this is the main aim when keeping the Torah and the *mitzvot*. As everyone knows, this is stated explicitly in the book of Deuteronomy.

R. Hayim[31] takes up this theme of love and fear because it is the most typical of the new emphases introduced by Hasidism. Landau says little about these matters. In the traditional rabbinic scheme the study of the Torah and the performance of the *mitzvot* *is* the love and fear of God.[31] But in the mystical approach of the Hasidim love and fear have to be cultivated as separate and main aims and this, according to R. Hayim but not according to other Hasidic leaders,[33] can only be done if the Kabbalistic 'intentions' are in the mind when the precepts are carried out. R. Hayim writes:

> This is certain. There is a man whose love for his God is so strong and faithful that he carries out each *mitzvah* with superlative excellence, strength and marvellous power, waiting in longing to perform the *mitzvot*, his soul expiring in yearning. For, in accordance with his spiritual stage, his heart and soul know the gracious value of the *mitzvot* and the splendour of tremendous glory and beauty, infinitely higher than all values. And how much

more so the dread and fear, the terror and trembling, which fall upon such a man when he performs a *mitzvah*, knowing as he does with certainty that he stands before the name of the Holy One, blessed be He, the great and terrible King before whom 'all the inhabitants of the earth are reputed as nothing; and He doeth according to His will in the host of heaven' [Dan. 4: 32], who stands over him always, seeing his deeds, for His glory fills the earth. Such a man is always in a state of shame and lowliness so intense that the world cannot contain it, especially when he carries out the *mitzvot*. Such a man's *mitzvot* are those which fly upwards in joy and satisfaction to draw down from there every kind of blessing and flow of grace to all worlds. Such a man belongs in the category of the 'righteous (Zaddik) is an everlasting foundation'[34] [Prov. 10: 25] 'under whose shadow we shall live' [Lam. 4: 20]. For it is he who sustains and establishes the whole world by the power of the blessing and flow of grace which result from the performance of the *mitzvot* in love and fear which are a source of satisfaction for Him at whose word the world came into being. As for those who perform the *mitzvot* like a lifeless figure of clay, without soul or vitality, but solely with the bodily motions, behold, it is stated in the *Tikkune Zohar*, Tikkun 10, that any *mitzvah* carried out without love and fear of man's Maker does not fly upwards. For love and fear are the two wings. They are like the wings of a bird by which it flies in the whole of the sky beneath the heavens. But no bird can fly upwards if it has no wings or if its wings are broken. So, too, *mitzvot* performed without love and fear are as if they have no wings. How, then, can they fly upwards?

R. Hayim[35] now adds another typical Hasidic idea. Some men are incapable of attaining to the proper degree of love and fear, either because they have been endowed with an inferior soul or because their sins have created a barrier between them and God. Since all Israel is as one body, even these need not despair, for as the *mitzvot* of the Zaddik rise upwards they elevate with them the *mitzvot* of their followers.[36] But this only applies if the effort of love and fear is made. A company travelling on the way will carry along with them one of their number who has fallen sick, but if one of them dies they will leave him where he is. R. Hayim's conclusion[37] is that, contrary to Landau, it is essential to recite the *le-shem yihud* formula, and this applies even to one who cannot grasp its meaning, since the letters themselves fly upwards.

In addition to his fear of mystical heresy, Landau's slighting reference to the 'seer' to whom the gates of heaven are open shows that he was disturbed at the Hasidic claim that the Zaddik was especially endowed with the gift of performing the unification. R. Hayim, far from denying the charge, proudly embraces the Hasidic doctrine regarding the special role of the Zaddik.[38] R. Hayim concludes:[39]

> Who can fathom the mind of the Zaddikim who walk before God and in whose heart there is wisdom? Their heart burns constantly as with a consuming fire to give satisfaction to the Creator, One and Unique, by means of the unification of His great and holy name and by uniting the lower world with the upper world and so uniting all worlds. Hardly for one moment do these matters depart from their mouth. One who admits that he does not know cannot act as judge in the matter and his judgements are null and void. So may all judgements and all prosecutors be rendered null and void for us and for all His people the house of Israel.

If we try to discover the reasons behind Landau's vehement opposition we have not far to look. In addition to the general rabbinic opposition to Hasidism and to the role of the Zaddik, which Landau shared with his rabbinic contemporaries, the distinguished rabbi, by virtue of his official position in Prague, was especially suspicious of any trace of Sabbatian heresy. (It is significant that Landau's voice is the only one of note raised against the recital of *le-shem yihud*.[40]) The effects of the Sabbatian movement and that of the Frankists were still keenly felt in that part of the world. At that period, too, the first stirrings of the modernists, led by Moses Mendelssohn, were bound to force a rabbi of Prague in an age of transition into an attitude which instinctively recoils from religious innovation.[41] Every Kol Nidre night there was repeated in Prague in Landau's day the declaration of a ban against the Sabbatians. Other Jews were forbidden to marry those suspected of Sabbatian leanings. The Prague community was always on the look-out for prayer-book innovations which could be read as Sabbatian hints such as the introduction of Psalm 21.[42] It is also relevant to point out that the reason some of Sabbatai Zevi's followers believed in him even after his conversion to Islam was because they argued that his apostasy was a trick wherewith to deceive the denizens of the 'Other Side' and thus perform the complete 'perfection' of the Shekhinah.[43] Moreover, Scholem[44] has established a close connection between Sabbatianism and the rise of Hasidism. Against such a background there is nothing surprising about Landau's opposition to a formula so mysterious in meaning, particularly when adopted so enthusiastically by the Hasidim.

An important observation of Landau on the two challenges of modernism and Hasidism is to be found in his commentary to the Talmud.[45] Here he refers to two dangerous trends, those of the 'philosophers' and the Hasidim. He accuses the Hasidim of speaking brazenly of the divine mysteries in order to impress the masses. Landau here concludes:

> Do not worry that you will receive some kind of punishment for failing to pray in accordance with the mysteries, as the Hasidim of our time imagine. It is not so. There is no punishment. On the contrary, you will be rewarded for separating yourself from these matters and as a result you will inherit eternal life.

On closer examination it can be seen that there is, in fact, a direct connection between the *le-shem yihud* formula and the Sabbatian heresy (although, chronologically, the former antedates the latter). In Sabbatianism En Sof is not the Governor of the world, but 'the God of Israel' (= Tiferet) is the true Governor of the world and the Messiah is an incarnation of 'the God of Israel'. Thus the very terms 'the Holy One, blessed be He' and the Shekhinah lend themselves very readily to Sabbatianism. The older formula may well have been adopted by the Sabbatians for their own purpose. Nor is the sexual element in the formula to be overlooked.[46]

Quite remarkable is the refutation of Landau by R. Hayim Joseph David Azulai (d. 1804), the renowned Sephardi traveller and scholar. Azulai writes:[47]

> A man should train himself to recite *le-shem yihud*, as is the practice in Turkey, for by so doing he demonstrates explicitly that his deeds are for the sake of God alone and then there will be no stranger in his studies or in the *mitzvot* he performs. Take no notice of that which Rabbi Ezekiel Segal Landau writes in his

Noda Biyudah, Yoreh Deah, No. 93, in which he attacks and
denigrates the recital of *le-shem yihud.* His anger at the Hasidim of
his country led him into error. It is certain that he did not have
in mind those who study the true science [the Kabbalah] in
holiness and humility, but he generalised. He continues to expound
the idea that no special intention at all is required and that all the
perfections occur automatically above as the result of our deeds. In
this he deliberately disagrees with R. Simeon b. Yohai and his
associates, the elevated holy ones, and with our Master the Ari, of
blessed memory, in whom the spirit of the Lord has spoken and
with whom Elijah, may be he remembered for good, conversed
as a man speaks to his neighbour. It is undoubtedly true that
whoever carries out the precepts for the sake of heaven certainly
performs the perfections above, but there is no comparison at all
between him and one who has the correct intentions. This is clear
and obvious.

The reference to Turkey in this passage should be noted. Turkey
was, of course, the home of the Sabbatians. The extraordinary
parallels between Azulai and R. Hayim of Czernowitz are too
close to be coincidental. Possibly, R. Hayim had read Azulai's
book and adopted his actual words.

The crisis of modernism was met by the Hasidim through a
much greater emphasis on mysticism and the Kabbalah. Revealing
is the report[48] of a conversation between the Hasidic master R.
Simhah Bunam of Pzhysha (d. 1827) and his disciple R. Hanoch
of Alexander (d. 1870). R. Simhah Bunam is alleged to have said
to R. Hanoch:

> I am astonished at the incredible degeneration in Jewish observance
> in the city of Prague [!], a city renowned for its men learned in
> the Torah, since we have been taught by the rabbis that the Torah
> shields against sin both at the time when one studies it and at other
> times as well. But the matter can be explained as follows. In
> former ages the revealed part of the Torah was enough. Now,
> however, in the time of the 'heels of the Messiah', the secret Torah
> [the Kabbalah] is essential. We observe that just before a lamp
> goes out its flame become stronger and flares up. So, too, the
> evil inclination did not prevail to the same extent in former times
> and the revealed part of the Torah was strong enough an antidote.
> But now, just before the redemption, the evil inclination is very
> powerful and as an antidote one requires the force provided by the
> secret doctrines.

CHAPTER XIII

Hasidic Prayer in the Responsa

In the previous chapter we examined in detail the Responsum of R. Ezekiel Landau against the Hasidic adoption of the *le-shem yihud* formula. As the Hasidic movement grew in strength and numbers the Halakhic (legal) aspects of some of the Hasidic practices began to be discussed in the Responsa of several prominent rabbis, some of whom, like R. Ezekiel Landau, were opposed to Hasidism, some of whom were neutral. The Halakhists among the Hasidim naturally took part in the debates. In this chapter we examine the Responsa bearing on Hasidic prayer.

We begin with the two Responsa on the Hasidic practice of wearing only garments other than woollen for prayer,[1] by R. Moses Sofer (1763–1839), the leader of Hungarian Orthodoxy,[2] and the Responsum on the same subject by the Hasidic master R. Moses Teitelbaum[3] (d. 1841), disciple of the 'Seer' of Lublin and of R. Elimelech of Lizensk. R. Moses Teitelbaum settled in the town of Ohel in Hungary where he became the leader of Hungarian Hasidism. R. Moses Sofer was no Hasid but neither was he opposed to the movement. In his youth in Frankfurt one of his teachers was R. Phinehas Horowitz (d. 1801), Rabbi of Frankfurt, who had had a close association with the Maggid of Meseritch. Another of R. Moses Sofer's teachers in Frankfurt was R. Nathan Adler (1741–1800) who adopted a Hasidic approach of his own.[4] These three Responsa are also important for their discussion of the adoption by the Hasidim of the Lurianic Prayer Book.[5]

R. Moses Sofer's first Responsum is addressed to Abraham Zevi Katz, who asked whether there is any warrant in Jewish law for those who refused to allow the prayer-leader to wear garments of wool. Their argument is that since they use the Sephardi (= Lurianic) Prayer Book, this version is so sacred that one who wears wool (so that there is a remote fear that there may be in the garment some linen, too, and he offends against the prohibition of wearing a mixed garment as in Deut. 22: 11) is not worthy enough to lead the prayers. R. Moses knows that some especially pious folk do avoid wearing garments of wool at any time for the reason given, but he cannot see what this has to do with prayer. He cannot see at all, he remarks, the alleged claim that there is a special 'mystery' according to which the Sephardi version cannot 'bear' one who wears wool. In an interesting and oft-quoted aside, R. Moses Sofer declares that his teachers R. Phinehas and R. Nathan both informed him that all the versions of the Prayer Book have the same effect. The Lurianic Prayer Book was compiled by the Ari as a Sephardi. If a man of similar stature had arisen among the Ashkenazim he would have made the necessary Kabbalistic improvements and corrections to the Ashkenazi Prayer Book. The Lurianic Prayer Book should be used by those who understand its meaning (i.e. the kavvanot), but otherwise it is advisable to use the Ashkenazi Prayer Book. R. Phinehas and R. Nathan both used the Lurianic version for themselves but did not encourage its use for others. R. Moses Sofer concludes:

> It follows from what we have said that those who use the Sephardi version can be assumed to have been initiated into the mysteries of the Lord. They know the secret and understand what they say and so have a right to use that version. But as for those, like us, who have not reached this stage, our prayers, which follow the Ashkenazi version, are also heard. One must not say that one prayer is different from another so that it cannot tolerate garments of wool. That is a nonsensical view.

From R. Moses Sofer's second Responsum (dated 1833), addressed to a Rabbi Meir, we learn that R. Moses' reply had been sent to R. Moses Teitelbaum, who was critical of the decision that there is no objection to wearing wool for those who use the Lurianic version. R. Moses Sofer refers, however, to his rival in very respectful terms. R. Moses Sofer makes the observation that just as the prophetic vision is expressed by each prophet in his own style so, too, prayer is for all, but should be recited by each group according to its own particular tradition. Prophecy comes from 'above to below' and it is all one, yet Isaiah speaks differently from Amos. By the same token, prayer, which is from 'below to above', is all one, yet Ashkenazim should be true to their own version and should not seek to substitute for it the Sephardi version. As for R. Moses Teitelbaum's contention that the Sephardim have taken upon themselves the obligation to avoid wearing wool when they offer their prayers, this would, indeed, be binding as a kind of vow if it were true, but where and by whom was such an obligation undertaken? The Sephardim hailing from Spain and Portugal and now residing in Amsterdam, London and Hamburg evidently do not know of any such obligation since all of them, and this includes their teachers, see no objection to wearing wool when they pray. If R. Moses Teitelbaum refers to the Ashkenazim who use the Sephardi Prayer Book, i.e. the Hasidim, it is up to him to produce evidence that such an obligation was undertaken by them. There is no evidence at all for such a contention. As for the Hasidic work *Likkute Amarim*, in which it is stated that the Maggid of Meseritch had argued that, nowadays, when no one is aware of which tribe he belongs to, the Lurianic version is a gate to heaven for all,[6] R. Moses Sofer admits that he has never seen this book. If the argument of the book is correct, why do Kohanim and Levites use the Lurianic rite and not that of their own tribe, since these do know to which tribe they belong? Moreover, already in the time of the Talmud the identity of the different tribes was no longer known and yet it is hard to believe that all the Talmudic sages used the 'Sephardi' version. The great French and German medieval scholars used the Ashkenazi rite even though they no longer knew to which tribe they belonged. Can we imagine that the prayers of these renowned scholars did not ascend to Heaven? R. Moses Sofer adds, however, that if R. Abraham Zevi (mentioned in the first Responsum) does recite his prayers among the Hasidim he should wear garments of linen or silk in order to avoid unnecessary conflict. This is a far worse offence than the possibility of wearing a garment of mixed stuff. R. Moses remarks that the word for 'mixed stuff' is *shaatnez* (Deut. 22: 11) and the letters of this form the words *satan az*, 'Satan the brazen'. Controversy is the brazen Satan who 'dances among us' today and should be avoided at all costs. Therefore, R. Abraham Zevi should not wear garments of wool when he prays with the Hasidim, not because the law demands it but because nothing is worse than strife and contention. The conciliatory attitude of R. Moses Sofer is very different from that of the Mitnaggedic rabbis who tried to prevent the Hasidim themselves from wearing garments made of other stuff than wool.

R. Moses Sofer's Responsum concludes with a note that sheds light on the Hasidic practice in this matter. The questioner had asked him why he had given an approbation to the *tallitim* ('prayer-shawls') manufactured in Pressburg (i.e. they were completely free from *shaatnez*), while giving no such approbation to cloth in general manufactured there. R. Moses replies that the *tallitim* factory is owned by Jews and these wish to have an approbation so that the Hasidim, too, can use their wares. But the cloth manufacturers are non-Jews and have no interest in obtaining an approbation from rabbis. From this we learn that for all their objection to wearing wool at prayer, the Hasidim did insist on wearing woollen *tallitim* (this is advocated by many Halakhic authorities), but they saw to it that these were completely free from any suspicion of *shaatnez*. R. Moses Sofer himself gave his approbation for this purpose. In all probability, where such an approbation was not forthcoming, the Hasidim still used woollen *tallitim* on the grounds that there was a real risk of *shaatnez* in woollen suits and the like manufactured in those days, but none in plain woollen *tallitim*.

R. Moses Teitelbaum's Responsum on the wearing of wool during prayer is brief and can be quoted in full. The editor's note at the end calls attention to the two Responsa of R. Moses Sofer on the subject. R. Moses Teitelbaum, too, refers to the pun on *shaatnez* and *satan az* but interprets it in his own way. R. Moses Teitelbaum writes:

You asked about someone in your town who declared that there is room for objecting to one who wears wool leading the congregation in prayer because there is a risk of mixed stuff, and that when he prays he should don other garments. It is perfectly true that a real risk exists that woollen garments may contain a strand of linen since, as everyone knows, this happens frequently. Happy is he who is careful in this matter and wears no wool. In Poland no God-fearing person wears wool. Also in this country [Hungary] many have removed their woollen garments from the time I came here. May they be blessed for so doing. We have no power, however, to compel the masses not to wear wool. Now with regard to the wearing of wool by one who leads the congregation in prayer, it is true that if there is, God forbid, any *shaatnez* in the garment he wears, that is to say, if a strand of linen is mingled in that garment, it does great harm to the prayer, even if he himself is not conscious that he is wearing *shaatnez*. Apart from the fact that a Biblical prohibition is involved, there is great impurity in a garment of *shaatnez*. Those fond of such expositions have pointed out that the letters of the word *shaatnez* form the words *satan az*. The force of Satan is strong and very powerful and is extended over one who wears it. And, moreover, *az* can be read as *ez* ['goat'] which is the satyr, as in the verse, 'And satyrs shall dance there' [Isa. 13 : 21]. How, then, can it be right for him to awaken compassion on the congregation when he is clothed with the garments of the 'Other Side'? Consequently, if the congregation wishes to introduce a rule that (even though they themselves do wear wool and have no fear of the risk of mixed stuff) the prayer leader at all events should not wear wool (since he is their deputy and because he is required more than they to awaken compassion and he has to be more scrupulous) it is certainly a sound rule and may they be blessed for it. But if the congregation have no concern for this, because the majority of them and all the ordinary members wear wool and it is only an individual who protests, then it does not seem right to me that an individual has the right to interfere in a congregation which uses the Ashkenazi version and not the version of the Ari, may the memory of the righteous and holy be for a blessing. No individual has the right of introducing a new rule, and even if it is a sound rule the individual has no standing to compel others to do as he does. But if they use the version of the Ari, may the memory of the righteous and holy be for a blessing, which is the version used by those who conduct themselves in piety [*Hasidut*], the law is certainly with the individual. For it is known that all who use this version in their prayers have taken it upon themselves to flee from ninety-nine gates of permissiveness in order not to risk a single, unclean gate of prohibition, God forbid, and they do not wear wool. It is possible that if an individual enters the synagogue to pray and he wears wool that they should not investigate too closely. But it has never been heard that one who wears wool should lead the prayers in a congregation in which the version of the Ari, may the memory of the righteous and holy be for a blessing, is used. For this would involve a contradiction, his prayer contradicting his garments, and by so doing he awakens a great accusation, God forbid. Consequently, where they use the version of the Ari, may the memory of the righteous and holy be for a blessing, no one wearing wool, in which there is a risk of *shaatnez*, should act as the prayer-leader. As for that which you write that it will lead to people scoffing at him, the Shulhan Arukh, Orah Hayim 1: 1, in the notes of my great-grandfather the Rama [R. Moses Isserles], may the memory of the righteous and holy be for a blessing, records, 'He should not be embarrassed because people laugh at him when he serves God'. The truth is that he will not be scoffed at. Even if the scoffers do mock him once or twice, they will be ashamed to do so after a while and they will close their mouths if his intention is for the sake of heaven. It will be to the honour of God and he, too, will be honoured. We have been given a promise that no one who trusts in God will be put to shame. With this I conclude and send the greetings of a faithful friend.

Another Responsum of R. Moses Teitelbaum[7] of relevance to Hasidic prayer deals with the prohibition of eating before the morning prayers. The author is very strict and forbids even a mere tasting of food before the morning prayer, but he does permit the drinking of tea or coffee. Although he does not refer specifically to the Hasidim,[8] it is clear that he is thinking of the Hasidic custom when he writes that the practice of drinking coffee or tea before the morning prayers is 'a custom of the pious' (*minhag vatikin*). It is also, he remarks, 'very helpful towards cleansing the bowels before prayer'.[9]

In the Responsa of the late Hasidic master and legal authority R. Hayim Halberstam of Zans in Galicia (d. 1876), disciple of the 'Seer' of Lublin, R. Naftali of Ropshitz (d. 1827) and R. Shalom of Belz (d. 1855), there are a number of references to Hasidic prayer. R. Hayim also has a lengthy Responsum on the substitution of the Lurianic Prayer Book for the Ashkenazi.[10] R. Hayim's Responsum, dated 1870, is addressed to 'the renowned Hasid, Rabbi Abraham Isaac, Rabbi of Kleinvardein'. The question is formulated in connection with the ruling of R. Moses Sofer:

> Your honour has asked whether it is permitted to change over
> from the Ashkenazi version and adopt the version of the Ari, of
> blessed memory, since in the *Hatam Sofer* it is stated that the Ari,
> of blessed memory, arranged the *kavvanot* because he was a
> Sephardi but the mysteries are hinted at also in the Ashkenazi
> version.

R. Hayim begins with a historical note. The Lurianic version is not identical with the Sephardi version.[11] Luria made a number of changes to suit the *kavvanot*. The Lurianic version is the most suitable for anyone who does not know to which tribe he belongs, as is stated in the work *Likkute Amarim*. This work is in any event based on the sound Lurianic tradition, says R. Hayim, and he fails to understand R. Moses Sofer's abrupt dismissal of the work. After subjecting R. Moses Sofer's remarks about the Talmudic rabbis to a critique, R. Hayim continues:

> Consequently, all the words of this Responsum [of R. Moses
> Sofer] are strange and whoever has good taste can rely on the
> great ones of the generation, the elevated holy men, who did
> change over from the Ashkenazi version to the Sephardi. I do
> not, God forbid, disagree with our master, the head of all the sons
> of exile, the Hatam Sofer, of blessed memory, for I do not even
> understand his secular conversation [i.e. and still less his Torah]
> except that I have stated that which I have seen and received from
> the elevated holy men, great in both the revealed things of the
> Torah and in the mysteries thereof. May the good Lord lead me
> in the way of truth.

As for R. Moses Sofer's complaint that the great medieval sages used the Ashkenazi version, even though they did not know to which tribe they belonged, the answer is that these sages were Kabbalists and did know the root of their own soul, i.e. to which tribe they belonged. True, the ordinary folk, who obviously did not have this knowledge, still used the Ashkenazi version but, then, the Lurianic version was not intended for these, only for the masters of prayer. The Baal Shem Tov, however, saw by the power of his holy spirit that his generation required the Lurianic version and so he ordained that his followers should use the Lurianic version.

The holy leaders of the generations who came after him [the Baal Shem Tov], his disciples and their disciples, scholars great in both the revealed things of the Torah and in the mysteries thereof, followed this practice. Consequently, whoever believes in the Baal Shem Tov and his disciples should grasp hold of the version of the Ari, of blessed memory, and should not depart from it. These are the words of one of low estate who is submissive to the disciples of the Baal Shem Tov in order to understand their holy words.

In two other Responsa[12] R. Hayim discusses the Hasidic objection to prayers being conducted with an officiating Hazan (Cantor) and a choir. Although the Hasidim attached much significance to melody in prayer,[13] they did not take kindly to the practice in large synagogues of the prayers being led by a Hazan and choir. In the Hasidic synagogues the prayer-leader was either the Zaddik himself or a devout member of the congregation with a pleasant voice. Even in the few Hasidic synagogues which did have a choir, this was composed of ordinary congregants who were gifted in this direction. The formal Hazan and choir smacked, for the Hasidim, of officialdom and lack of spontaneity. They held his efforts to be more in the nature of a musical performance than an act of worship and saw in the whole institution an attempt by Jews to copy Church worship. R. Hayim's first Responsum on this topic is addressed to an anonymous elderly president of a community who failed to protest when a Hazan and choir were introduced to lead the congregation in prayer. R. Hayim writes:

I have heard that in the Hasidic synagogue in your community a Hazan [shatz = shaliah tzibbur, 'deputy of the congregation'] with a choir has been appointed and I am greatly astonished. What can they have been thinking of! Our forefathers struggled so hard until they succeeded in removing this scab from the children of Israel. Thank God in Hasidic congregations there are none who pray accompanied by an arrangement of song and pleasant melody as in the theatre. Rather do they choose a worthy man who pours out his heart in prayer in the presence of the Lord. Even in all the other Galician communities, though they do not use the Sephardi version, yet they take care not to bring songsters into the synagogue in the manner of the theatre, God forbid. In your community, too, they used to pray, as in all other Polish cities, in love and fear without uncouth cries. And for the Days of Awe [Rosh Ha-Shanah and Yom Kippur] you used to choose a God-fearing perfect man to pray on your behalf before the Lord of all. How, then, could your hearts have changed so to bring an idol into the house of our God? It is especially hard to understand since the Hazan you have chosen has a bad reputation, as a sinner. I am especially surprised at your honour who has been strongly opposed to the innovators all your life and who refused to allow any wicked hands to touch the honour of God's house and His Torah. How can it have happened that in your old age your hands should have become so weak as to allow innovators who have just arrived on the scene to satisfy their lust in the courtyards of the Lord and to think of their nonsense at the time of prayer, of the love songs that are sung in the theatre? Woe to these fools, uncircumcised of heart, in whom there is no understanding. But an old man like you who behaved uprightly in his youth, how can you be embarrassed in your ripe old age and so put the days of your youth to shame? Why do you fail to rebuke them with words of uprightness and to exercise force and coercion against the wicked who wish to profane God's name? The little serenity they have found is when they pour out their souls in prayer. For during the rest of the day, for our sins, they are immersed in numerous occupations and are among strange folk with peculiar opinions. Their drinking is not lawful and who knows if their food is prepared according to the law? And there are other things they do as they move about in the streets of the town. All that they have left is the short time they have for prayer, to pray together with the God-fearing, and led by a God-fearing prayer-leader. How could they have become turncoats? . . . I want to urge you, therefore, to recall the days of old when you used to visit the Zaddikim whose words entered your heart. Now, too, let the fear of God be awakened in your heart to smite the crown of the wicked and to drive out of the house of the Lord the Hazan and his helpers.

The second Responsum on the same theme is dated 1864 and is addressed to the leaders of the community of Miskolcs. R. Hayim begins by stating the question:

I have your letter in which you ask me whether it is permitted to have a house of prayer that is exactly the same as the house of prayer of others [i.e. of non-Jews] and to have a prayer-leader and a choir who sing songs other than our own and who bow down as is their [the non-Jewish] way.

R. Hayim states that there are laws binding on all Jews and, in addition, there are local customs. Local custom is also binding upon the members of a community and the custom in Galicia is opposed to any alteration in the synagogue and its services. This applies all the more when the motive for change is in order to ape Christian worship. They must not be embarrassed by the taunt that their form of worship is uncouth. Every religion has practices which seem bizarre to outsiders, yet the adherents of these religions do not change their ways because others ridicule them. R. Hayim sees in the attempt at introducing such innovations an attraction for the views of the Reformers, on whom he pours scorn. It is useless, he says, to try to prove that there is a prohibition by quoting rabbinic sources since the Reformers do not accept rabbinic authority. A new *motif* is here added to Hasidic opposition to innovations in prayer. The rise of the Reform movement made the Hasidim, themselves originally innovators in prayer, become bitterly opposed to the slightest change. R. Hayim concludes, 'Therefore, my friends, do as the Torah ordains and do not go in the way of those who hate our holy Torah and keep far from their opinions. Then it will be well with you'.

Finally, in an important Responsum,[14] addressed to the Rabbi of Mosichisk, R. Hayim deals with a problem that must have exercised many Hasidic communities: whether it is permitted for the members of a Hasidic conventicle to divide up into groups, i.e. for some of the members to organise separate services in another conventicle. The Rabbi of Mosichisk observes in his question that, twenty years before, a *klaus* had been established in which the Lurianic version was used and in which the most respected members of the community prayed. Some of the members now wish to build another *klaus* but the Rabbi is not happy about this. On the one hand, it is true that the original *klaus* has become too small to accommodate all the worshippers. But, on the other hand, he has heard R. Shalom of Belz and his brother, the Rabbi of Kaminka, advise against such separation because it leads to 'a division among the people', i.e. in all probability it would weaken Hasidic loyalties. R. Hayim replies that there is obviously no legal objection, since it is the custom 'in all the cities of the diaspora' to build more than one House of Learning. Nevertheless, he bows to the wisdom of the two Hasidic masters mentioned and he refers to a similar opinion given by R. Naftali of Ropshitz. The general Hasidic practice was, in fact, to have only one *klaus* or *stiebel* for the followers of a particular Hasidic master.

One of the most famous Respondents in the nineteenth century was the Rabbi of Lemberg, R. Joseph Saul Nathanson (1808–75).[15] A Responsum of R. Joseph Saul,[16] relevant to the theme of Hasidic prayer, concerns the recitation of the Hallel on Passover eve. The Hallel consists of Psalms 113–18 and is recited on festivals during the morning service. According to the Mishnah[17] it was the practice in Temple times to recite the Hallel at the time when the Paschal lamb was offered on the eve of Passover. The Sephardi custom is to recite the Hallel on Passover eve as a reminder of the Temple practice, but the Ashkenazim do not recite it then.[18] Together with some other Sephardi customs, the Hasidim adopted this one and, as a result, even a number of non-Hasidic communities introduced the custom of reciting the Hallel on the first and second nights of Passover. The basic legal question, as in connection with the Hasidic adoption of the Lurianic Prayer Book, was the prohibition of departing from local custom. The Polish rite did not have the Hallel as part of the service on the first and second nights of Passover and to depart from the custom was illegal.

Nathanson's Responsum on this topic is addressed to his pupil, R. Joseph Meises. The Rabbi of Meises's community (the community is not mentioned by name) ordered the Hallel to be recited on the first and second nights of Passover. When the lay leaders and the ordinary members protested that this was contrary to the custom, the Rabbi retorted that the conduct of services in the synagogue was his responsibility not theirs and that, in any event, this was not a matter to be decided by custom since early sources refer to the practice of reciting the Hallel on these occasions. Meises debated the matter and turned to Nathanson for his ruling. Nathanson begins his reply by noting, 'What reply can I give and how can I answer? For our sins the plague in these matters has spread, especially since decisions in these matters win for them [the rabbis] popularity and honour among the masses.' Nathanson adds that even in Lemberg in that very year they recited the Hallel in the Central Synagogue on Passover eve despite the definite ruling that it should not be recited given by his great-uncle R. Jacob Meshullam Ornstein (d. 1839), a former Rabbi of Lemberg. It is clear that by the middle of the nineteenth century the Hasidic movement had become so well established in Galicia that rabbis were tempted to introduce Hasidic rites into the official services in order to win the approval of the masses. Interestingly enough, in the course of his elaborate discussion of the legality of the practice, Nathanson quotes the Talmudic passage[19] that, just as it is a duty to speak when people will listen, it is a duty not to speak when people will not listen. It is probably more than a coincidence that this is the passage, in the same context of lack of power in the face of Hasidic opposition, quoted by R. Ezekiel Landau.[20] The difficulties in this kind of situation faced by the Rabbi of Prague at the end of the eighteenth century were even more severe when faced by the Rabbi of Lemberg in the middle of the nineteenth. (In this very Responsum Nathanson quotes from Landau's Responsa collection, *Noda Biyudah*.) Nathanson advises Meises not to protest because this is precisely what the rabbi who permitted it wants, his aim being to acquire fame as an innovator. Punning on the verse (Exod. 14: 8), 'The children of Israel went out with a high hand' (*be-yad ramah*), Nathanson remarks that when the time comes when they will have the power of enforcing the old customs, then 'The children of Israel will go forth by the hand of Rama' (= R. Moses Isserles, the great sixteenth-century legal authority who established the forms of the Ashkenazi customs for the Jews of Poland).[21]

In the course of his discussion in this Responsum, Nathanson refers to a much earlier Responsum of his on the other question of changing from the Ashkenazi to the Lurianic version of the

Prayer Book. He remarks that in the year 5656 (= 1856) he was approached by R. Michael Hibner, Rabbi of Niznib. It was the custom in this town for the Rabbi to be invited to pray in the Great Synagogue on the sabbath but on week-days in the new House of Learning. In the latter the Sephardi rite was followed but in the Great Synagogue the old Ashkenazi rite was followed. The Rabbi asked Nathanson whether, on his visits to the Great Synagogue, he should use his own (the Sephardi) version or follow the congregation in using the Ashkenazi version. Furthermore, what would the law be if the whole congregation wished to change over from one rite to the other? Again Nathanson quotes the Talmudic dictum that just as it is a duty to speak when people will listen, it is a duty not to speak when people will not listen.

In another (undated) Responsum,[22] addressed to R. Jonathan Benjamin Pollack, Nathanson takes up further the question of substituting the Sephardi Prayer Book for the old and established Ashkenazi Prayer Book. Nathanson remarks here that the people of his country and of Hungary are the descendants of the Ashkenazim and should use the Ashkenazi rite, 'except that the Hasidim from the days of the Baal Shem Tov, may his memory be for a blessing, began to establish the custom of introducing the Sephardi version'. He observes that basically this is improper, since in all ritual matters the Ashkenazim follow the decisions of R. Moses Isserles and it is forbidden to depart from the custom. Once again Nathanson remarks, 'There is much to be said on this question but just as it is a duty to speak when people will listen it is a duty not to speak when people will not listen.' Consequently, Nathanson advises his questioner to keep to the Ashkenazi version. If, however, he is called upon to lead the prayers in a synagogue which uses the Sephardi version he, too, should use it, reciting his prayers from the Sephardi Prayer Book. 'The main thing', Nathanson concludes, 'is to behave always with humility and never to quarrel over these matters. The Lord who searches all hearts knows full well that your intention is for the sake of Heaven.'

Notes

Chapter II

1 *Keter Shem Tov* (Jerusalem, 1968), p. 22b
2 'Contemplative Prayer in Hasidism', *Studies in Mysticism and Religion presented to G. Scholem* (Jerusalem, 1967), p. 209
3 Schatz, p. 210
4 Ber. 21a; Sukk. 38a, but see Maimonides *Yad, Tefillah* 1:1 and *Kesef Mishnah* ad loc.
5 Shabb. 10a
6 Shabb. 11a
7 D. Z. Hillmann, *Iggerot Baal Ha-Tanya* (Jerusalem, 1953), no. 21, pp. 33–4
8 *Maor Va-Shemesh* (Tel Aviv, 1965), *va-yehi*, to Gen. 49: 22, p. 56b
9 Ber. 32b
10 *Maor Va-Shemesh, va-yetze*, to Gen. 28: 16–17, p. 30b. The Midrash quoted is in the *Yalkut* to Gen. 28:16
11 (n.p., n.d.), pp. 8–9
12 'Devekuth, or Communion with God' and now reprinted in his *The Messianic Idea in Judaism* (New York, 1971), pp. 203–27
13 Solomon of Lutzk, *Maggid Devarav Le-Yaakov* (Jerusalem, 1962), pp. 134–5, s.v. *ve-etz ha-hayim be-tokh ha-gan*
14 *Tzavaat Ha-Ribash* (Jerusalem, 1948), p. 2
15 *Ben Porat Yosef* (Koretz, 1781), p. 53a, in the name of R. Nahman oⱼ Kosov but on p. 23b in the name of 'R.I.'? In *Toledot Yaakov Yosef* (Warsaw, 1881), p. 176b, *va-ethanan*, he simply says that he 'heard this'. Cf. A. J. Heschel, 'R. Nahman of Kosov', Harry A. Wolfson Jubilee Volume (Jerusalem, 1965), p. 130 and *Sefer Baal Shem Tov* (Sotmar, 1943), vol. 1, p. 143 note 9
16 *Toledot, va-ethanan* p. 176b
17 *Degel Mahane Efrayim* (Jerusalem, 1963), *haftarah ki tetze*, p. 253
18 Avot 1: 3
19 *Keter Shem Tov*, p. 9a
20 *Keter Shem Tov*, pp. 14a–b
21 *Degel Mahane Efrayim, toledot*, p. 34

22 *Degel Mahane Efrayim*, p. 283
23 *Toledot, kedoshim*, pp. 100b–101a
24 *Maggid Devarav Le-Yaakov*, p. 101
25 *Maggid Devarav Le-Yaakov*, p. 84
26 *Or Ha-Meir* (Jerusalem, 1968), vol. 2, *derush le-rosh ha-shanah*, p. 258a. The same comment in shorter form is given in *Maggid Devarav Le-Yaakov*, pp. 16–17
27 *Ha-Hasidut Ke-Mistikah* (Jerusalem, 1968), Chapter 6, pp. 78–95. This is the same author as the Rivka Schatz quoted earlier
28 *Enthusiasm* (Oxford, 1957), p. 254
29 *Tzav Ve-Ziruz* (Jerusalem, 1962), pp. 6–7
30 See e.g. the section on this theme in R. Arele Roth's *Shomer Emunim* (Jerusalem, 1966), vol. 1, pp. 95a–98a
31 R. Moses of Koznitz, *Beer Moshe* (New York, 1964), *shemini atzeret*, p. 195a

Chapter III

1 Horodetsky, ed., *Shivhe Ha-Besht* (Tel Aviv, 1960), p. 95. Cf. Heschel, p. 130
2 *Maggid Devarav Le-Yaakov*, p. 62
3 This idea is not original with the Maggid but was advanced in the Lurianic school itself. For details see H. J. Zimmels, *Ashkenazim and Sephardim* (London, 1958), pp. 116–17. Zimmels refers to the passage in the Zohar (II, 251a) that a synagogue should have twelve windows. On the basis of this the Shulhan Arukh (Orah Hayim 90: 4) rules, 'It is proper for a synagogue to have twelve windows'. The commentator R. Abraham Gumbiner (*Magen Avraham* ad loc.) refers to the passage in the Zohar. A source for the idea as applied to the different rites, as given by Zimmels, is Jacob Hayim Zemah, *Nagid U-Metzaveh* (Amsterdam, 1712), p. 18a
4 For details see the excellent analysis by A. Rubinstein in his review of A. Wertheim, *Halakhot Ve-Halikhot Ba-Hasidut* (Jerusalem, 1960) in *Kiryat Sefer*, vol. 36, no. 3 (June 1961), pp. 280–6
5 *Sefer Hamishah Maamarot* (Jerusalem, 1966), *Maamar Nusah Ha-Tefillah*, pp. 159–86, quoted by Rubinstein
6 *Sefer Hamishah Maamarot*, p. 159
7 See M. Wilensky, *Hasidim U-Mitnaggedim* (Jerusalem, 1970), vol. 1, p. 45 note 10 for a list of these sources
8 S. Dubnow, *Toledot Ha-Hasidut* (Tel Aviv, 1967), pp. 119–23; Wilensky, vol. 1, pp. 44–9
9 The technical rabbinic term for altars erected outside the Temple, applied here to the Hasidic conventicles
10 *Minyan* ('number') is the quorum of ten required for public prayer; hence a *minyan* is a group of worshippers (plural *minyanim*)
11 A Talmudic metaphor, see Hag. 14b, used here for mystical heresy, i.e. misunderstanding the Kabbalistic mysteries to which Luria refers
12 For this letter together with an Introduction and notes see Wilensky, vol. 1, pp. 168–76

13 R. Joseph Karo (1488–1575), author of the Shulhan Arukh and the great legal authority for the Sephardim
14 R. Moses Isserles (d. 1572), Rabbi of Cracow, author of notes to the Shulhan Arukh and the great legal authority for the Ashkenazim
15 Cf. Wilensky, vol. 1, pp. 40–1 note 26
16 On the Hasidic *stiebel* see Wertheim, pp. 68–71; Y. Alfasi, *Ha-Hasidut* (Tel Aviv, 1969), pp. 94–9. The latter chapter seems to have been based on the former without acknowledgement
17 *Responsa* (Warsaw, 1882), *Radbaz*, III, no. 772 (no. 910), also printed in Rokotz, *Siah Sarfe Kodesh* (New York, 1954), 1, p. 4. Rokotz remarks that R. Aaron of Kerlin, disciple of the Maggid of Meseritch, urged God-fearing men to copy out this Responsum and to memorise it!

Chapter IV

1   See Wertheim, pp. 88–93; Alfasi, *Ha-Hasidut*, pp. 184–91
2   Ber. 5: 1
3   Ber. 23a
4   Orah Hayim 92: 1 and 93: 1–3
5   Ber. 22a but see L. Ginzberg, *Commentary to the Palestinian Talmud* (New York, 1971), Introduction, that the Babylonian and Palestinian Talmuds differed on this
6   See Wertheim, pp. 66–8
7   Sabb. 10a
8   Orah Hayim 91: 2
9   *Menahem Tzion, tetze*, quoted by A. I. Sperling, *Taame Ha-Minhagim* (Jerusalem, 1957), p. 40
10 Pp. 193–5
11 Wilensky, vol. 1, p. 275
12 See the sources quoted by Wilensky, vol. 1, p. 38 note 19
13 Wilensky, vol. 1, p. 54
14 Wilensky offers no comment on this but perhaps it refers to the Hasidic practice of drinking coffee before praying
15 i.e. smoking their pipes. Cf. Wilensky, Index: *ishun be-mikteret*; Sperling, p. 102; Wartheim, pp. 224–5. A reliable source (R. Samuel of Shinov, *Ramatayim Tzofim* (Jerusalem, 1970), p. 51a note 13) reports that the 'Seer' of Lublin used to take snuff *during* his prayers as an aid to concentration
16 Wilensky, vol. 1, pp. 38–9
17 Wilensky, vol. 2, p. 207
18 Wilensky, vol. 2, p. 195
19 *Nefesh Ha-Hayim* (Bene Berak, 1958), iv, 4, p. 36a
20 *Nefesh Ha-Hayim*, iv, 8, p. 37b
21 *Toledot Yaakov Yosef*, p. 142b, *shelah*
22 *Maggid Devarav Le-Yaakov*, p. 27
23 *Lebensgeschichte*, ed. J. Fromer (Munich, 1911), pp. 204–5
24 *Likkute Torah*, (Israel, n.d.), *shavuot*, p. 54b
25 Satan, the 'Other Side'

26 A pun on the law that when a sacrifice is brought the priest must not have in his mind any thought of offering it outside the allotted space and time set aside for it, otherwise the sacrifice is invalidated
27 *Tiferet Shelomo* (Jerusalem, 1963), *moadim*, p. 8a
28 For details of later Zaddikim who recited their prayers after the times fixed for them see Sperling, p. 27; Alfasi, *Gur* (Tel Aviv, 1954), pp. 156–9
29 See R. Schatz Uffenheimer, pp. 103, 150
30 *Keneset Yisrael* (Warsaw, 1910) p. 10a, on Israel of Ruzhyn and family
31 *Sefer Torat Avot* (Jerusalem, 1971), part 2, *Torah U-Tefillah*, no. 26, pp. 160–1
32 See *Amud Ha-Emet* (Tel Aviv, n.d.), p. 82

Chapter V

1 Ber. 34a
2 Ber. 34a–b
3 Ber. 31a
4 See the letter in defence of Hasidism by this teacher in Wilensky, vol. 1, pp. 84–8
5 III, 218b–219a
6 II, 79–80
7 Orah Hayim 48: 1
8 *Shelah*, part 2, *inyane tefillah*, p. 79
9 *Magen Avraham* to Orah Hayim 48: 1, note 4
10 Quoted, as a tale current among the Hasidim, by Wertheim, p. 103 note 82
11 Ber. 10b
12 *Noam Elimelekh* (Jerusalem, n.d.) to Lev. 23: 6, p. 99
13 *Noam Elimelekh* to Lev. 19: 4, p. 94; to Lev. 23: 6, p. 99; to Exod. 30: 12, pp. 78–9
14 *Likkute Maharan* (Bene Berak, 1965), no. 156, p. 105b
15 On R. Abraham of Kalisk see the notes in my translation of *Tract on Ecstasy* by Dov Baer of Lubavitch (London, 1963), pp. 34–5. R. Shneor Zalman of Liady, in a letter to Abraham of Kalisk (D. Z. Hillmann: *Iggerot Ha-Rav Baal Ha-Tanya* (Jerusalem, 1953), p. 175) reminds him of the Maggid's displeasure and the Maggid's rebuke to him in 1772 precisely for the practice of turning somersaults. For R. Hayim Haikel of Amdur see S. Dubnow, *Toledot Ha-Hasidut* (Tel Aviv, 1967), pp. 132, 367–72. Dubnow, p. 132, quotes the saying of the Hasidim defending the practice of turning somersaults, '*Az es kumt zu menschen gadlus azoi mus er sich übervarfen.*' ('When a man is afflicted with pride he must turn himself over.')
16 See Knox, pp. 558 f.
17 *Mitpahat Sefarim* (Altona, 1768), p. 31
18 Ber. 32b
19 Yev. 105b; Shulhan Arukh, Orah Hayim 95: 2

20 Evidently referring to Shulhan Arukh, Orah Hayim 125:1, 'One should raise the eyes on high when reciting the Kedushah', see *Ture Zahav* ad loc. who quotes the Tanhuma and argues that the eyes should be closed

21 R. Menahem Azariah of Fano, *Responsa* (Venice, n.d.), no. 113

22 i.e. when the angels stood their wings did not move and so, too, when man stands in prayer there should be no bodily movement

23 See this chapter, note 15

24 H. M. Hielmann, *Bet Rabbi* (Berditchev, 1903), p. 16a, note 2

25 Hillmann, pp. 33–4

26 That prayer is 'service of the heart' is stated in Taan. 2a

27 In the Prayer Book, see Singer's Prayer Book, new ed. (London, 1962), p. 40

28 The *Pirke Hekhalot* are late Midrashim on the angelic hosts and their praises. The Piyutim are the liturgical poems composed in the Middle Ages

29 *Likkute Torah* (Israel, n.d.), *Hadrakhah* 7, p. 8a

30 *Keter Shem Tov*, pp. 24a–b

31 *Keter Shem Tov*, p. 3b

32 This interpretation of Job 19: 26, that man can know God by observing his own physiological and psychological make-up and processes, was first put forward in the Middle Ages (for the details see A. Altmann, 'The Delphic Maxim in Medieval Islam and Judaism' in his *Studies in Religious Philosophy and Mysticism* (London and Ithaca, 1969)) and was very popular with the Hasidim.

33 *Tzavaat Ha-Ribash* (Jerusalem, 1948), p. 7b; *Likkute Yekarim* (Lemberg, 1865), p. 1b; *Sefer Baal Shem Tov* (Sotmar, 1943), vol. 1, p. 145 note 65

34 Lemberg, 1864, p. 40a (wrongly printed as '50'), note 7

35 Jerusalem, 1962, no. 42, p. 411

36 *Yad, Teshuvah*, 10

37 *Major Trends in Jewish Mysticism*, 3rd rev. ed. (New York, 1954; London, 1955), pp. 226–7

38 I, 21b–22a

39 *Mishnat Ha-Zohar*, 2nd ed. (Jerusalem, 1957), vol. 2, pp. 280–301

40 I, 49–50a and 230a

41 See David Knowles, *Western Mysticism*, 3rd ed. (London, 1967), pp. 110 f.

42 On the position of women in Hasidism see S. A. Horodetzsky, *Ha-Hasidut Ve-Ha-Hasidim* (Tel Aviv, 1951), vol. 4, 67–71; H. Rabinowicz, *The World of Hasidism* (London, 1970), pp. 202–10

43 *Keter Shem Tov*, p. 25b

44 *Keter Rosh*, printed at end of *Siddur Ishe Yisrael*, no. 29, p. 527

45 See note 8 above

46 *Keter Shem Tov*, p. 26a

47 *Yalkut Moshe*, quoted in *Sefer Baal Shem Tov*, vol. 2, p. 31a

48 *Or Ha-Meir, terumah*, pp. 68b–69a

49 For these details see M. H. Kleinmann, *Or Yesharim* (Jerusalem, 1967), p. 84b

50 Hielmann, part 2, p. 4 note 3

51 *Sippurim Noraim* (Lemberg, 1875), no pagination

52 Alfasi, *Ha-Hasidut*, pp. 141–2
53 Alfasi, *Gur*, p. 157
54 *Nine Gates* (London, 1961), pp. 6–8
55 *Nine and One Half Mystics* (New York, 1969), p. 209
56 *Shomer Emunim*, vol. 2, p. 291a
57 *Iggerot Shomer Emunim* (Jerusalem, 1942), no. 44, pp. 63a–64b
58 See M. S. Geshuri, *Ha Niggun Ve-Ha-Rikkud Ba-Hasidut* (Tel Aviv, 1955);
    T. Ysander, *Studien Zum Beschtschen Hasidismus* (Uppsala, 1933), pp. 317–
    320; Wertheim, pp. 103–6; Rabinowicz, Chapter 20, pp. 192–201
59 *Kunteros Ha-Hitpaalut*, in Hillel ben Meir of Poritch, *Likkute Biurim*
    (Warsaw, 1865), pp. 11a–b, pp. 76–7 in my translation
60 See below, pp. 98–103 for the Habad view on ecstasy
61 In the letter of his son Eleazar printed at end of *Noam Elimelekh* in various
    editions
62 Quoted from a MS. of R. Yitzhak Eisik of Komarno in R. Arele Roth's
    Shomer Emunim, vol. 1, p. 33b note 37
63 *Beer Moshe* (New York, 1964), *mishpatim*, p. 57a
64 The remarks in this passage follow Geshuri, pp. 249–60
65 *Magen Avot, yitro*
66 *Magen Avot, va-yikra*

Chapter VI

1 Ber. 5: 1
2 Ber. 31a
3 Ber. 31a
4 Ber. 34b
5 Ber. 30b
6 Tos. to Ber. 34b
7 Mishnah Ber. 2: 4
8 On this topic see H. G. Enelow, 'Kawwanah: the Struggle for Inwardness
    in Judaism', in *Studies in Jewish Literature in honor of Kaufmann Kohler*
    (Berlin, 1913)
9 *Duties of the Heart*, VIII, 3
10 *Guide of the Perplexed*, trans. S. Pines (Chicago, 1963), III, 51, pp. 622–3
11 See above, pp. 21–3
12 *Yad, Tefillah* 4: 15–16
13 *Yad, Tefillah* 10: 1
14 Orah Hayim 101; Shulhan Arukh 101:1 in *Rama*
15 'The Kavvanoth of Prayer in Early Hasidism', *Journal of Jewish Studies*, vol.
    ix (1968)
16 *Ha-Hasidut Ke-Mistika*, Chapter 10, pp. 129–47
17 p. 178
18 *Tzavaat Ha-Ribash*, p. 8b; *Or Torah* to the verse; *Sefer Baal Shem Tov*, vol.
    I, pp. 118–22. Cf. the elaboration of this theme in *Degel Mahane Efrayim*,
    noah, p. 9
19 *Keter Shem Tov*, p. 48a–b; *Sefer Baal Shem Tov*, vol. 1, p. 122

20 *Divre Emet* (Germany, 1947), *noah*, p. 12
21 *Keter Shem Tov*, p. 24b
22 *Maor Va-Shemesh, nitzavim*, end, p. 238
23 *Shaar Ha-Tefillah* (Sudlikov, 1813), Introduction, pp. 1a-2b

Chapter VII

1 For a detailed account of Habad thought together with some of the more important sources see my translation with an Introduction and notes of *Tract on Ecstasy* by R. Dov Baer
2 See Sperling, pp. 37-8
3 *Ramataim Tzofim* (Jerusalem, 1970), p. 29a note 19
4 The *Kunteros Ha-Hitbonanut* was published during the author's lifetime as Part 2 of his *Ner Mitzvah Ve-Torah Or* (Kopust, 1820), under the title *Shaar Ha-Yihud* ('Gate of Unification'). It was also printed as an Appendix to R. Shneor Zalman's *Torah Or* (Lemberg, 1851) under the title *Kunteros Ha-Hitbonanut*. The edition used here, and to which page numbers in the notes refer, is the photograph edition of the Lemberg edition, published in New York in 1948. (The number mentioned first is that of the author's division into sections. The number mentioned second is that of the page.) A Commentary on some of the chapters of the work was published as part of R. Hillel ben Meir of Poritch's collected works, known as *Likkute Biurim*, published in Warsaw in 1868 (this is referred to in the following notes as LB). R. Hillel was a disciple of R. Dov Baer
5 i, 2a-3a
6 LB, 2b
7 ii and iii, 3a-4b
8 LB 5b
9 iv, 4b-5a
10 v, 5a-6a
11 vi, 6a-7a
12 xii, 11b

Chapter VIII

1 *Keter Shem Tov*, p. 18b. On the subject of this chapter see Ysander, pp. 209-24, but he has ignored completely the aspect of *hitpaalut*.
2 *Avodat Yisrael*, p. 51b
3 For this and the following about R. Levi Yitzhak see the biographical essay printed at the end of the Jerusalem edition (1964) of his *Kedushat Levi*, pp. 537-8. For the legends concerning R. Levi Yitzhak see J. S. Minkin, *The Romance of Hasidism* (New York, 1935), Chapter 7, pp. 152-177
4 *Avodat Yisrael, behukotai*, p. 55b
5 See I. M. Rabbinowitz, *Ha-Maggid Mi-Koznitz* (Tel Aviv, 1947), p. 64
6 Rabbinowitz, pp. 65-73
7 Cf. the remarks of R. Solomon of Radomsk, *Tiferet Shelomo* (Jerusalem, 1963), vol. 2, p. 34b that the fear of God exercises a powerful attraction for man, unlike other, 'external', fears, and there is joy in it. This is, of

173

course, Otto's famous definition, in his *Idea of the Holy* (London, 1953), of the numinous as *mysterium tremendum et fascinans*

8   M. H. Kleinmann, *Zikkaron La-Rishonim* (Jerusalem, 1959), pp. 22–7; W. Rabinowitsch, *Ha-Hasidut Ha-Litait* (Jerusalem, 1961), p. 18

9   S. Sevin, *Ishim Ve-Shittot* (Tel Aviv, 1952), p. 68

10 B. Landau and N. Uretner, eds: *Ha-Rav Ha-Kadosh Mi-Belza* (Jerusalem, 1967), p. 218

11 See the sources quoted by Dubnow, pp. 208–9 and Dubnow's remarks on this

12 These rules have been printed in a number of works, recently in *Torat Ha-Maggid*, ed. Israel Klepholtz (Tel Aviv, 1969), vol. 1, pp. 3–9

13 *Torat Avot*, no. 72, p. 164

14 *Torat Avot*, no. 77, p. 165

15 *Torat Avot*, no. 78

16 This subject has been examined in detail in my translation of *Tract on Ecstasy* (*Kunteros Ha-Hitpaalut*) by R. Dov Baer and in my study of R. Aaron of Starosselje, *Seeker of Unity* (London, 1966). The following outline is based on these two works

17 Quoted by Hielmann, p. 88 note 1

18 This letter is printed as the Introduction to R. Dov Baer's *Kunteros Ha-Hitpaalut*. See my translation, Appendix I, pp. 177–87

19 In my translation of the tract. The page numbers following are those of the Hebrew edition, Warsaw, 1868

20 p. 4b

21 p. 9b

22 pp. 10a f.

23 Second volume entitled *Shaare Avodah* ('The Gates of Divine Worship') (Shklov, 1821). See my *Seeker of Unity* for further details

24 *Shaare Avodah*, Introduction

25 Hielmann, Part I, p. 134

26 Hielmann, Part II, p. 4

Chapter IX

1   The origins of this doctrine have been acutely traced, by J. G. Weiss, 'The Beginnings of Hasidism', to the pre-Hasidic groups influenced by underground Sabbatianism. According to Weiss, the Baal Shem Tov and his associates used the Sabbatian principle of the descent of the Zaddik in order to redeem the 'holy sparks' from the domain of the evil, but applied it not in action, as in Sabbatianism, but in thought, especially in prayer

2   Weiss, op. cit., pp. 92–6

3   See I. Tishby and Y. Dan, 'Torat Ha-Hasidut Ve-Sifrutah', offprint from *Hebrew Encyclopedia*, vol. 17 (Jerusalem, 1966), pp. 783–4

4   *Toledot, va-yakhel*, p. 75b

5   See I. Tishby's *Torat Ha-Ra Ve-Ha-Kelipah Be-Kabbalat Ha-Ari* (Jerusalem, 1968) for the idea of the breaking of the vessels as a cosmic catastrophe, a doctrine which the later Kabbalists softened. Cf. Tishby and Dan, op. cit.,

pp. 772–4 that in Hasidic thought the 'breaking of the vessels' is for the purpose of crossing the abyss between the Infinite and the finite and is hence itself part of the *tikkun* ('perfection'). Tishby and Dan quote the parable of the Maggid of Meseritch in which the 'breaking of the vessels' is compared to a tailor who first has to cut the cloth into pieces before he can sew the pieces together again to make a suit

6   *Toledot, ekev,* p. 181a

7   *Keter Shem Tov,* p. 6a. Cf. *Maggid Devarav Le-Yaakov,* p. 18, that the beauty of a woman is a spark from above and man is not permitted to attach himself to that beauty. If, however, 'it comes suddenly to meet him' then 'he should attach himself through this beauty to the beauty above'. In the same work, p. 24, it is said that as a result of struggling with 'strange thoughts' and rising above them a man can attain to an even loftier stage of *devekut*

8   *Peri Ha-Aretz* (Jerusalem, 1965), *va-yiggash,* p. 11a

9   *Likkute Torah* (Israel, n.d.), *Hadrakhah* 7, p. 9a

10 *Degel Mahane Efrayim,* p. 131

11 Wilensky, vol. 2, pp. 239–50

12 Wilensky, p. 147

13 Wilensky, p. 159

14 *Tanya* (Vilna, 1930), part 1, Chapter 28, p. 35a

15 *Likkute Maharan* (Bene Berak, 1965), no. 233, p. 115a

16 Op. cit., pp. 789–98

17 *Tanya* (Vilna, 1930), *Iggeret Ha-Kodesh,* no. 26, p. 144b. Tishby and Dan quote *Tanya, Kunteros Aharon,* but, unless the bracket is a later addition, there R. Shneor Zalman states explicitly (p. 154b) that when a prayer is recited without *kavvanah,* that is with 'strange thoughts', the elevation can be effected by even one prayer recited later with *kavvanah,* or, rather, by means of parts of prayers throughout the year being recited with *kavvanah.* This has nothing whatsoever to do with the elevation of 'strange thoughts' as advocated by the early masters. It should, however, be noted that the idea of a single prayer with *kavvanah* elevating the 'strange thoughts' in other prayers is found in the *Toledot* of R. Jacob Joseph, *shelah,* p. 143c, end of page, with reference to the prayers of Rosh Ha-Shanah

18 *Likkute Maharan,* no. 96, p. 96a

19 'The Kavvanoth of Prayer in Early Hasidism', note 47, pp. 186–7

20 pp. 19–20

21 *Derekh Pikkudekha* (Jerusalem, n.d.), Introduction, no. 7, 6–8, pp. 25–6

22 In fact, of course, the early Hasidic sources do not confine the doctrine to the Zaddikim but urge its application on all the Hasidim

23 *Derekh Pikkudekha,* Introduction, no. 7, 8, pp. 25–6

24 These works were not accessible to me and I have had to rely on quotations from them in *Sefer Baal Shem Tov,* vol. 1, pp. 159–63. This section should be consulted for other works in the same vein advocating the doctrine. Cf. Tishby and Dan, pp. 799–800, and for R. Yitzhak Eisik see the full-scale but uncritical biography, *R. Yitzhak Eisik Mi-Komarno* (Jerusalem, 1965) by H. J. Berl

25 *Otzar Ha-Hayim* (Lemberg, 1858), *hukkat*, p. 167c

26 *Hekhal Ha-Berakhah* (Lemberg, 1871), *mikketz*, p. 248c

27 Ber. 33b, interpreted by the early Hasidim to mean that he repeats the words of the prayers because the first time he recited them with 'strange thoughts' in his mind. Rather than repeat the words, he should accept the first utterance, even though it is with 'strange thoughts', and he should elevate these thoughts. By repeating the words he demonstrates that his belief is that the thoughts invalidate his prayers

28 *Hekhal Ha-Berakhah*, *va-yehi*, p. 131b

29 *Keneset Yisrael*, p. 20a

Chapter X

1 See, for example, Knox, *Enthusiasm*, Index: 'Tongues, gift of'

2 See M. Sabar, *Mikhlol Ha-Maamarim Ve-Ha-Pitgamim* (Jerusalem, 1962), vol. 3, p. 1771

3 See Rivka Schatz Uffenheimer, pp. 118–21

4 *Lebensgeschichte*, p. 203. Cf. the eye-witness account of R. Zeev Wolf of Zhitomer, *Or Ha-Meir*, *tzav*, pp. 95c–d, quoted by Schatz Uffenheimer, p. 120

5 Quoted by Schatz Uffenheimer, pp. 118–19, from *Maor Va-Shemesh*, New York, 1958 (not the edition used in this book), p. 51a. Cf. the remarks of R. Elimelech of Lizensk, the teacher of R. Kalonymus, in *Noam Elimelekh* to Exod. 25:2 (p. 71 bot.), 'When the Zaddik wishes to explain some Torah or some verse he shakes his head as he begins to speak and the explanation comes to him from his root (in Heaven)'. Cf. the critique by R. David of Makov (*Shever Posheim*, Wilensky, vol. 2, pp. 165–6) for a similar description of the Zaddik waiting for inspiration with his hand over his face. He does not prepare his discourses but relies on the holy spirit which 'speaks from out of his throat'. This preacher makes the extremely important observation that in this the Hasidim are like the Mennonites and the Quakers in their worship! See Wilensky's note (277) on the comparison of the Hasidim to the Quakers

6 Quoted by Schatz Uffenheimer, pp. 119–20 from *Tiferet Uziel* (Tel Aviv, 1962), pp. 53b–c

7 Ber. 7a. In the context the meaning is that God prays to Himself that His mercy will prevail over His judgement, but here the turn is given to the saying that when the Zaddik prays it is really God speaking through him and so, as it were, praying to Himself! Cf. the story told in *Shivhe Ha-Besht*, on p. 85 of R. Jacob Joseph of Pulnoye, who once prayed in such a lofty state of mind that he 'clothed his needs so that it was as if the Shekhinah offered something similar to those needs in Her prayer to the God of Israel'

8 Translating the verse, 'My mouth shall [merely] *speak* the praises of the Lord' (which He Himself utters through me)

9 See above, pp. 93–7

10 Printed at the end of the *Noam Elimelekh* in various editions

11 See above, p. 23

12 This has to be qualified slightly in that there are a (very) few new prayers composed by the Hasidic masters. See Wertheim, pp. 97-100
13 no. 156, p. 105b
14 *Ramataim Tzofim*, part 2, p. 23a note 30

Chapter XI

1 On this see Wertheim, Appendix I, pp. 231-4; Ysander, pp. 102-15
2 M.K. 16b. For the oft-quoted Hasidic interpretation see e.g. Levi Yitzhak of Berditchev *Kedushat Levi* (Jerusalem, 1964) *rosh ha-shanah*, p. 275
3 *Shivhe Ha-Besht*, p. 53
4 *Or Ha-Meir, tetzaveh*, p. 70b. The author refers here to his commentary to *noah*, p. 5a where he clearly identifies the role of the prayer leader as stated in this passage with the role of the Zaddik
5 See above, p. 171 note 32
6 On this theme see the penetrating comments of G. Scholem, *On the Kabbalah and Its Symbolism* (New York and London, 1965), pp. 139-53
7 *Peri Ha-Aretz* (Jerusalem, 1965), *noah* and *lekh lekha*, pp. 2b-3a
8 *Kedushat Levi, shir ha-shirim*, pp. 193-4
9 *Noam Elimelekh* to Exod. 23: 19, p. 70. The idea of the Zaddik as the 'channel' is found in very early Hasidic teaching. See the quotations from the works of R. Jacob Joseph of Pulnoye in Samuel H. Dresner, *The Zaddik* (New York, n.d.), p. 277 note 33 and p. 378 note 34
10 *Noam Elimelekh* to Gen. 18: 1, p. 13, and freq. The Talmudic saying is, 'Raba said, "Life, children and sustenance depend not on merit but on *mazzal*"' (M.K. 28a). *Mazzal* is, of course, destiny, luck, fate, and there are obvious astrological implications. R. Elimelech's interpretation is to take *mazzal* as referring to the 'upper worlds' which can only be influenced by the prayers of the Zaddik
11 *Noam Elimelekh* to Exod. 38: 21, p. 80. Cf. to Num. 18: 8, pp. 120-1. On the basis of passages such as these, Dubnow, pp. 182-3, sees R. Elimelekh as the Hasidic teacher who, more than any other, stressed the material side of Zaddikism
12 *Noam Elimelekh* to Lev. 19: 10
13 *Noam Elimelekh* to Lev. 16: 1, pp. 91-2
14 *Noam Elimelekh* to Gen. 30: 36, pp. 23-4
15 *Noam Elimelekh* to Gen. 47: 28, pp. 40-1
16 Talmudic saying (Yev. 64a; Hull. 60b). See *Noam Elimelekh* to Exod. 10: 1, pp. 53-4, that, at times, God issues a decree for the sole purpose of having it annulled by the prayer of the Zaddik
16a *Noam Elimelekh* to Lev. 23: 4, p. 98
17 *Noam Elimelekh* to Gen. 32: 4, p. 27
18 *Noam Elimelekh* to Gen. 37: 1, pp. 31-2
19 Here described as the Maggid of Rovno. The Maggid lived in Rovno in his youth and returned there after his sojourn in Meseritch. See A. Kahana, *Sefer Ha-Hasidut* (Warsaw, 1922), pp. 143-4; Dubnow, p. 178 note 1
20 Nidd. 31a

21 *Noam Elimelekh* to Deut. 1: 1, p. 133
22 *Toledot, yitro*, p. 58a
23 See above, pp. 36–42
24 This is rabbinic interpretation, see: Sifre *ekev*, 49. For the Hasidim 'cleaving' to God means *devekut* (see above, pp. 21–3), and this is achieved through the help of the Zaddik. Rabbinic references to 'scholars' (*talmide hakhamim*) are interpreted generally in Hasidic literature as referring to the Zaddikim
25 On this see Wertheim, pp. 161–4; Ysander, pp. 324–6
26 p. 161
27 See the suggestion of Kamelhaar, quoted by Wertheim, p. 163 note 39, that, as 'old Hasidim say', the practice is based on Nahmanides' comment to Num. 1: 45
28 *Shever Posheim*, Wilensky, pp. 66–7
29 The 'keys' of rain, childbirth and the revival of the dead (see Taan. 2a), i.e. the Zaddik can perform these miracles
30 *Tiferet Shelomo*, vol. 1, to Gen. 1: 16, pp. 5a–b
31 *Tiferet Shelomo*, vol. 1, *noah*, p. 9a
32 *Tiferet Shelomo*, vol. 1, *va-yera*, pp. 16b–17a
33 See Landau and Uretner
34 This prayer has been printed at the beginning of a number of Prayer Books but recently a different and, it is claimed, a more authentic version has been published in D. M. Rabinowitz, ed., *Haggadah Shel Pesah* (Jerusalem, 1962). Where the text of this version differs from the standard text it is quoted in the notes prefaced by HP=*Haggadah Shel Pesah*
35 HP 'the great fire of the evil inclination'
36 HP 'We are in great distress, O our Father'
37 HP 'as it is Thy benevolent will'
38 HP 'We take delight always in Thee, in Thy greatness', etc.
39 HP adds here a further lengthy supplication in which prayers are offered for sustenance on behalf of those who have to beg for money that the donors give them without putting them to shame, and on behalf of those who earn their own living. This addition includes, too, a prayer that 'we should have the merit of serving Thee with all our heart, with both our inclinations, the good and the evil, so that our evil inclination will also be coerced into Thy perfect service'. God is also entreated to save from 'forbidden food, forbidden drink, forbidden garments and forbidden sexual practices'. There is also a reference to finding favour 'in the eyes of the Zaddikim of the generation that they may teach us the good way that is upright in Thy presence'. This addition seems on the whole to reflect later conditions, so that the claim that this version of the prayer is more authentic is more than a little doubtful.
40 See S. A. Horodetzsky, *Ha-Hasidut Ve-Ha-Hasidim* (Tel Aviv, 1951), 2, p. 82, note 16; Wertheim, p. 101
41 *Kinderlech*, lit. 'toddlers', 'little children'

Chapter XII

1 *Noda Biyudah* (Zolkiew, 1823), *Yoreh Deah*, No. 93. Benjacob lists the

first edition of the *Noda Biyudah* as Prague 5336 (=1776) but the letter in question is dated Sivan 22, 5536 (=1776) which leaves insufficient time lapse between the writing of the letter and the publication of the book. In fact, as the colophon to the first edition clearly states, the work was published a year later in 1777

2 On this theme see Scholem, *On the Kabbalah and Its Symbolism*, pp. 104-9; Tishby, *Mishnat Ha-Zohar*, vol. 1, pp. 219-63; Tishby, *Torat Ha-Ra Ve-Ha-Kelipah*

3 Zohar III, 51b, given by Elijah de Vidas, *Reshit Hokhmah* (Tel Aviv, n.d.), *Shaar Ha-Ahavah*, Chapter 9

4 See Zohar III, 83a, 'because you laboured in the Torah and the precepts in order to unite the Holy One, blessed be He, and His Shekhinah'

5 Beg. p. 2. Vital, however, does not refer to an actual formula but simply states that when a man performs a *mitzvah* he should have the intention to unite thereby the name of the Holy One, blessed be He, with His Shekhinah

6 e.g. Isiaiah Horowitz, *Shelah, Shaar Ha-Otiot*, 1, p. 44a, quoting from de Vidas; Elijah of Smyrna, *Midrash Talpiot* (Warsaw, 1875), s.v. *yihud*, p. 238, also quoting de Vidas

7 e.g. on p. 32 and on pp. 96-103

8 R. Arele Roth, *Shomer Emunim*, vol. 2, Chapters 16-21, pp. 278-98, gives three different versions, the one quoted and two more elaborate ones. Interestingly enough, in one of the versions, he provides the following optional addition, 'And in the name of all the Zaddikim and in the name of the Zaddik of the generation in whom all the souls of Israel are included'

9 i.e. as a formula. The words themselves, however, are early and occur, e.g. in the *Shelah*, Introd., beginning, p. 2a

10 See the explanation given in R. Zevi Elimelech Spira of Dinov, *Igra De-Pirka* (Zolkiew, 1861), no. 26, 'This is the meaning of, "For the sake of the unification of the Holy One, blessed be He, and His Shekhinah" (that is to say, we do this *mitzvah* so as to prepare the Male and Female for their unification, and the idea of their unification is) "through that Hidden and Concealed One". For when they have been made ready, the flow from the Hidden and Concealed One illumines them that they might be united as one.' Cf. Hillel Zeitlin, *Be-Pardes Ha-Hasidut Ve-Ha-Kabbalah* (Tel Aviv, 1965), p. 49

11 *Toledot, shelah*, p. 248

12 *Noam Elimelekh, bo*, p. 56; Deut. beginning, p. 133

13 *Kedushat Levi, likkutim*, p. 311, referring to the formula as *nusah ha-ari*, i.e. instituted by Luria

14 *Tanya*, I, 41, p. 114. For further references to the formula in early Hasidic literature see *Sefer Baal Shem Tov*, vol. 1, pp. 178-9 (from *Likkute Yekarim*, 4a, and *Keter Shem Tov*, 2b) and vol. 2, pp. 160-1. Cf. R. Kalonymus Kalman Epstein, *Maor Va-Shemesh, terumah*, beg. p. 94b

15 Yev. 65b

16 Wertheim, pp. 71-2

17 Zev. 2b

18 Zev. 2b
19 First ed. Sudlikov, 1813, Responsum printed at beg. of the work, pp. 3–10
20 See above, p. 81
21 Ber. 13a
22 On the general question of a conflict in law between the Talmud and Kabbalah see *Encyclopedia Talmudit*, vol. 9, pp. 254–5
23 p. 4
24 Shulhan Arukh, Orah Hayim, 25: 5
25 Shulhan Arukh, Orah Hayim, 8: 91
26 See above, pp. 74–80
27 Cf. the very revealing remarks of Landau in his *Tzion Le-Nefesh Hayah* (Prague, 1791), *Berakhot*, Introduction, that in his youth he had heard from R. Nathan ben. Levi of Brody that we cannot really understand how ideas such as the Sefirot and Right, Left and Centre, or Lovingkindness, Judgement and Mercy, can be applied on high, but these terms are like the alphabet a child learns. This is to enable him to carry on his studies when he grows older. These Kabbalistic terms are solely for the purpose of equipping us to understand the divine mysteries in the Hereafter!
28 Zohar III, 152a
29 p. 5b
30 R. Hayim possibly hints at the Kabbalists' description of their science as 'wisdom', *hokhmah*
31 p. 7b
32 See e.g. Sifre, Deut. 33, and above, p. 20
33 See above, pp. 74–80
34 R. Hayim translates the verse, evidently, as 'foundation of the world' (*olam*)
35 p. 7b
36 See above, pp. 126–32 on the prayers of the Zaddik
37 p. 8a
38 pp. 9b–10a
39 p. 10a
40 It features in none of the famous anti-Hasidic polemics collected by Wilensky in his *Hasidim U-Mitnaggedim*
41 See S. Wind, *Rabbi Yehezkel Landau* (Jerusalem, 1961)
42 Wind, pp. 19–20
43 See Scholem, *Shabbatai Zevi* (Jerusalem, 1957), pp. 734–7 and *The Messianic Idea in Judaism*
44 *Major Trends in Jewish Mysticism*, pp. 334–7; cf. above, pp. 107–8
45 *Tzion Le-Nefesh Hayah*, *Berakhot*, to Ber. 28b, p. 39b
46 For a bizarre application of the doctrine in later Hasidism see Baruch of Medziboz *Botzina Di-Nehora* (Pietrikov, 1889), section 6, where it is said that Moses of Ludomir visited R. Baruch, the grandson of the Baal Shem Tov, and found the master quarrelling with his wife. This was said to be a representation on earth of the debate on high between 'the Holy One, blessed be He' and His Shekhinah and was done for the purpose of *tikkun*. Cf. the following from the secret diary of R. Yitzhak Eisik Judah Jehiel of Komarno, *Megillat Setarim*, ed. N. Ben-Menahem (Jerusalem, 1944)

605 [= 1845], the 20th day of the Omer. I happened to be in the town of Dukla. I arrived there at night when all was dark so that there was none to offer me hospitality until a certain tanner took me into his house. I wished to recite the evening prayer and to count the Omer but was unable to do so there. So I went to the House of Learning and I recited my prayers there. From this happening I came to appreciate the idea of the descent of the Shekhinah and Her pain when She had to endure a stay in the street of the tanners. I wept many tears before the Lord of all over the pain of the Shekhinah and I fainted from my great distress and slept for a while. I saw in a vision a great and splendid light in the form of a virgin with her adornments, and she illuminated all with her brightness but I did not have the merit of seeing her face. More than this one should not record. Her light was brighter than the sun at noon

47 *Simhat Ha-Regel*, Ruth (Livorno, 1782), p. 5a
48 Introduction to the Tel-Aviv edition(1960) of Hayim Vital's *Etz Hayim*

Chapter XIII

1 See above, pp. 48–9
2 Responsa, *Hatam Sofer, Orah Hayim*, nos 15 and 16. On R. Moses Sofer as a Respondent see S. B. Freehof, *The Responsa Literature* (Philadelphia, 1959), pp. 89–91
3 Responsa, *Heshiv Moshe, Orah Hayim*, no. 7. On R. Moses Teitelbaum as a Hasidic master see Dubnow, *Toledot*, pp. 442–3 and on these Responsa see Wertheim, *Halakhot*, pp. 193–5
4 On R. Nathan Adler and his relationship to Hasidism see Dubnow, pp. 434–1 and Wilensky, vol. 1, pp. 324–6
5 See above, pp. 36–42
6 See above, pp. 38–9
7 *Heshiv Moshe, Orah Hayim*, no. 6
8 Cf. above, p. 169 note 14
9 Cf. above, p. 46
10 *Divre Hayim* (Lemberg, 1875), part 2, *Orah Hayim*, no. 8
11 Cf. above, pp. 38–9
12 *Divre Hayim*, part 2, *Orah Hayim*, nos 17 and 18
13 See above, pp. 67–9
14 *Divre Hayim*, part 2, *Orah Hayim*, no. 21
15 On R. Joseph Saul Nathanson as a Respondent see Freehof, pp. 91–3
16 *Shoel U-Meshiv* (Lemberg, 1865–79), Second Series, part 4, no. 135. Cf. H. J. Zimmels, *Ashkenazim and Sephardim* (London, 1958), pp. 110–20
17 Pes. 5: 7
18 Shulhan Arukh, Orah Hayim 487: 4
19 Yev. 65b
20 See above, p. 144
21 It is just possible that R. Joseph Saul by quoting this verse is thinking of its application by the grandson of the Baal Shem Tov to his grandfather, through whose teachings the redemption of the Jewish people will be

brought about (see *Degel Mahane Efraim* to this verse, p. 101). R. Joseph Saul may be hinting that it is not the vindication of the Baal Shem Tov that he wishes to see but of R. Moses Isserles, whose opinion had been challenged by the Hasidim. In 1870 R. Joseph Saul gave his approbation to the reprinting of the *Degel* and was probably familiar with the work even before this time. R. Joseph Saul gave his approbation to a number of Hasidic works printed in Lemberg. To some extent he was an admirer of Hasidism and was held in great esteem by the Hasidim. But where Hasidic practice seemed to him to be contrary to the law he naturally sided with the latter

22 *Shoel U-Meshiv*, Third Series, part I, no. 247

Bibliography

Only works referred to in the book are listed

I   Hasidic works (in alphabetical order of titles)

Amud Ha-Emet (Tel Aviv, n.d.), on Mehahem Mendel of Kotzk
Avodat Yisrael, Israel of Koznitz (Lemberg, 1858)
Beer Moshe, Moses of Koznitz (New York, 1964)
Ben Porat Yosef, Jacob Joseph of Pulnoye (Koretz, 1781)
Botzina De-Nehora, Baruch of Medziboz (Pietrikov, 1889)
Degel Mahane Efrayim, Moses Ephraim of Sudlikov (Jerusalem, 1963)
Derekh Emet, Meshullam Phoebus of Zharabaz (n.p., n.d.)
Derekh Hasidim (Jerusalem, 1962)
Derekh Pikkudekha, Zevi Elimelech Spira of Dinov (Jerusalem, n.d.)
Iggerot Shomer Emunim, Arele Roth (Jerusalem, 1942)
Igra De-Pirka, Zevi Elimelech Spira of Dinov (Zolkiev, 1861)
Imre Binah, Dov Baer of Lubavitch (Shanghai, 1946)
Haggadah Shel Pesah, ed. D. M. Rabinowitz (Jerusalem, 1962)
Hekhal Ha-Berakhah, Yitzhak Eisik Judah Jehiel of Komarno (Lemberg, 1971)
Kedushat Levi, Levi Yitzhak of Berditchev (Jerusalem, 1964)
Keneset Yisrael (Warsaw, 1910), on Israel of Ruzhyn and family
Keter Shem Tov (Jerusalem, 1968)
Kunteros Ha-Hitbonanut, Dov Baer of Lubavitch, part 2 of his *Ner Mitzvah Ve-Torah Or* (New York, 1948)
Kunteros Ha-Hitpaalut, id., in *Likkute Biurim* (see below)
Leshon Hasidim (Tel Aviv, 1961)
Likkute Amarim, see below *Maggid Devarav Le-Yaakov*
Likkute Biurim, Hillel ben Meir of Poritch (Warsaw, 1865)
Likkute Maharan, Nahman of Bratzlav (Bene Berak, 1965)
Likkute Torah, Mordecai of Tchernobil (Israel, n.d.)
Likkute Yekarim (Lemberg, 1865)
Magen Avot, Solomon Zalman of Kopust (Berditchev, 1902)
Maggid Devarav Le-Yaakov (or *Likkute Amarim*), Solomon of Lutzk (Jerusalem, 1962), teachings of the Maggid of Meseritch

183

Maor Va-Shemesh, Kalonymus Kalman Epstein of Cracow (Tel Aviv, 1965)
Megillat Setarim, Yitzhak Eisik Judah Jehiel of Komarno, ed. N. Ben-Menahem (Jerusalem, 1944)
Noam Elimelekh, Elimelech of Lizensk (Jerusalem, n.d.)
Or Ha-Meir, Zeev Wolf of Zhitomer (Jerusalem, 1968)
Otzar Ha-Hayim, Yitzhak Eisik Judah Jehiel of Komarno (Lemberg, 1858)
Peri Ha-Aretz, Menahem Mendel of Vitebsk (Jerusalem, 1965)
Ramataim Tzofim, Samuel of Shinov (Jerusalem, 1970)
Sefer Baal Shem Tov (Sotmar, 1943)
Shaare Avodah, Aaron of Starosselje (Shklov, 1821)
Shaar Ha-Tefillah, id., Gate III of *Shaare Avodah* (Miskolc, 1940)
Shaar Ha-Tefillah, Hayim ben Solomon of Czernowitz (Sudlikov, 1813)
Shivhe Ha-Besht, ed. S. A. Horodetsky (Tel Aviv, 1960)
Shomer Emunim, Arele Roth (Jerusalem, 1966)
Tanya, Shneor Zalman of Liady (Vilna, 1930)
Tiferet Shelomo, Solomon of Radomsk (Jerusalem, 1963)
Tiferet Uziel, Uziel Meisels (Tel Aviv, 1962)
Toledot Yaakov Yosef, Jacob Joseph of Pulnoye (Warsaw, 1881)
Torat Avot (Jerusalem, 1971), sayings of the Lechovitz—Kobryn—Slonim dynasties
Torat Ha-Maggid, ed. I. Klepholtz (Tel Aviv, 1969), teachings of the Maggid of Meseritch
Tzavaat Ha-Ribash (Jerusalem, 1948)
Tzav Ve-Ziruz, Kalonymus Kalman Spira of Piatzina (Jerusalem, 1962)
Zikkaron Zot, Zot Zikkaron, Divre Emet, Jacob Isaac of Lublin (Germany, 1947)

II Works on Hasidim and other books

Alfasi, Y., *Gur* (Tel Aviv, 1954)
Alfasi, Y., *Ha-Hasidut* (Tel Aviv, 1969)
Altmann, A., 'The Delphic Maxim in Medieval Islam and Judaism' in his *Studies in Religious Philosophy and Mysticism* (London and Ithaca, 1969), pp. 1–40
Azulai, C. J. D., *Simhat Ha-Regel* (Livorno, 1782)
Baer, I. F., 'The Social and Religious Aim of the *Sefer Hasidim*' (Heb.) in *Zion*, III (Jerusalem, 1938), pp. 1–50
Bahya Ibn Pakuda, *Duties of the Heart*, various editions
Berl, H. J., *R. Yitzhak Eisik Mi-Komarno* (Jerusalem, 1965)
Buber, M. *Tales of the Hasidim* (New York, 1947–8)
De Vidas, Elijah, *Reshit Hokhmah* (Tel Aviv, n.d.)
Dresner, S. H., *The Zaddik* (New York, n.d.)
Dubnow, S., *Toledot Ha-Hasidut* (Tel Aviv, 1967)
Elijah of Smyrna, *Midrash Talpiot* (Warsaw, 1875)
Emden, J. *Mitpahat Sefarim* (Altona, 1768)
Enelow, H. G., 'Kawwanah: The Struggle for Inwardness in Judaism' in *Studies in Jewish Literature in honor of Kaufmann Kohler* (Berlin, 1913), pp. 82–107

Freehof, Solomon B., *The Responsa Literature* (Philadelphia, 1959)
Geshuri, M. S., *Ha-Niggun Ve-Ha-Rikkud Ba-Hasidut* (Tel Aviv, 1955)
Ginzberg, L., *Commentary to the Palestinian Talmud* (New York, 1971)
Halberstam, Hayim, *Divre Hayim*, Responsa (Lemberg, 1875)
Hayim of Volozhyn, *Nefesh Ha-Hayim* (Bene Berak, 1958)
Heschel, A. J., 'R. Nahman of Kosov' in the Harry A. Wolfson Jubilee Volume (Jerusalem, 1965), Heb. section, pp. 113–41
Hielmann, H. M., *Bet Rabbi* (Berditchev, 1903)
Hillmann, D. Z., *Iggerot Baal Ha-Tanya* (Jerusalem, 1953)
Horodetzsky, S. A., *Ha-Hasidut Ve-Ha-Hasidim* (Tel Aviv, 1951)
Horowitz, I. *Shelah* (*Shene Luhot Ha-Berit*) (Jerusalem, 1963)
Ibn Abi Zimra, David, *Responsa* (Warsaw, 1882)
Jacobs, L., trans., *Tract on Ecstasy* (London, 1963)
Jacobs, L., *Seeker of Unity* (London, 1966)
James, W., *The Varieties of Religious Experience* (London, 1905)
Kadanir, J. *Sippurim Noraim* (Lemberg, 1875)
Kahana, A., *Sefer Ha-Hasidut* (Warsaw, 1922)
Kleinmann, M. H., *Zikkaron La-Rishonim* (Jerusalem, 1959)
Kleinmann, M. H., *Or Yesharim* (Jerusalem, 1967)
Knowles, D., *Western Mysticism*, 3rd ed. (London, 1967)
Knox, R. A., *Enthusiasm* (Oxford, 1957)
Landau, B. and Uretner, N., eds, *Ha-Rav Ha-Kadosh Mi-Belza* (Jerusalem, 1967)
Landau, Ezekiel, *Noda Biyudah* (Zolkiev, 1823)
Landau, Ezekiel, *Tzion Le-Nefesh Hayah* (Prague, 1791)
Langer, Jiri, *Nine Gates* (London, 1961)
Maimon, Solomon, *Lebensgeschichte*, ed. J. Fromer (Munich, 1911)
Maimonides, Moses, *Yad Ha-Hazakah*, various eds
Maimonides, Moses, *Guide of the Perplexed*, trans. S. Pines (Chicago, 1963)
Menahem Azaraiah of Fano, *Responsa* (Venice, n.d.)
Minkin, J. S., *The Romance of Hasidism* (New York, 1935)
Nathan of Hanover, *Shaare Tzion* (Zhitomer, 1848)
Nathanson, Joseph Saul, *Shoel U-Meshiv* (Lemberg, 1865–79)
Newman, L. I., *The Hasidic Anthology* (New York, 1944)
Otto, R., *The Idea of the Holy* (London, 1957)
Perl, J., *Megalleh Temirin* (Lemberg, 1864)
Philo, see Yonge
Rabinowicz, H., *The World of Hasidism* (London, 1970)
Rabinowitsch, W., *Ha-Hasidut Ha-Litait* (Jerusalem, 1961); also published as *Lithuanian Hasidism* (London and New York, 1971)
Rabbinowitz, I. M., *Ha-Maggid Mi-Koznitz* (Tel Aviv, 1947)
Rokotz, J. K. K., *Siah Sarfe Kodesh* (New York, 1954)
Rubinstein, A., Review of Wertheim, *Halakhot* in *Kiryat Sefer*, vol. 36, no. 3 (June, 1961), pp. 280–6
Sabar, M., *Mikhlol Ha-Maamarim Ve-Ha-Pitgamim* (Jerusalem, 1962)
Schatz, Rivka, 'Contemplative Prayer in Hasidism' in *Studies in Mysticism and Religion Presented to G. Scholem* (Jerusalem, 1967), pp. 209–226
Schatz Uffenheimer, Rivka, *Ha-Hasidut Ke-Mistikah* (Eng. title, *Quietistic*

Elements in 18th Century Hasidic Thought) (Jerusalem, 1968)
Scholem, G., *Major Trends in Jewish Mysticism*, 3rd. rev. ed. (New York, 1954; London, 1955)
Scholem, G., *Shabbatai Zevi* (Jerusalem, 1957)
Scholem, G., *On the Kabbalah and Its Symbolism* (London and New York, 1965)
Scholem, G., 'Devekuth or Communion with God' in *Review of Religion*, vol. 14 (1949–50), pp. 115–39
Scholem, G., *The Messianic Idea in Judaism* (New York, 1971; London, 1972)
Sevin, S., *Ishim Ve-Shittot* (Tel Aviv, 1952)
Siddur Hare Besamim (Warsaw, 1933–4)
Siddur Ishe Yisrael (Tel Aviv, 1968)
Singer, S., *Authorised Daily Prayer Book*, new ed. (London, 1962)
Sofer, Moses, *Hatam Sofer*, Responsa (Pressburg, 1855)
Spira, Hayim Lazar of Munkacs, *Sefer Hamishah Maamarot* (Jerusalem, 1966)
Sperling, A. I., *Taame Ha-Minhagim* (Jerusalem, 1957)
Teitelbaum, M., *Ha-Rav Mi-Ladi* (Warsaw, 1913)
Teitelbaum, Moses, *Heshiv Moshe*, Responsa (Lemberg, 1866)
Tishby, I., *Torat Ha-Ra Ve-Ha-Kelipah Be-Kabbalat Ha-Ari* (Jerusalem, 1968)
Tishby, I., *Mishnat Ha-Zohar*, 2nd ed. (Jerusalem, 1957)
Tishby, I. and Dan, Y., 'Torat Ha-Hasidut Ve-Siftrutah', offprint from *Hebrew Encyclopedia*, vol. 17, pp. 769–822 (Jerusalem, 1966)
Vital, H., *Etz Hayim* (Tel Aviv, 1960)
Vital, H., *Shaar Ha-Mitzvot* (Tel Aviv, 1962)
Weiner, H., *Nine and One Half Mystics* (New York, 1969)
Weiss, J. G., 'The Beginnings of Hasidism' (Heb.) in *Zion* (1951), pp. 46–106
Weiss, J. G., 'The Kavvanoth of Prayer in Early Hasidism' in *Journal of Jewish Studies*, vol. 9 (1958), pp. 163–92
Wertheim, A., *Halakhot Ve-Halikhot Ba-Hasidut* (Jerusalem, 1960)
Wilensky, M., *Hasidim U-Mitnaggedim* (Jerusalem, 1970)
Wind, S., *Rabbi Yehezkel Landau* (Jerusalem, 1961)
Yonge, C. D., ed., *Works of Philo Judaeus* (London, 1854–5), vol. 4
Ysander, T., *Studien Zum Beschtschen Hasidismus* (Uppsala, 1933)
Zangwill, I., *Dreamers of the Ghetto* (Philadelphia, 1943)
Zeitlin, Hillel, *Be-Pardes Ha-Hasidut Ve-Ha-Kabbalah* (Tel Aviv, 1965)
Zemah, Jacob Hayim, *Nagid U-Metzaveh* (Amsterdam, 1712)
Zimmels, H. J., *Ashkenazim and Separdim* (London, 1958)

Index